FERRIES
OF THE
LOWER THAMES

FERRIES

OF THE
LOWER THAMES

Joan Tucker

AMBERLEY

The illustrations in this book are the property of the author unless otherwise stated.

The map references in this book are to Ordnance Survey Explorer series at 1:20 000 scale (2½ inches to 1 mile). The modern spellings of place names are taken from these maps.

First published 2010

Amberley Publishing Plc
Cirencester Road, Chalford,
Stroud, Gloucestershire, GL6 8PE

www.amberley-books.com

Copyright © Joan Tucker 2010

The right of Joan Tucker to be identified as the Author of this work has been asserted in accordance with the Copyrights, Designs and Patents Act 1988.

ISBN 978 1 84868 968 8

British Library Cataloguing in Publication Data.
A catalogue record for this book is available from the British Library.

Typeset in 10pt on 12pt Sabon.
Typesetting and Origination by FONTHILLDESIGN.
Printed in the UK.

Contents

Preface

Ferries of the Thames are worthy of a volume to themselves, an undertaking which as far as our knowledge extends, has never yet been attempted. There is a lingering charm about these watery ways that makes them far preferable to a rigid bridge, and a certain spice of adventure is always possible to the ferry-farer.

West London Sketcher Magazine in 1888-89.

The scope of this book covers the Thames between Staines and Yantlet Creek in the estuary. Many books have been written about the River Thames, some of them devoted to bridges, most of which replaced a ferry, but not one has been concerned specifically with ferries, which are the means of crossing the river from bank to bank by boat from one set point to another. Due to the nature of evolution of ferries, archive material is rare, but a pattern can be observed. The king owned the Thames and its fords. Initially, a crossing would occur at a natural outcrop of rock which formed a pavement and became a ford. When the bed of the river was deepened to improve navigation, ferries became necessary at the same place or close by. Rights of ferry were given by the king to a servant or the local Lord of the Manor. From being an ad hoc affair, the transaction became legal and binding. From then on the history of each ferry differs. Many eventually were superseded by bridges and later still, as civil engineering developed, by tunnels as well. By then the provision of crossings had become the responsibility of public or corporate bodies, instead of private enterprise on a small scale. However, ferries on less important routes lasted into the twentieth century. Eighteen were shown in a street directory of about 1930. *The Authentic Map Directory of London & Suburbs – New & Revised Edition* included a ferry near Harrods' Depository at Castelnau (Barnes), possibly for the use of their employees. By the end of the Second World War, most of the eighteen were discontinued. Only three are still running in 2010, two in summer and weekends only, the other being Woolwich Free Ferry, the traffic on which is phenomenal.

Ferries were disregarded by historians generally. Even the compilers of antiquarian county histories seem to have overlooked their significance, so for information we turn to legal documents, leases, Acts of Parliament, account books and court cases. Travellers' tales, including poetry, are rewarding, if they can be tracked down, for the personal observations they give. Occasionally, such diaries and accounts of tours are illustrated by the early topographers with drawings and watercolours. Some repositories have kindly allowed such images in their possession to be reproduced here.

Two books are particularly notable in the history of the river. Henry Humpherus, the secretary of the Company of Watermen and Lightermen searched through his Company's records in his spare time and noted significant details year by year to produce *The History of the Origin and Progress of the Company of Watermen and Lightermen* in three volumes between 1874 and 1886. Fred S. Thacker not only produced *The Thames Highway* in two volumes in 1914 and 1920 by studying the records of the Thames Conservators, but walked the length of the river from Cricklade to Kew. For monographs on particular ferries, transactions of local history societies, where they exist, have been invaluable.

Although many ferries had disappeared before the invention of the portable camera, the work of two photographers in particular has been outstanding. Grateful thanks are given to the National Monuments Record for the opportunity to reproduce images from the collection of Henry Taunt of Oxford, whose prodigious output from the 1880s onwards is of outstanding quality. He specialised in the River Thames, mainly above the tidal reaches. S. W. Rawlings worked for the Port of London Authority and took opportunities to record the life of the river in the tidal reaches between 1945 and 1965. His large collection is also held by the NMR.

Following the *Princess Alice* disaster, the popularity of the River Thames as a pleasure resort was curtailed. The commercial aspect also declined with more and more vessels not able to access the London Docks because of size. Trade was diverted to other ports. By the 1930s the London Thames, which had been a valuable highway, was neglected, its assets ignored. A. P. Herbert, aided by Rt Hon. John Burns and others led a campaign to bring the river back to life. In his book *No Boats on the River*, he advocated installing water buses and Thames taxis. Progress was halted during the war and afterwards when focus was on the development of new towns and infrastructure. Following increased prosperity in the 1970s and the installation of the Thames Barrier, which gave security for riverside properties to be developed, the Thames is becoming once again a vital artery in the life and prosperity of London, aided by the forward-looking policies of the department of the Mayor of London.

In the early hours of Saturday 27 May 1732, the painter William Hogarth, his fellow artist Samuel Scott and three other friends on a whim set out on an exploration. They hired a Gravesend Boat at Billingsgate. There was a strong wind and it was raining: 'Straw was our bed and a Tilt our covering.' They passed Purfleet and at Gravesend had difficulty getting ashore. For the next four days they walked to Rochester, explored the Isle of Grain, and stayed at the Chequer alehouse there. Because no ferryman would take them over the Medway to reach Sheerness, they hailed a passing boat. A good time was passed by all in ribaldry, horseplay, singing and mock fighting with cow dung. On the Wednesday, they returned to Billingsgate, then took a wherry to Somerset Water Gate and walked back to Covent Garden, whence they had started. *Hogarth's Peregrination* by Charles Mitchell reproduces the diary kept by the friends. The Chequer is now called Hogarth Inn in commemoration of the visit long ago. It is to be hoped modern-day ferry farers will get as much pleasure and spice of adventure in a jaunt on the river to places mentioned in this book.

Introduction

Staines. Ask a man or woman in the street the whereabouts of the London Stone, they do not know. Likewise the manageress of the pub in the former Town Hall, where the original stone was once housed, who was born and brought up in the town and she does not know. The stone has been a symbol of the town for hundreds of years. It marks the western boundary of the jurisdiction of the Lord Mayor and Corporation of the City of London over the River Thames.

The Thames is one of the four royal rivers of England. The others are the Severn, Trent and Yorkshire Ouse. Originally, it meant that the monarch had full control over the water and navigation. In 1197 King Richard I returned from an expensive crusade and sold the care and rights of the river to the City for 1,500 marks, a large amount of money.[1] Mainly the charter was concerned with abolishing the weirs across the river to give free access for navigation. Unfortunately, it did not specify the exact part of the river to be sold, thus leading to some complications in future years. Gradually it became apparent that it covered the course of the river between Colne Brook at Staines and Yantlet Creek in north Kent. King John confirmed the charter in 1199 and Henry III in 1227. The London Stone (the City Stone) was erected in 1285 close to the river, marking the tidal reach at that time. Since navigation was improved and bridges built further downstream, the tidal limit is now below Teddington Lock.

In 1619 the stone was moved higher up the bank, further from the river, and later still to a place higher up where it remains behind iron railings set on four graduated plinth stones in Ashby (Lammas) Recreation Ground on Wraysbury Road on the western outskirts of Staines. However, the top part, about two feet high, which resembles a Roman milestone and may even have been one, is in a glass case in a lobby outside the Spelthorne Museum at the back of Staines Library. A glass-fibre replica is on the plinth and bears the initial inscription, 'God preserve ye City of London'.

Traditionally, the Lord Mayor and Aldermen would travel upriver periodically, in their ceremonial barges and shallops (covered wherries) rowed by licensed watermen, to touch the stone with a sword, thus confirming their rights, such as charging tolls and levying taxes. Some of these visits were recorded on the plinths. The Lord Mayor in 1781 supplied the pedestal;[2] Sir Claudius Stephen Hunter, renowned for reviving ceremonious events, in 1812; William Venables in 1826; the Conservators of the River Thames in 1857, after the City had lost jurisdiction; and 1957 when they paid their last visit. Crowds would gather on these occasions to watch the custom of bumping the Sheriffs and Aldermen who had not been made 'free of the waters'. Coins were thrown to the crowd, speeches made and toasts were drunk.

As Conservator of the River Thames, the Lord Mayor had charge of its lower course, its embankments, weirs, creeks, etc. and supervision of the fisheries, navigation and watermills. But overall control was still with the Crown, which meant an Act of Parliament must be obtained before any major improvements could be made. An Act of 1751 set out to improve and complete the navigation of the Thames and Isis from

The London Stone situated on the riverbank at Staines. (Engraving from Mr and Mrs S. C. Hall's *The Book of the Thames*, 1859)

The London Stone before it was moved further up the bank. Photo 1883 by Henry Taunt. (Reproduced by Permission of English Heritage)

London to Cricklade in Wiltshire. It was not successful, as the preamble to the Act of 1771 in the reign of George III states that the Commissioners vested by the former Act did not have proper powers 'to prevent certain abuses and exactions being committed by owners of several towing paths, locks, weirs, turnpikes (meaning barriers put to prevent cattle entering the water, watergates or a particular type of lock constructed to allow for change in gradient), dams, floodgates and other engines'.[3] Also several barge-masters and their servants had offended. Therefore, the costs of carriage had increased and the 'navigation much damaged'. A survey and estimate had been made for making proper turnpikes, cleaning and embanking certain parts, purchasing land for making towing paths, building bridges across streams and other purposes.

Commissioners were to be appointed from each of the six districts through which the river ran. The first was the lower, or tidal reach. Each Commissioner was to hold lands in his own right of annual value of at least £100, except the Mayor of Guildford and the Bailiffs of Godalming. Commissioners had powers to purchase locks, ferries and lands for the use of the navigation and to make towing paths, banks, roads, bridges, ferries and ways for towing, haling or drawing boats (with horses or otherwise). For each of these new works, they were allowed to make charges. Some charges were already being made under the previous Act, but compensation would be paid if an owner lost income by the alterations. If men who were halers (i.e., bow-haulers) were put out of work by the horse-towing paths, they could apply for relief if they could not get work and be given not more than 4s per week. Vessels must not draw more than three feet of water, and a line one inch wide was to be painted in white on the hull to indicate this restriction. An annuities scheme could be set up.

Another Act was passed in 1768, similar to the above, but with specific reference to the area from the London Stone to London Bridge. The City would allow £10,000, if necessary out of their own estates, without increasing tolls or duty on persons navigating the river in order to improve navigation on that stretch. Much of the printed Act is taken up with points of law. Additionally it states, 'Nothing in the Act authorises the Mayor to compel the owner of any garden, lawn, orchard etc which have been used as such for six months before the Act was passed (except where towing paths are now used) or pull down any such messuage already begun, to make any new towing path, bridge, road, tollgate etc without the consent of the owner.' This Act has special clauses for towing by horses. The Mayor and Corporation shall determine the prices of carriage and rates and fares for horses between Staines and the City. Such prices are to be displayed at public places on the riverbanks. If, after twenty days of the notices being posted, any owner of a vessel shall take more payment for horses employed, he shall pay £20 for each offence, one half to the informer, the other to the aggrieved party.

By 1774 there were still problems, so a new Act was passed 'more effectually to improve and complete the navigation of the Thames westward of London Bridge within the Liberties of the City of London'.[4] It transpired that the £10,000 earmarked by the Corporation was not enough to carry out the improvements. Therefore, the part of the 1771 Act which stipulated that the Commissioners then should not take away any rights of the City, nor could they erect weirs, locks, turnpikes or toll-gates within the Liberties, that is District 1, should be repealed.

The regulations concerning the gauging of vessels caused problems, resulting in an amendment to the 1771 Act in 1775. The law was found to be prejudicial to bargemasters and tended to enhance the price of carriage. The white lines often got rubbed out. By this Act no person was to be fined for drawing more than three feet between 5 May and 1 November or for more than 3 feet 8 inches in the rest of the year in districts beyond the flux of the tide. The white line was abolished for frames,

King George III (reigned 1760-1820).
During his reign many Acts were passed for
regulating navigation on the River Thames.
Mezzotint after Zoffany, 1771. (Reproduced
via Wikimedia Commons)

gauges, etc., in each district. Pieces of lead or tin were to be fixed instead. A corollary stated that lock owners shall not act as Commissioners for settling watermarks on their own lock.

A further Act of 1777 ratified the jurisdiction of the Mayor and Corporation.[5] Its aim was to enable them 'to purchase the present tolls and duties payable for navigating' on the River Thames west of London Bridge within the Liberties of the City and for levying a small toll in lieu therefore for the purpose of more effectually completing the navigation. Already the Mayor had completed some works which had considerably reduced the costs of navigation on his stretch, but the expenditure was higher than the £10,000 estimated. A further £8,000 would be needed to complete the works in addition to the annual costs of repair.

The City wished to purchase the tolls and duties being charged by private owners, thus making the process of navigation free. This would alleviate hold-ups and other inconveniences. Instead, the City wanted to make a charge on tonnage for their part of the river. The tolls would include charges for hire of horses. Toll-houses and toll-gates would be erected. The charges were set by the Act. Barges between London Bridge and Brentford would pay ½*d* per ton; to Isleworth or Richmond 1*d*; to Chertsey or Laleham 3½*d*; to Staines and upwards 4*d* per ton. Tolls would not be charged on vessels less than three tons, nor on pleasure boats. All owners of vessels shall have their name painted in white capital letters six inches high and one inch wide on each side at their own expense. It was to be higher than the watermark when the boat was fully laden, and renewed when defaced. The authority would pay for the gauging and tons being marked.

However, the Act did have drawbacks for the City. No toll-gates or houses were to be erected on any part of lands lying between the garden of Dudley Montague at Richmond and the road leading from the Ham to Twickenham ferry, or upon ground granted by the Crown to Lord Cholmondely and then in the possession of Georgina, Countess Dowager Cooper. In some places it would not be lawful for the Mayor to make use of horses for towing on the Surrey side between His Majesty's bargehouse at Kew and the site of his ancient Palace of Richmond. On the Middlesex side horses could not be used from Isleworth to the upper end of land then in the occupation of the Earl of Buckinghamshire in Twickenham. The City would have to approach the respective owners for dispensation.

It was stated in the Act that King George III had provided 'a commodious public footwalk' alongside the river from the late horse ferry at Kew to the site of the palace for the benefit of the people of Richmond, Kew and adjacent towns. Another one extended the whole length of the site of the palace, and if used as a towing path by horses, the footwalk would be greatly injured, becoming dangerous. As it was of 'public utility' for barges to be towed by horses, rather than man, the Mayor should make a proper towing path for horses from the bargehouse at Kew to Water Lane in Richmond. It should not be raised higher the whole length of the footwalk than absolutely necessary for horses to tow with safety in times of spring tides and land floods. In those circumstances horses could be used.

As the Port of London became more important, trade and subsequent troubles increased. Thieving was rife but was not brought into control until the River Police Force was set up in 1798. An Act passed in 1762 sought to prevent thefts committed by persons navigating bum boats and other craft on the Thames.[6] Bum boats were small boats which would come alongside to sell goods to ships at anchor. They could satisfy every need – vegetables, rope, sail cloth, beer, pitch, etc. 'Many ill-disposed persons ... under pretence of selling liquors of different sorts, also slops, tobacco, brooms, fruit, greens, gingerbread and other such-like ware' to sailors and labourers employed on the ships, 'do frequently cut, damage and spoil the cardage, cables, buoys, buoy ropes, etc belonging to the ships and fraudulently carry them away' for profit. Some seamen and labourers are complicit with this practice.

Henceforth, any person using a bum boat for selling or bartering among seamen (except those employed by Trinity House) shall be guilty of a misdemeanor and have the boat forfeited on conviction. Therefore, every bum boat owner on the Thames operating for those purposes from London Bridge downstream to Lower Hope Point (at the edge of the Cliffe Marshes in Kent) shall be registered with Trinity House. They will pay 5s for the registration which will be published in the *London Gazette*. Notices will also be posted up at Iron Gate Stairs, The Hermitage, Execution Dock, Shadwell Dock, Rotherhithe Old Stairs, Deptford, Radcliffe Cross and Blackwall. Trinity House had powers to stop, search and detain any suspected bum boats. Stiff penalties would ensue.

Magna Carta, signed by King John at Runnymede just above Staines in June 1215 included clauses meant to regularise control of the Thames, particularly that the City of London shall still have all the old liberties and customs which it had been used to. No town or freeman shall be distrained to make bridges or banks but such as were accustomed to make them 'in the time of King Henry, our grandfather'. Likewise, no banks to be defended except those in the same places in his time. All wears (weirs or kidells) shall be utterly put down by the Thames and Medway and through all England, keeping only those by the coasts. This last continued to be a moot point for hundreds of years. There were revisions to Magna Carta in 1216, 1217 and 1225, but the above clauses remained.

At the beginning of Queen Victoria's reign, the proposed Victoria Embankment was being planned. The Crown then disputed the right of the City and Corporation to the bed and soil of the Thames in its tidal stretch. (F. S. Thacker was of the opinion[7] the Queen herself was behind the lawsuits which ensued). The City fought the claim but suffered a setback when a petition from residents of London was presented asking for the City to relinquish their rights. A Thames Conservancy to cover the whole river from Cricklade to Yantlet Creek was proposed. Increasing costs of maintenance and falling revenue due to competition from railways made the proposal inevitable. On 15 January 1857 the City finally gave up all claims to the river, thus ending nearly 700 years of its association with the river.

The Thames Conservancy Act was then passed, which gave control over the river below Staines only to a Board. Eleven Conservators were appointed, some of whom were members of the Corporation of London, and it was deemed that one third of future rents and fines were to be paid to Her Majesty's credit. In 1866 another Act added the responsibility for the upper Thames from the Thames Commissioners to the Thames Conservancy. It was a large and important body and as such published 'The Thames Bye-laws' in *The Times*, covering several columns, on 13 July 1907. Mostly they concerned regulations for navigation, for instance, lights to be shown particularly by the increasing number of steamers. The area specified was from Cricklade to Yantlet Creek but the following year in 1908 the Port of London Act transferred jurisdiction of the tidal river to the Port of London Authority.

The limit of their area was set at 265 yards below Teddington Lock where a stone pillar was erected on the Surrey bank by the PLA (Exp. 16361 71912). Some powers over the Lower Thames, like freshwater fishing, were returned to the Conservators by the PLA who retain responsibility for the Lower Thames to the present. The area covered by the Authority is ninety-five miles of river from Teddington to the estuary.[8] It now concentrates on managing safety, being responsible for river channels, moorings, lights and buoys, also providing a wide range of services for shipping, including pilotage.

CHAPTER ONE
Staines to Shepperton

STAINES

'Ad Pontes' was the Roman name for Staines (Exp. 160 031 713) when they set up supply routes following the invasion by Emperor Claudius in AD 47. It was nineteen miles from London and reputedly the first place upriver where the Thames could be bridged. The plural name suggests there were two or more bridges, possibly over the Colne Brook, to the ait (island in a river), or the River Ash. When the Saxons took over they called the town 'Stana' perhaps because of the stone bridge left by the Romans, or a ford made using stones. Barons travelling to Runnymede[1] in 1215 would have used a ford. Clause twenty-three of Magna Carta removed the responsibility for the upkeep of bridges from individual owners to districts. By 1222 the town of Staines had built a wooden bridge below the present one, close to the market place.

During the Civil Wars there were skirmishes on Staines Moor in 1642 and 1648[2] and the bridge was destroyed. Until it was replaced in 1687, a ferry was operated by the bridgemasters to take traffic across this important road. Horses too had to be taken over when they drew up the barges to Windsor because the towing path crossed over.[3] This was given as evidence of the necessity for increasing tolls on barges passing upstream in an enquiry dated 1672. The tolls had been raised from 4d to 7d per barge. Repair of Egham causeway was another reason.

The ferry seems to have been kept as a semi-permanent service because of the bridge being damaged. John Gay, author of *The Beggar's Opera*, in a poem about his journey from London to Exeter about 1714 refers to this.

> Thence o'er wide shrubby heaths, and furrowed lanes,
> We come, where Thames divides the meads of Staines,
> We ferry'd o'er, for late the winter's flood
> Shook her frail bridge, and tore her piles of wood.

When Staines acquired a more substantial bridge, it seems a ferry still operated further downstream and crossed diagonally beneath the railway bridge of 1856. Thacker describes the access to it as down steps close to Messrs Timms' boatyard. Joseph and Elizabeth Pennell describing their journey down the Thames in *The Stream of Pleasure* published in 1891 note the 'ugly railway bridge crossed the river just here, we could look under it to the still busier ferry, [they had seen one already by the road bridge] where the punt, crossing every minute, was so crowded with gay dresses and flannels that one might have thought all Staines had been out for an outing.'

In his book *The Historic Thames*, Hilaire Belloc sets the scene of the river at Staines, describing it as 'a boundary between the maritime and the inland part of the river'. The London Stone is a tangible symbol of this, but from here downstream, it is a more serious grown-up river. This is apparent about 2 km downstream at Penton Hook (Exp. 190 045 693) where the river has almost made an oxbow.

Staines. Looking downriver towards the railway bridge. Postcard posted from Staines, August 1919.

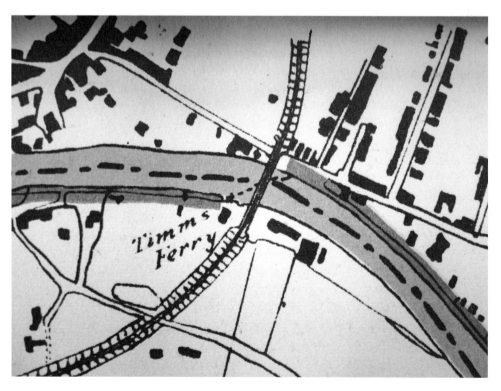

Timms' Ferry marked on the south (right) bank below Staines. From the book of plans produced for the Draft Report published in 1984 for establishing the Thames Path. It allowed for a continuous path along the whole length of the river, to exclude the use of ferries. The plans show the Horse Towing Path on which the new National Trail was based. (Courtesy Gloucestershire Archives)

LALEHAM

Another 0.5 km further downriver is Laleham (Exp. 160 046 685), site of an ancient ferry crossing to the opposite bank in the parish of Chertsey. There was a prehistoric ford here, guarded by an earthwork on the Surrey bank. Spearheads have been found in the bed of the river. The ferry was owned by Chertsey Abbey (founded in 666) about 2 km to the south-west, to which it was connected by Ferry Lane, a straight road across Laleham Burway. It is still a bridleway which crosses the M3 by a bridge. The pasturage on the Burway,[4] formerly an island, is part of the manor of Laleham. An Exchequer deposition of 1696 describes 'the communable customs of this pasture'. For example, the herdsman had a boat separate from the Laleham ferry boat, in which he took the milkers to and fro, although they are sometimes reputed to have waded across.

A well-known legend, *Blanche Heriot and the Curfew Bell of Chertsey*[5] involves Laleham Ferry. During the Wars of the Roses there was a fierce battle at Barnet in April 1471 when Edward IV defeated the Earl of Warwick to regain the crown. One of the Lancastrians fled to Chertsey Abbey where he sought sanctuary close to his lover, Blanche. In the battle he had spared the life of an important Yorkist and was given a ring as a token of gratitude. However, he was captured at the Abbey and sentenced to death the next day at curfew. A friend was dispatched to London with the ring to seek pardon from the King. On his return he was held up at the last moment at Laleham Ferry. Meanwhile, Blanche managed to stop the curfew bell from tolling by climbing the bell tower and hanging on to the clapper. The messenger arrived with the King's pardon just as the soldiers were checking what was happening. There are several versions of this story, which is commemorated by a statue of Blanche Heriot near Chertsey Bridge.

An agreement was made in 1828 between George Hartwell Esq. of Laleham, Middlesex, and Richard Trotter of Chertsey, Surrey, ferryman.[6] Trotter was to take the ferry house and garden together with the ferry across the Thames with all tolls and fixtures, except any trees growing on the premises, for one year and thenceforth from year to year. Trotter was already in occupation. The rent was £25 per quarter with Trotter keeping the premises in good order and paying all taxes.

Laleham Ferry. The ferry boat is being punted across to the ferry house on the Surrey bank. (From Halls' *The Book of the Thames*, 1859)

One special clause was that Trotter shall ferry across, backwards and forwards free of all charges whatsoever, not only George Hartwell, but his heirs, assigns, servants, labourers and workmen, plus whoever shall be in occupation of his premises at Laleham. To provide this service Trotter had to keep boats with some skilful persons constantly on the spot for ferrying other persons too 'who shall require the same and not charge more than the usual and accustomed charge of one penny each going or returning'. Attached to this document is a small 'billet' handwritten and signed only by Trotter. 'Commencing Michaelmas 1841 I agree to be paid £6.50 per annum by the Earl of Lucan in lieu of ferry for the whole of his family … indoors and stable servants and his visitors – his farming bailiff shepherd or man in charge of stock'. Another part dated 11 October 1841 titled 'A Contract for the ferrey' is obviously written by the ferryman himself. 'For the Erl of Luking and Lady and Hall the family and the goviness when they plese to com over – to ferrey the Housekeeper Buttler Trotman Dixson Hedgcock Bowers Gamekeeper And Gorge the Sheppard when on your Lordships Biseness … And the men that coms to work on the medow land to and from theire work from six in the morning and at six at night for the sum of six pound … If the medows is Cut for hay to Be extery charge for the haymakers.' Added in another hand is 'If Trotter is to look after Lord Lucan's boat … he is to be paid £1 a year for so doing'.

The Lucan family had bought land in the area, including the Manors of Laleham and Chertsey at the beginning of the nineteenth century. In 1888 the Third Earl,[7] Field Marshall George Charles Bingham, in charge of the Heavy Brigade in the Crimean War, leased Laleham Ferry to William Harris. The indenture gives the dimensions of the ferry house with garden as 26 perches, with another garden nearby of 1 rood 7 perches. Harris was to take over from Alfred Trotter and to keep all profits running the ferry for twenty-one years at £30 each half year and to pay all taxes and insurance of £200 each year. Once in every three years he was to paint the outside wood and ironwork with two coats of 'good oil colour' also to make good the stucco. Inside whitewash and colour every seven years with the usual colour. The premises were not to be underlet or assigned without the written permission of the lessor, Lord Lucan. Again, he is to ferry all inmates of the lessor's house at Laleham, his visitors and work people free of charge.

Attached to this lease is a letter handwritten a few days later by Lord Lucan to his solicitor H. E. Paine in Chertsey.[8] 'Dear Sir, Everything was settled definitely between me and Harris as I thought I had fully explained to you. If he has foolishly and wrongly taken up the ferry house in an untenable state of repair he has done so at his own risk and at his own responsibility. I had let him the ferry for seven years certain but I undertook to secure him 14 years to cover any repairs he might have to make. I will not allow him one farthing, however may be the roof or the guttering and I do not think the better of him for seeking anything, so specific and precise was my arrangement with him.'

These legal documents were drawn up in October 1888, Harris and Lucan having made an informal agreement in September whereby Harris would pay all legal fees and take over the ferry at Michaelmas 'when Trotter quits'. Nowhere does the condition of the house appear in writing.

Mr Paine received a letter from the solicitor at the General Post Office, London, in October 1890 concerning William Harris.[9] It was the law for the Royal Mail to be taken over a ferry free of toll. This meant that anyone carrying the mail whether by horse or carriage, and since 1869 carrying telegrams, should not pay for going to fetch mail or bringing it back. Harris had been seen by an officer who explained there was a penalty of £5 for non-compliance. Harris persisted in refusing the ferry to a PO Telegraph Messenger without paying toll. The Post Office solicitor asked if Mr Paine as Lord Lucan's solicitor could draw Harris' attention to the matter 'to remove any doubt in his mind upon the point'.

Differences must have been patched up, because the same Earl gave a lease on 25 April 1910 to Joseph Harris, boatbuilder of Laleham[10] of the ferry house and right of ferry plus an osier bed of 9 acres bordering the Thames on the right bank. (This may be the area marked on the latest map as reservoir.) The rent was £70 half yearly, otherwise the terms were the same as previous leases, except for two clauses. J. Harris was allowed to make tennis courts for the use of his customers, besides boathouses and slipways. He may not fell, top or lop any trees, except pollards in the due season. This reflects the increase in pleasure boating from the 1880s until the First World War.

Thacker records a chain ferry being permitted for use in 1867, but in 1911 VCH states it was a punt. While walking in January 1915, Thacker spoke with a fisherman, Arthur Harris, who recalled ferryman Trotter from an old Thames family. The ferry served a useful purpose when the Burway became a famous cricket ground. Some principle laws of the game were settled here, including the width of the bat. Later a golf club was established when George Knight,[11] who was ferryman between 1936 and 1972, took many golfers over for tuppence each way. Among them were Bob Hope and Bing Crosby.

The ferry ran from by the ferry house on the Surrey side, seen in old photographs side-on to the river where teas would be served to visitors. Built in the traditional Georgian style at the beginning of the nineteenth century, it burnt down in the 1990s. A new large house was built on the site in 2004 by a Cheltenham architect using similar features. The name has been kept, but the ferry operates no longer. On the Laleham shore the landing place was straight at the end of the lane to the village, as it turns the corner towards the car park and recreation ground. Now it is a concrete slipway almost hidden by trees, where once it was bare land, as described by Matthew Arnold, born here in 1822 and buried in the churchyard in 1888. The quotation is from *Sohrab and Rustum*.

Laleham. View of the ferry. 1880s. From an album. (Reproduced by Permission of English Heritage)

Through the black tents he pass'd, oe'r that low strand,
And to a hillock came, a little back
From the stream's brink – the spot where first a boat,
Crossing the stream in summer, scrapes the land.

CHERTSEY

From Laleham the Thames Side Road leads to Chertsey Bridge (Exp. 160 055 665). The first bridge was built of timber about 1410. Before that the crossing of the Thames at this point was by ferry, first mentioned in the wardrobe accounts[12] of Edward I in 1299 when 3s was paid to 'Sibille, the ferrywoman of Chertsey' and her six men for wafting the King and his family over the river when they were travelling to Kingston. The ferry was in the gift of the Crown and granted at times as a sinecure to retired members of the Royal Household. In 1340 Edward III gave it to William de Altecar, yeoman of the chamber, for life.[13] A reference was made to the ferry of Redewynd by Chertsey in 1368. John Parker took over the ferry in 1376 in succession to William Debenham. John Palmer and Thomas Armner, two gentlemen of the Chamber received the ferry with 'the barge, boat and all fees' from Richard II in 1395.

Henry IV recognised the necessity of a bridge for the busy road to London, and granted a licence to build one in 1410.[14] Not until 1780 was a new bridge, just upstream of the old one, started, built in stone, and opened in 1785. Although altered several times it is the same bridge today carrying the A375 and listed Grade II.

PHARAOH'S ISLAND

After Chertsey Bridge the river turns in an easterly direction and after several bends comes to Dockett Point. About halfway between that and Shepperton Lock is an ait called Pharaoh's Island (Exp. 160 068 658). From the roadside verge a small rowing boat ferry runs to the island to serve the twenty or so houses there, to which it is the only access. All of them have Egyptian names, like Osiris and Ishta. The island was given to Lord Nelson to use as a fishing retreat, after the Battle of the Nile in 1798. A bell is there to summon the ferry person, but the little boat is already moored on the mainland side. Is it a private ferry? Are there two boats available?

SHEPPERTON-WEYBRIDGE

A few yards further on where the road turns towards Shepperton itself is a ferry still in operation to Weybridge on the Surrey shore (Exp. 160 075 660). However, the ancient ferry, which was held with the manor, was in operation from by Shepperton Church by the fourteenth century or before. Jervoise quotes a mention of a ferry at Scheperton in the Calendar of Inquisitions for 1317, when it was held by John de Bello Campo. It crossed to land on the Surrey side which is now Desborough Island, made when a cut to replace meanders was made in 1935. It was much used in the seventeenth century. Charles Dickens Junior in his *Dictionary of the Thames 1887* suggests there was a former church built on stilts in the river, the debris of which was used when the present church was built in 1614. The Old Ferry House built in the mid-nineteenth century stands in Church Square. Listed Grade II, it is now a bed and breakfast establishment.

Fred S. Thacker gives the circumstances by which there came to be two ferries operating in Shepperton. The lock was opened by the City of London in 1813

Shepperton. Church Ferry. From a print *c.* 1850. (Courtesy of www.old-england.com)

with a lock house beside it. The first lock-keeper was William Hatch, a carpenter from Winston Green, Ditton Marsh, who was paid 28*s* a week. William Downton contacted the Corporation in June 1815, claiming to be the owner of Shepperton Ferry and legally bound to maintain it. He was suffering much reduced income from his Church Ferry because Hatch was providing a ferry from the lock. Hatch was told to desist, but in 1820 he was accused again of depreciating the ancient ferry by 'ferrying over horses etc to the injury of the established ferry'. One George Winch of an influential Shepperton family of barge owners deposed that 'if the ferry at the lock was discontinued it would delay the barges very materially and the horses would be obliged to go a considerable distance round. That ferry is of great public utility and can be used at all times, which the old one cannot; he has himself about twenty horses weekly going over the ferry in the summer and about five in winter.' The Winch family no doubt arranged for the last part of the straight road from the village now called Ferry Lane to be laid out in 1843 to accommodate their own relays of barge horses to take over at the lock.

Hatch was told to keep an account of the horses he wafted over, and not to take any passengers who must still use the original ferry. His wages were increased to 32*s* in 1835 as lock-keeper and ferryman. He was still in employment in 1859 when he was admonished for using bad language and discourteous behaviour, but the next year he was pensioned off at the age of eighty after spending forty-eight years in the job. Purdue, who operated the old ferry, complained in 1861 that the lock ferry was taking passengers, to his loss. A local petition in 1863 asked that the ancient ferry be removed to the lock. The Thames Conservancy agreed, and the parish road was made up as Ferry Lane after the Inclosure Awards. In fact, the Church Ferry did continue and was still running in the mid-1950s, known as Wilsons and charging one penny.

The name of Purdue is noted on the Thames for many generations. In the fifteenth century, Shepperton Ferry was kept by one. The complaint in 1861 is noted. The Old

Bailey Archive records that James Purdue, ferryman using a punt at Shepperton, gave evidence in a court case concerning arson in 1896.[15] George Purdue owned a boatshed by the Church Ferry about 1900 where he offered to take care of clients' boats and house them for the season.

Duntons owned the boatyard and operated the ferry by the lock in the 1920s. They also hired out boats and kept a riverside café, but the lock ferry was closed in 1960. Proposals were made for a footbridge, but came to nothing. Instead, the ferry restarted in 1986, possibly when new owners took over the adjacent boatbuilder's yard. Messrs Nauticalia now own it and run the ferry at regular times by request. A bell is to be rung by potential passengers on each quarter hour. The fare is £1, with more for cycles. Trade is brisk because the ferry is part of the Thames Path, a National Trail. Some children cross the river to attend school in Weybridge. The alternative is a long diversion round by Walton Bridge. Asked what the name of the ferry is, Shepperton or Weybridge, the ferryman answered, 'When I'm here at Shepperton, it's called Weybridge Ferry. In five minutes time when I'm at Weybridge, it's called Shepperton Ferry.'

H. G. Wells in *The War of the Worlds*, 1898, describes the ferry. 'We remained at Weybridge until mid-day and at that hour we found ourselves at the place near Shepperton Lock where the Wey and Thames join. Part of the time we spent helping two old women to pack a little cart. The Wey has a treble mouth and at this point boats are to be hired, and there was a ferry across the river. On the Shepperton side was an inn with a lawn and beyond that the tower of Shepperton Church … rose above the trees.' After this, in chapter twelve, he describes the battle with the martians, who attacked the people who were trying to escape across the ferry.

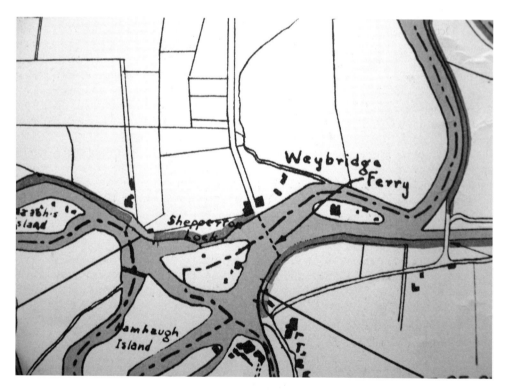

Shepperton-Weybridge. The ferry still operates from the same spot. Plan from the Thames Path Draft Report 1984. (Courtesy Gloucestershire Archives)

CHAPTER TWO
Walton to Kingston

COWAY STAKES

Much controversy has been exercised for at least 200 years about the form, function and actual whereabouts of the area known as Coway or perhaps Causeway Stakes. Undoubtedly, the Thames has changed course in the vicinity of Walton-on-Thames (Exp. 160 094 666) where shoals allowed for shallow water and fording in earlier times. Julius Caesar's account[1] of his conquest of Britain in his second invasion about 54 BC relates how the Britons inserted sharpened stakes into a riverbed to prevent his legions crossing. He does not say where this happened. The common belief among historians was that it was at the ford between what is now Walton and Halliford at a bend in the river, because that was the easiest place to cross above London. They had not considered London itself, across the Kent/Essex marshes, or, what is most likely, Brentford.

Large stakes have been drawn out of the riverbed just above Walton Bridge. Thacker saw one in the British Museum bearing this inscription: 'This stake was on 16th October 1777[2] drawn out of the bottom of the River Thames, in which at least five-sixths of its length were imbedded; it stood with several others which (the water being uncommonly low) were then easily to be seen, about one-third of the river's breadth from its south bank, a quarter of a mile above Walton Bridge.' Archaeological evidence has shown they were made of young oaks and stood four feet apart in two rows across the river. Bede, writing about 800 years after the event said they were cased with lead. Geoffrey of Monmouth said they were put to stop Caesar's boats. Authorities have questioned the age of the wood.

A more likely explanation is derived from the name Coway or Cow Way, being a ford where cattle being driven to or from London would cross the river and the stakes would prevent them from straying from the causeway. (Duxford on the upper Thames, still in use in recent times has marker posts in the water beside the metalled causeway). Additional evidence is supplied by the position of a piece of land called Coway of about nine acres beside the river on the Weybridge side but which is part of the parish of Shepperton. Above Weybridge to the south on St George's Hill, about two miles away from the supposed ford, is a large fortified enclosure which would have sheltered droves of cattle. To clinch the matter, if the stakes were intended to impede the Romans, they would have been planted along, rather than across the river. Coway Stakes used to be marked on old maps but modern maps do not show it, there being nothing to see now.

WALTON FERRY AND BRIDGE

Before the first bridge was built at Walton-on-Thames in 1750, the crossing was made by ford and later ferry, which both belonged to the manor of Shepperton. The road

Walton-on-Thames. The Riverside. The ferry was still remembered when this postcard was produced in the 1950s. The building on the left became the Anglers public house.

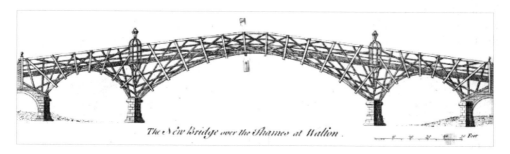

Old Walton Bridge. From a drawing in *The Gentleman's Magazine*, 1750. Designed by William Etheridge, who also designed the Mathematical Bridge at Queen's College, Cambridge, in 1749. (via Wikimedia Commons)

from Gaston Bridge north of the town to Walton Ferry (A244) was made in the Middle Ages. In 1676 Sir William Boreman petitioned for a public horse ferry. The manor was sold in 1741 together with the ferry, which was let then at £17 per annum. Because of the increasing importance of Walton and the ferry being potentially dangerous, a petition for a bridge was presented to Parliament in 1747. An Act providing for a bridge was passed, one clause stating that permission must be obtained first from the owner of Shepperton Ferry. The bridge, designed by William Etheridge and paid for by Samuel Dicker MP, was of a remarkable design. *The Gentleman's Magazine* described it as composed of 'timbers tangent to a circle of one hundred feet diameter'. Known as a mathematical bridge, it was constructed so that any timber if faulty could be taken away and replaced without disturbing the overall structure. Several artists painted it including Canaletto, whose famous painting hangs in the Dulwich Art Gallery. The bridge was taken down in 1783 on the advice of the engineer John Smeaton and a ferry operated until 1788 when a new bridge was built. That collapsed, so a ferry was in service from 1859. The present bridge is the fifth on the site, with another in the planning stage.

SUNBURY-ON-THAMES

The Thames was the mainstay of Sunbury (Exp. 161 106 688) in early times with wharves lining the shore and connected to the main street by short alleys.[3] One ferry which was conveyed with the manor in 1604 was located here and crossed to meadows on the Surrey side to the north of Walton or West Molesey. At the beginning of the twentieth century, it was known as Clarke's ferry after the family who owned it, and operated a large boat with a chain. In the mid-1950s the fare was tuppence, when there were two ferries operating. Trade had long since gone from the river because of silting. After Sunbury weir and lock were constructed, the ferry would cross to the island, then perhaps by footbridge over the lock to the Surrey side.

In 1865 one E. Clark (*sic*) of Sunbury had applied for a piece of land opposite Sunbury Church, which was on Thames Street parallel with the river, to build a boathouse, presumably on Rivermead Island in the middle of the river. Someone called F. Wilson from Chertsey took over as lock-keeper at Sunbury in 1892, and in 1910 he won first prize for the best lock garden between Bray and Teddington. Wilson may have been related to George Wilson[4] who bought the Ferry House and the boatbuilder's business carried on from it. He was succeeded in 1936 by his son George Frederick Wilson who set up the company of George Wilson & Sons (Boatbuilders) Ltd in 1944. He died in 1968 when his son George Sidney Wilson, who was born in the Ferry House in 1933, took over.

Sunbury Locks. From Tombleson's *Views on the Thames and Medway*, 1830s. Steel engraving. The Sunbury Locks are now positioned further downstream.

Sunbury. Site of the ferry, near the weir, photographed from approximately the same point as the engraving of Sunbury Locks. From an album *c.* 1880. (Reproduced by Permission of English Heritage)

Behind the Ferry House, which must have been side-on to the foreshore, was a boathouse and beside them was a strip of land about sixty feet long running down to the Thames from Thames Street. A lorry could have been driven down, but most of it was prone to flooding. All the boatbuilding business was carried on in premises held on lease since 1907 on the island. This land was used for transporting materials across to the island, for storing boats in summer and for mooring against. The Company claimed it had acquired a right to title by possession, although in 1968 they had registered the land as Common Land. An inquiry was held at Guildford by the Commons Commissioner in 1979 when he dismissed the claim. He declared the land was 'an accessway to a public ferry from and to Sunbury to and from the island and possibly beyond to and from the other side of the river'. It was not a part of the Ferry House. His conclusion was that the land 'is land in which the public have, or are reputed to have, some sort of interest as being ferry land and/or available for launching boats'.

Charles Dickens often passed through Sunbury on his way, sometimes by river, to visit friends. He describes the ferry house in an incident in *Oliver Twist* when Bill Sikes is travelling through to commit a burglary at Chertsey. 'As they passed Sunbury Church, the clock struck seven. There was a light in the ferry house window opposite, which streamed across the road, and threw into sombre shadow a dark yew-tree with graves beneath it.'

HAMPTON

Hampton Ferry situated by the church (Exp. 161 141 695) is one of only a few ferries still working above London on the Lower Thames and crosses to what was known as Molesey Hurst, north of West Molesey in Surrey. Although rumoured to date from Domesday, the earliest reference is to Henry VIII, who granted Stert Mill and two ferries from East and West Molesey to Hampton Court and Hampton just upstream

Hampton. The ferry site near the church. Painting by Robert Gallon (1845-1925) reproduced in black and white as a postcard. Gallon specialised in landscapes in oils and painted several scenes on the Thames.

to Sir Thomas Heneage. By Letters Patent of 1585[5] ferries were granted to Elizabeth Crane of Molesey Prior for twenty-one years at a rent of 20s each. Her husband, Anthony Crane, had been the tenant of the Manor of East Molesey. The grant also included Stert Mill.

Both ferries were granted together in the reign of James I to Lady Dorothy, wife of Sir Christopher Edmondes, Lord of the Manor of Molesey Malham. Her tenure was for forty-one years from 1606 at the same rent, but she sublet to three ferrymen, Greensmith, Crane and Budbroke. They passed the lease to Sir John Lytcott, whose widow sold it to Henry Pickering of London. Pickering obtained a new lease in 1646 and sold it to James Clarke.

On the advice of his cousin and counsellor Augustus Henry Fitzroy, Duke of Grafton, and his counsellor Charles Townshend, George III sold his manor of East Molesey in 1767 to Baker John Littlehales Esq. for £1,300.[6] The sale included the mill and 'all that passage over the Thames between West Molesey and Hampton called Hampton Ferry and the boats to the said passage belonging and all customs and profits to the said passage and boats in any wise belonging and appertaining of our manor of East Molesey'. Hampton Court Ferry was also included.

Hampton increased in population after the exodus from London at the time of the Plague, and the Great Fire of 1666, then became a place for commuters who used the river as a highway. Thomas Marling, a banker[7] of the affluent Marling family of Gloucestershire, owned mortgages on many new houses in Hampton when he died in 1884. But the ferry drew most of its custom from transporting passengers over to Molesey Hurst for Hampton races, cricket matches, duels and boxing. The house there was included with the ferry when the manors of East and West Molesey were offered for sale in 1820.[8] The area then became known as Hurst Park. Races were established there in 1892 and continued until recent times. The large punt-like ferry boat could carry up to thirty people a time, propelled by four big ferrymen. It is said that for safety those at the edges of the boat would link arms to prevent anyone falling overboard.

Hampton. The ferry landing is in front of the church, across a busy road. It is still in operation. Postcard sent from Hampton in 1958.

Inevitably others tried to take part in this lucrative business to the detriment of the owner of the ancient ferry. A court case was reported at length in *The Times* on 3 August 1895. Four defendants were likely to be committed to prison for disobeying an injunction granted in 1893 restraining them from ferrying passengers or goods near to the ancient ferry, so as to disturb the plaintiff from his possession and enjoyment of it. When the races were on, other ferrymen would come to Hampton and ply for trade, thus depriving the plaintiff of his profits and forcing him to go to law. At the first hearing there were twenty-eight defendants. Two of them, Benn and Waldock, who owned boats and a boatbuilding yard, came to an agreement with the plaintiff, whereby, despite the injunction, they would be able to carry their friends and business customers in their own boats from their own wharf close to the ferry free of charge. Now the pair had broken that agreement and had ferried people across for hire. The judge said that Benn and Waldock might have adhered to the injunction, but it did not entitle them to carry people back from the south side to the north for payment, which is what they had done. To get around the clause forbidding them to carry anyone for hire, they had hired one of their boats to an employee called Francis, who had used it to convey customers across to the grandstand, the judge considered he would not do this for nothing. On this occasion, Mr Justice Stirling would not imprison them but they had broken the injunction and must pay all the costs of the application.

When Hurst Park Racecourse was closed and housing built there, the ferry was seemingly not needed. Richmond Borough Council offered a lease on Hampton boatyard and the ferry rights. Some local inhabitants set up a Ferry Partnership to keep it open. They acquired an army assault vessel and with an outboard motor fitted, it plies for hire from April to October to a timetable on weekdays, and on demand at weekends. Most of the regulars are commuters, but cyclists, walkers and clients of Hampton pubs also use the ferry.[9] Access is difficult as it is from a busy stretch of road by the church.

TAGG'S ISLAND FERRY

Between Hampton and Hampton Court Bridge is Tagg's Island (Exp. 161 148 688) named after a family who had a boatyard there. Originally called Walnut Tree Island, it was part of the Manor and Honour of Hampton Court. The only access was by ferry from the Middlesex bank. Squatters were cleared from the island in Victorian times by developers and it became a place of entertainment with a hotel. Many famous people were visitors and the history of the island in its heyday provides interesting reading. Not until about 1965 was a bridge of sorts provided and the crossing by ferry was somewhat precarious. 'The ferry used to chug sideways on chains across the river and there were anxious moments when the car had to drive off across a gap'. The Bailey Bridge was replaced in 1982, approached from the A308. To quote L. T. C. Rolt, 'it is a curious psychological fact that no island hotel on the Thames which has had to depend on a ferry, however efficient the ferry service, has ever prospered.' Today the island is a houseboat community.

HAMPTON COURT FERRY

Hampton Court Ferry (Exp. 161 154 684) was in existence, it is thought, in the Middle Ages, but it was not of much importance until Henry VIII took over the court from Cardinal Wolsey and made it into a palace, when the ferry became a valuable means of communication. The King had an African grey parrot that would call ferrymen across the water.[10] The Manor of East Molesey on the Surrey side of the river was leased by the Crown, together with the two ferries to various tenants. A Crown Lease of 1634[11] between Charles I and Edward Sidenham, his paid servant, gives to Sidenham and his wife Anne, in fee-farm (rent charge) lands of the rental annual value of £5,000 for an annuity of £200. The lands were in Datchet Mead in New Windsor, but included 'the ferries of Hampton and Hampton Court and fishing from Cobham Bridge to a place in the Thames abutting upon the parishes of Thames Ditton and East Moulsey'.

By 1667 James Clarke held the Manor of East Molesey together with Hampton Court Ferry. He was a servant to the Crown, holding posts including Chief Clerk of the Kitchen to William and Mary and to Queen Anne. The ferry was to remain in the Clarke family for several generations. The ferries were valuable holdings and the ferrymen worked hard for their wages, about 10s a quarter. One Thomas Taylor[12] at Moulsey had a head servant named Joseph who had jilted Elizabeth Stapleton and was father of her child. Joseph was arrested in 1739.

Lady Mary Clarke was the only daughter of James Clarke and married Sir James Clarke. He was Lord of the Manor and lessee of the ferry, which had been renewed for ninety-nine years in 1677. An interesting collection of letters[13] written by Lady Mary to her legal advisor Samuel Joynes at his chambers at Lamb's Buildings in Middle Temple between 1749 and 1752 gives details of the working of the ferry and the building of a bridge. Her son, James Clarke MP, was then Lord of the Manor.

During the period previous to the passing of the Act, Samuel J. Joynes wrote to Lady Mary on 30 March 1750, 'The Bill has gone through Commons and is now with the Lords.' He enclosed the preamble to the Act. It stated it would be of great benefit to the public in general 'if a bridge were built cross [sic] the River of Thames from Hampton Court … to the opposite shore at East Moulsey.' It goes on to say that there are about twenty-six years left of the lease granted by Letters Patent in 1677. James Clarke was asking His Majesty George II to grant him leave to build a bridge at his own expense. Joynes wrote to Her Ladyship at (West) Drayton on 8 April to explain

Hampton Court Bridge. The first bridge designed by Samuel Stevens and built at the entire expense of James Clarke. It opened in 1753. (Reproduced from a commemorative booklet issued for the opening of three new Thames bridges on 3 July 1933)

that her consent to the Bill was not required. He said that when the subscribers to the bridge had paid he would ensure she had payment. (Was this regarding compensation for the ferry?) In a letter written the day before he said, 'Before the bridge can be built every person interested must have satisfaction made to them and that satisfaction must be secured to the parties now interested in the ferry'.

The Act received Royal Assent on 15 April 1750. James Clarke was allowed to build the bridge of timber and to make roads and bridges leading to it if necessary. During the term of the lease then in force as granted to his grandfather he could charge tolls. When it expired he could try to renew unless the Crown wished to buy the structure from him to make the bridge toll-free. Some Articles of Agreement for the construction exist in Surrey Record Office. The first, dated 15 August 1752 is between Clarke and the two carpenters who were to build the bridge, Samuel Stevens and Benjamin Ludgator. It was a flimsy affair with seven steep arches, rather like a willow-pattern bridge, and opened in December 1753. After twenty-five years it was replaced by another timber bridge on the same site where the ferry was, with The Toye, a famous sixteenth-century tavern, adjoining the south-west corner of the Outer Green Court of the Palace on the Middlesex side.

Tolls were vested in James Clarke forever, but he still kept the ferry rights. Although a document of 1767 states that 'Hampton Court Ferry has been annihilated or disused', there are indications that it continued. Indeed, it would have been necessary when the first bridge was dilapidated and rebuilt. The ferryman had forecast he would not be able to pay £70 for rent once the bridge was built, but somehow the money was found.

Lady Mary had problems with the ferryman. On 10 August 1750[14] she wrote, 'I was so uneasy that Corbett the ferryman had not paid the £50 promised both me and Mr. Johnson [agent] so faithfully to pay before Lady Day. I writ him word that I had heard from you and that you was very uneasy and would not stay longer. He came here soon after Mrs. Kien was gon. I was not at home but he told my daughter that he had been very ill or he had don it according to his promis, but that he would sertainly pay it at michaelmas and the other 50 as soon as ever his father in law [step father?] had sold a house which he was about doing. I think for it would be proper for you to write to him and tell him that he has failed so much in his payment he promised, that you cannot nor will not stay longer, without his father in law will joyn in a security with him to you.

'I believe the man is very honest and industrious but all my fear is as he is in such a state of health he should dye so pray try if you can git better security, for I am vastly uneasy.'

Corbett was still alive when Lady Mary sent again to Joynes on 31 March 1752. 'Mr. Corbit called here the other day but I was not up, he sent me word he had had so bad a time and got so little at the ferry that he hoped I would ??? and then have the whole year together. I send him word I was sorry I could not, but that I must desire him to pay you the half year and that please when you see him to tell him for I have so much to pay I must git in all I can'. Lady Mary Clarke died in 1754, aged sixty-nine.

THAMES DITTON

Very little is known about Thames Ditton Ferry (Exp. 161 162 673), although it is even now marked on maps. Thacker does not mention it, nor do any other books, except to say it was by the Swan Inn in a picturesque village. At the time of Domesday 'Dictun' was owned by the Bishop of Bayeux in Normandy but there seems not to have been a manor. The church dates from the thirteenth century, so does the Swan Inn, now listed Grade I. Perhaps the ferry's main claim to fame is the part played by it in Charles I's escape in 1647 from Hampton Court Palace where he was imprisoned on lenient terms after his defeat by Cromwell's army. Colonel Whalley, Cromwell's cousin, was his gaoler. The King was attended by his own servants, two of whom arranged for the ferry to cross to meet the King, and horses to be ready to take him to nearby Oatlands House, then to the Isle of Wight where he was soon recaptured at Carisbrooke Castle. The Governor there had betrayed him.

The ferry ran to the Hampton Court bank from the present slipway beside the inn. Henry VIII, it is said, was a frequent visitor to the inn, which is testified by his seal of approval in the British Museum. The usual way from London by carriage to the palace was via the High Street at Thames Ditton, then by fording the river at the site of the slipway or, if the tide were up, the ferryman would row over. Usually the King would be brought upriver by boat. To allow for an easier journey apparently he arranged for the river to be straightened, thus creating the three islands now off the Surrey shore. Two of the islands remained part of Middlesex until the local government reorganisation of 1972.

On the smallest, Swan Island, was a ferryman's hut, recently restored. He was kept busy with a dual role, either taking people across the width of the river, or to the largest island, Thames Ditton Island. When trade on the river was at its peak, this was an important shipment point. Many of the Royal Household had houses in the village. One ferryman, Robert Harrison,[15] was prosecuted in 1729 for working the ferry boat, not being a licensed waterman. The same year, a certificate of good repair was given in respect of the highway leading from East Molesey Common to Thames Ditton ferry.

Mary Lloyd in *Sunny Memories*, 1880, recalls how the ferryman was deprived of a fare one day. Towards the end of his life, J. M. W. Turner (1775-1851), who spent much time on the Thames, was staying with a house party at the house in Thames Ditton of the Carrick Moore family. The ladies planned to go over the ferry to visit Hampton Court gardens. Turner, having his boat with him, said, 'I will row you.' There was some difficulty landing on the sedgy bank but the ladies did not mind. He insisted on taking them further on to a more convenient place, 'because,' he said with a shrug, 'none but the brave deserve the fair'.

Thames Ditton. Photograph taken in the 1880s showing a fishing punt. From an album.

Thames Ditton. The Swan, well known to fishermen. The ferry would leave from the steps in the wall. Boyle Farm is the large house on the other side of the slip. (From Halls' *The Book of the Thames*, 1859)

Thames Ditton. The Swan. The landing stage and the busy slip. *c. 1900*.

After several years of negotiation and at Queen Victoria's wish, the Park of Hampton Court was opened to the public, as reported in *The Times* of 8 May 1893. Besides the normal entrance by Kingston Bridge, there was to be a new entrance near Thames Ditton Ferry and another opposite the ferry at Surbiton. People living in the village do not remember the ferry working in their lifetime, except there are a lot of old photographs in Ye Olde Swan.

Thames Ditton Island became popular as a riverside resort for picnics and camping in the early part of the twentieth century.[16] Gradually, it became covered with holiday chalets with private moorings for each. After the suspension bridge was built in 1939 (Pevsner, *Surrey*, puts 1914) more permanent houses were built. All of them had become private freeholds by 1963 when a limited company was set up to administer the island after the owner, the landlord of the Swan, sold it. The company maintains the footbridge, which is private, and provides a ferry when it is closed for repairs. The slipway is also their property, and it may be inferred that the ferry rights rest with the company. In fact it is most probable the ferry has always been the property of the Swan for the seven or more centuries of its existence. Which is why there are no records.

Ferrying on the Thames was a common rural occupation in Middlesex,[17] according to John Norden, surveyor and author of *Speculum Britanniae* in the late sixteenth century. Both fishing and ferrying were secondary products of the county's agriculture. He remarked on the type of person working in those activities. 'Not meddling with the higher sort, I observe this in the meaner and first of such as inhabit near the Thames; they live either by the barge, by the wherry or ferry, by the sculler or by fishing, all which live well and plentifully, and in decent and honest sort relieve their families.' A list of ferries in Middlesex was included with an edict issued in 1659 forbidding ferries to work between sunset and sunrise. They were the larger, more important ferries, like Brentford, Richmond, Twickenham, Hampton Court, Sunbury and Shepperton. Bridges at Kingston and Staines already existed.

There were several ferries in the vicinity of Kingston upon Thames, possibly each on lease from the Crown. Consequently, no deeds exist, or they are not currently available. Long Ditton had a ferry depicted on a postcard in 1911. Maybe it ran in opposition to Thames Ditton Ferry, but the only reminder is a pub called the Ferry.

PARKER'S FERRY

Postcards also exist, posted in the 1900s, of Parker's Ferry at Surbiton. The town, now a suburb of Kingston, was originally called Walford, indicating a ford was replaced by a ferry. Later it was known as Kingston New Town, then by a more apposite name, Kingston-by-the-Railway, after the line from Waterloo to Kingston was opened in 1840. The ferry to Hampton Court Park was only a short walk from the station. It is not clear whether Parkers was a boatyard in its own right or whether it was the same as we know now as Hart's Boat Yard (Exp. 161 175 678).

RAVEN'S AIT

Raven's Ait is a small island opposite Surbiton. The ferry which ran from Harts on the Queen's Promenade did go to the Hampton Court bank and also landed on the island, in ancient times called Raven's Arse. A white motorised ferry can land people on the island now in two minutes for a piece of silver. The place has been much in the news lately, since it was vacated by the Sea Cadets Corps. They were followed by a company who used the premises to hold weddings but they soon went bankrupt. An enterprising group of squatters then set up the Raven's Ait Island Occupation Ecological Community Centre to save the world. They claimed to be setting up an educational facility, which is what the Royal Borough of Kingston Council as owners had promised to do. The public were reminded that the 'man-made' island was common land and had not been registered as such in 1968 by the council. Following Magna Carta, then the death of King John when the barons had invited Prince Louis of France to become king, the Treaty of Kingston was signed on the island on 11 September 1217 by the barons and Prince Louis, who renounced his claim to the English throne. This gave back to English citizens their civil rights. The community claim they are fighting for those rights again. They will go to the High Court.

Meanwhile, the council wish to sell the island for £7 million to a developer for a hotel. Or Ossie Stewart, an Olympic gold medallist who owns Hart's Boatyard, now an extensive restaurant, would set up a school for sailing and canoeing. Whatever the outcome, Raven's Ait Ferry will continue for a time yet. The community did start up their own ferry before they were evicted, but there was opposition because they were not licensed boatmen and there were health and safety issues.

KINGSTON FERRY

A ferry is marked on the maps just upstream of the bridge at Kingston upon Thames almost opposite St Raphael's Church on the Portsmouth Road (Exp. 161 177 685). The bridge is recorded since the thirteenth century, being the first one upstream of London Bridge replacing a ford. Archaeological finds of axe-heads and Roman artefacts suggest a much older date for the bridge, which was defended, and a castle stood nearby. There is no explanation for a ferry here except it may have served the large household at Hampton Court Palace. Also a ferry would have been needed when

Kingston. This little chap is not a crossing sweeper, but a ferry-crossing sweeper. It must have been an important occupation. From an album *c.* 1880.

the bridge was under repair or renewal. Another factor for keeping the ferry was that the bridge was under toll until 1870.

An historical event took place here[18] in February 1554 during the reign of Mary I when Sir Thomas Wyatt roused the 'Men of Kent' to rebellion against the Queen's proposed marriage to King Philip II of Spain. Wyatt was encamped at Southwark in preparation to attack London, but when he heard he was about to be encountered there, he hastily retreated to Kingston to cross the river by the bridge. When the rebels arrived, the townsfolk had broken the bridge, but seeing the ferry boats lying unguarded in the river, he got all his (400) men across during the night and marched on London to attack it from the north. Meanwhile, Mary had appealed to the loyalty of her subjects and had mustered a force of 25,000 men by promising not to marry without the consent of Parliament. Wyatt and his associates were taken prisoner at Temple Bar and sent to the Tower, where they were executed. Four years later, Queen Mary was dead.

In more recent times people cross by ferry for leisure purposes. Pathé News[19] put out a clip in September 1936 featuring Miss Violet Pope, the only woman ferry owner working on the Thames. She had been an actress but gave up to take over her father's ferry. She was rowing a group of children to the paddling beach on the Middlesex bank. At present, the council has plans to enhance the ferry, café and other riverside features on Queen's Promenade to provide a 'recreation hub'.

CHAPTER THREE
Twickenham Ferries

TROWLOCK ISLAND

Above Kingston the Thames was noted for its fishing, and disputes over fishing rights are recorded from Tudor times. Trowlock Island, or Ait, (Exp. 161 178 708) is situated off the left bank at Teddington. It is a thin strip of land about one third of a mile long, separated from the mainland by a narrow channel of water which looks man-made. There is no derivation of the name Trowlock but it could be something to do with fishing. Why else would Mr Norwood of Hampton Wick persist in banking up the entrance of the channel until asked by the City to stop in 1785?

Today the island is home to a community living in twenty-nine small holiday-type houses, mostly wooden.[1] The Royal Canoe Club's headquarters and gym are also here. Trowlock Island Ltd manages the island under the chairmanship of John Bazalgette who is descended from Joseph Bazalgette, the eminent Victorian engineer who was the saviour of the River Thames and London as we know and enjoy them today. As expected, the island has an abundant wildlife.

It is approached from Teddington by Trowlock Way, a lane which runs through the grounds of Teddington School to the water's edge where there is a platform and a unique ferry which is strictly private for the use of the inhabitants. The chain ferry, which replaced a small wooden raft, runs on cables or chains which are connected to both banks of the water channel. It is operated by the passenger turning a handle on the vessel, which is then propelled by winching to the opposite bank. From paying tuppence for this facility, the islanders had to pay £3.77 in the 1970s to the Thames Conservancy. When the Environment Agency took over, they did a survey and demanded £7,000 per annum, asserting that 'the part of the river the ferry crossed was a ransom strip, and that the ferry chain rested on the river bed'. Angered residents said they would go to court, so EA took them to the High Court in January 2006.[2] The judge pronounced both parties should settle out of court, Bazalgette later announced the matter had been settled satisfactorily by negotiation. Trowlock Island Company now charges £200 p.a. service charge per property and provides the ferry, maintenance of the attractive gardens and parkland, which make up half the island, and other services.

TEDDINGTON

Scant evidence is available for the existence of the ferry at Teddington (Exp. 161 167 715), the most obvious indication being the short Ferry Road leading to the river where now two footbridges cross to the island formed by three locks. James Brindley, the canal engineer, made a plan of the river in 1770 which showed the ferry crossing to Ham Fields from beside a mill on the left bank. A lease held at London Metropolitan Archives

Trowlock Island. The private ferry linking the island to the mainland at Teddington. (via http://en.wikipedia.org/wiki/File)

Teddington. Edwardian scene on the river near Teddington Locks. The western suspension footbridge, which crosses the weir stream, can be seen. (Courtesy www.old-england.com)

Teddington. Stone erected in 1908 to mark the upper limit of the Port of London Authority's control of the River Thames. Photo S. W. Rawlings. (Reproduced by Permission of English Heritage)

for properties in Teddington in 1801 includes a messuage and garden called the Ferry House.

Navigation in the Teddington stretch had always given problems, mainly from shifting shoals, so the City obtained permission to build four pound locks, of which Teddington lock was the first. It was built exactly over the line of the ferry. A notice dated 6 June 1811 appeared in *Jackson's Oxford Journal* stating that the lock was completed and would be opened for general use about 20 June. After that it would become dangerous to navigate down the old channel.

The ferry continued until after two more locks were constructed in 1854 and 1857. Then local residents and businesses considered that two footbridges would be more feasible, and they raised subscriptions for an engineer, G. Pooley, to construct them between 1887 and 1889.[3] One is a suspension bridge of elegant design which crosses the weir stream on the west side of the lock island, the other is less attractive, being of girder design, and crosses the lock cut, linking the island with Ham Fields. They both had steep steps up and down, but now wooden ramps have been added for the benefit of cyclists. Even after the footbridges were provided, there was still a clientele for the ferry, which continued to operate from beside the Angler's Inn until about 1950.

It was commonly thought that Teddington meant 'Tide End Town'. The tide does end below the locks now, but before the navigation improvements, it did reach only to Richmond. So that name is disproved, although a pub named Tide End Cottage is in Ferry Road. A stone marking the end of the tideway and the beginning of the jurisdiction of the Port of London Authority is set on the right bank below the locks.

TWICKENHAM

There have been three or perhaps four ferries at Twickenham. The oldest (Exp. 161 167 737) is known to have been in existence in 1659, when it was included in the list of ferries which must not operate during nighttime, but it may have started earlier. The ferry ran from the Middlesex bank just downstream of Eel Pie Island to the extensive Ham House estate on the Surrey side, being the nearest point from Twickenham village to reach the Surrey bank. Ham House was built in 1610 but soon after became the property of the Murray family. William Murray,[4] a 'whipping boy' to King Charles I when Prince of Wales, was created Earl of Dysart in 1643. He was succeeded by his daughter, who was Countess in her own right, being a Scottish title. She married Sir Lionel Tollemache who became the 3rd Earl, and the widespread estates have continued in that family ever since.

Lady Elizabeth Tollemache signed the first document extant linking the ferry with her family in 1692 when she granted a lease of Twickenham Ferry to Richard Blower[5] (1636-95) It enabled him to continue running the ferry at a rent of 40s a year. Blower's family had come to Twickenham about 1600 and were still around 150 years later. His widow took on the ferry until she died in 1704. The 3rd Earl Dysart leased the ferry to Thomas Love, whose wife also took on the ferry when he died until her death in 1744. About this time, a rival ferry started up nearby run by two local men, Treherne and Langley. Elizabeth's son, the 4th Earl, took them to court and was awarded damages of sixpence and sixpence costs against them for trespass. However, in 1746 the widow Margaret Langley and Samuel Kain gave Earl Dysart a bond for £100 in which Margaret recited she had ferried passengers 'as a publick ferry', despite the original ferry being only 100 yards away. She agreed not to do anything to the prejudice of the ancient ferry.

Lord Dysart gave a lease to Thomas Neale, son of a local waterman, in 1746, but withdrew it weeks later. Instead, William Tomlins became the ferryman with 'free liberty to have and keep a ferry boat upon the River Thames between the Town of Twickenham and the Manor of Ham for the passage of all foot passengers and for carrying them to and fro for the usual and accustomed toll rate or price of ½d each passenger'. The lease was renewed until Tomlins' death in 1762.

Teddington Ferry and Eel Pie Island were also in Earl Dysart's interest. Floods cut away part of the towing path near Teddington, so part of his private lands had to be used. For this he charged a toll of threepence per horse. This caused dissension with the barge owners; the towpath changed sides, and in 1809 the engineer John Rennie, in recommending a lock and weir, referred to 'Twickenham horse ferry.' Further trouble came in 1814 when Hector Phelps, who had been ferryman since 1780, started proceedings against a man called Redknap and others who had been ferrying illegally. (A daughter of Richard Blower had married a Benjamin Redknap.) The case was dropped but taken up the next year when an action was brought against Thomas Redknap and Wlliam Turner for infringing Phelps' rights by taking passengers across only 100 yards from his ferry (known as the Dysart Ferry). The defendants happened to be members of the Company of Watermen, who had strict rules about how their members should operate. The Company decided Redknap and Turner were not justified in carrying passengers and agreed to pay compensation to Phelps with his costs.

Demand for the ferry increased as Twickenham and Petersham became affluent with middle- and high-class society moving out of London. Charles Dickens in *Little Dorrit*, 1857, sets a scene in Twickenham. Mr Meagles had a cottage residence of his own there on the road by the river. It was converted from an old brick house, part of which had been pulled down and another part changed into the present cottage and surrounded by a garden and trees and spreading evergreens. There was a conservatory and a pleasant view of the river overlooking the ferry. Dickens reflected on 'the drifting of the boat, so many miles an hour the flowing of the stream, here the rushes, there the lilies, nothing uncertain or unquiet, upon this road that steadily runs away; while you, upon your flowing road of time, are so capricious and distracted.' Arthur Clennam strolled out there on a Saturday, and the next day took the ferry before breakfast for a walk. On his return he met for the first time Henry Gowan, who had just hailed the ferry from the Twickenham side. The ferryman came over without acknowledging the summons. Gowan and his dog got in the boat followed by Clennam, who had taken an instant dislike to them. Gowan stood with his hands in his pockets for the crossing, 'and towered between Clennam and the prospect'.

Following the setting up of the National Trust in 1895, there was increased public interest in the preservation of the countryside, and in particular the need to retain public access to the Thames riverside as new building developments were making this difficult. As a result, in 1902 the Richmond, Petersham & Ham Open Spaces Act was passed, which secured the large open space on the Surrey side. About the same time, the London County Council acquired the Marble Hill estate on the Middlesex side opposite. Visitors to these places found difficulties because coming from Richmond Bridge was inconvenient, and although they could use the Dysart Ferry, it meant a long walk. Here was an ideal opportunity for a rival ferry to be set up.

Meanwhile, the Dysart Ferry was doing well. Thomas Cooper, a large man called 'Gallant Tom the Ferryman', died in March 1891 after holding the post since about 1864. In his stead, the 9th Earl Dysart appointed thirty-five-year-old William James Champion. He was local to Twickenham and had been a watchman on the Dysart estate. The fact he was not a licensed waterman was of no concern as the Watermen & Lightermen Act of 1859 exempted existing ferries. At first, Champion lived in Sion Road, close to the ferry landing, but at the turn of the century Ferry Cottage was built for him on the bank adjoining the slipway. (Ferry House, Twickenham, was a gentleman's residence.)

Twickenham Ferry.

Twickenham Ferry. Landing place on the left bank, at the same site that Dickens knew, although the buildings are different. Postcard posted in London 1911.

Twickenham ferryman William Champion with a passenger and his assistant in the other boat. A Thames lighter with its sweep is in the background. From an album *c.* 1912. (Reproduced by Permission of English Heritage)

The ferry was so popular it had its own parlour song written by Theo Marzial in three verses, published in 1878. The last verse was painted on a board at the side of the cottage.

O hoi-ye, ho ho! you're too late for the ferry
(The briar's in bud, the sun going down),
And he's not rowing quick, and he's not rowing steady,
You'd think 'twas a journey to Twickenham Town,
O hoi and o ho! you may call as you will –
The moon is a-rising o'er Petersham Hill,
And with Love, like a rose in the stern of the wherry,
There's danger in crossing to Twickenham Town. [*sic*]

Champion, though, had a wife who served refreshments, paying rent of £1 a week, from a wooden shelter by the steps on the Surrey bank. The Thames Conservators had granted a licence for the steps on both sides, and for wooden sheds many years before. Trade was so good, Champion had three boats, each carrying twenty, or fifteen or eight passengers. He had 'a strong lad' to work for him, Abraham Moffat, who was paid £1 a week in summer, or 14s in winter. Sometimes another man was called to help. The lease of the ferry was £30 a year, but this may not have included the cottage. On Sundays Champion could take £3-4. His payments into the bank each year averaged £150.

Walter Hammerton (1882-1956) was a licensed waterman, who had won the Kingston Coat and Badge race.[6] An enterprising man, he made an agreement in 1908 with LCC to moor a large, floating boathouse near the Marble Hill towpath for three years, later renewed. He also had punts and skiffs for hire. On the other bank were some steps nearly opposite where Ham Street, which leads from Ham village, ends. A footpath led to the steps across a strip of land bought by Surrey County Council. If

Twickenham ferry landing showing the tea kiosk on the Surrey bank. Postcard, *c.* 1920.

people wanted to hire a boat, they would signal to Hammerton or his partner Samuel Jameson, who would come over to fetch them. Others would pay one penny for this service. Gradually, the business 'gambolled' and Hammerton painted FERRY on the side of the boathouse to be seen from both sides of the river. A flag was displayed and a sign put up at the corner of Richmond and Orleans road, a lane leading to the site, in 1912. The park-keeper at Marble Hill explained, 'if men are playing cricket perhaps wives might ask me the best way to get to the other side because the view is very pretty. Of course, I naturally direct them to this ferry which is nearest.'

Matters gradually grew worse. Hammerton declared he was receiving only about £12 a year in revenue from the ferry, by charging one penny a head. There was a feud between Champion's family and his own. Champion was making disparaging remarks about passengers, calling them 'butterflies and 'peculiar people'. Sunday evenings were particularly upsetting for him when young men would come 'with their pretty girls' and in the rain 'the powder-faced girls' would insist on being ferried immediately. Hammerton rejected offers of compromise from the Earl and prepared for an inevitable court case by selling his house and moving to live on the houseboat to save for the legal fees.

A summons was given and the case[7] Earl of Dysart v. Hammerton & Co. was held in the High Court of Justice, Chancery Division, before Mr Justice Warrington in April 1913, lasting several days. Champion joined the Earl as plaintiff. They claimed to hold an ancient ferry by prescription or by grant, both of which had been lost. Hammerton challenged their right and asserted he was establishing his own rights and those of his customers. He said, 'There is no other safe and convenient place for ladies crossing owing to the present state of Richmond Bridge [meaning increased motor traffic].' The judge put forward three points on which he had to pass judgement. Whether the plaintiffs was entitled to the franchise. If so, was theirs a ferry from 'point to point' or from 'vill to vill'? Thirdly, had the defendants been and were they now disturbing their ferry? As to the first two points the judge had no doubt they were entitled. On the third point he judged the ancient ferry was not being disturbed, in that it had not lost custom by the new ferry. Rather, Hammerton's had not set out to disturb the status quo, but had satisfied a need occasioned by new circumstances, in that an increased population and strangers visiting the public parks had demanded a new service. (Hammerton had claimed the only regular passengers were those going to church on Sundays.)

Before giving his verdict Judge Warrington cited a previous ferry case, that of Newton v. Cubitt in 1862-63 concerning a new ferry at Greenwich, where the definition of a ferry in law is given.

> A ferry exists in respect of persons using a right of way where the line of way is across water. There must be a line of way on land, coming to a landing place on the water's edge, or, where the ferry is from or to a vill or to one or more landing places in the vill. The franchise is established to secure a convenient passage and the exclusive right is given because in an unpopulous place there might not be profit sufficient to maintain the boat, if there was no monopoly. The ferry is unconnected with the occupation of land and exists only in respect of persons using the right of way. The questions whence they come and whither they go are irrelevant to the exercise of that right; and the ferryman has no inchoate right in respect of any of them, unless they come to his passage.

The judge applied this definition to this case by explaining a monopoly was created for the convenience of the public and it would be unreasonable to so extend it as to cause a substantial inconvenience to the public (i.e., to cause them to walk more than

500 yards to the old ferry and return back along the bank). This was new traffic. 'The area for the monopoly of a ferry would depend on the need of the public for passage.' When delivering his verdict the judge said, 'this was an action for nuisance.' But there was no nuisance, so the action was dismissed with costs awarded to the defendants, Hammerton and his sleeping partner, builder T. J. Messom. The plaintiffs managed to gain a legal 'indulgence' stating that a franchise ferry did exist in Twickenham from Point A on the roadside a little below the old town, and Point B at the end of a public footpath crossing a field belonging to Earl Dysart and running into another public highway called Ham Street.

In February 1914 Dysart & Champion went to the Court of Appeal[8] about certain parts of the judgement and this time Hammerton was involved in considerable expense, despite a grant of £100 from LCC. Dysart was still claiming a franchise ferry, and wanted to close down Hammerton, who said it was not one. Two of the three panel judges found in favour of Dysart and ordered Hammerton to pay costs and cease ferrying. But Lord Justice Buckley decided differently, pointing out that a public ferry was a public highway of a different kind, and its terminus must be in a place where the public had rights of way. On the Middlesex bank this was the case, but on the Surrey side the landing was on Dysart land where the public had no rights and never had had them. This meant it could not be an ancient franchise and no evidence of a lost Crown grant existed. Hammerton was now desperate and out of pocket. He wrote down all the circumstances in a batch of eight exercise books, now deposited in the Local Studies collection at Richmond.

Sir John Brunner, a rich chemical manufacturer, was waylaid by Hammerton as he was getting in his car in London.[9] As a result Brunner brought some influential people to a meeting on the barge and they agreed to underwrite the costs of an appeal to the House of Lords. The case was heard over five days in May 1915, with the support of Lord Parmoor of Cliveden. Hammerton's appeal was withheld and costs were awarded to him for this and the previous appeal. He was unsuccessful in finding a publisher for his story, but instead he issued his own song, 'Hammerton's Ferry – the Ferry to Fairyland', meaning Marble Hill Park, selling at tuppence. From then on, Walter Hammerton prospered; he acquired a steam launch, *The Amazon*, designed a lightweight punt and received the freedom of the City of London in 1923.

Both ferries operated fairly successfully for a time, serving people looking for a good day out in the countryside. In 1921 Earl Dysart agreed to lease his ferry and the cottage adjoining to Mr (Percy?) Smoothy.[10] In 1933 they took out a hire purchase agreement together to purchase a new ferry boat. The ferries continued in service during the Second World War, but Smoothy retired in 1946, leaving his son Harold in charge. However, there came great changes in 1948 when the 10th Countess of Dysart and the Tollemache family presented Ham House to the National Trust. It was not their main house, that being Helmingham in Suffolk, where the 6th Earl had given commissions for copying portraits to the young John Constable.[11] Buckminster Estates, the trustees for the family, sold the ferry rights and cottage to Smoothy. It was a declining asset.

By 1961 Harold Smoothy was still in business but it was costing £3,000 a year to run, still at a charge of tuppence a head. He was barely making a living, until in November he became ill. The ferry closed and some people approached the borough council to purchase it, but they would not guarantee to keep it open. Instead, in June 1962 Smoothy sold the ferry to Sidney Cole, a London Docks pilot, the cottage had already been sold separately. Cole ran the ferry giving a full service, using a motor-powered boat specially designed for his daughter Maisie to use. Soon the Coles ran into difficulties; the service was stopped on weekdays due to lack of trade, then it

Twickenham Ferry. The photographer, S. W. Rawlings, is the passenger facing the ferryman. Photo taken possibly in the 1950s. (Reproduced by Permission of English Heritage)

stopped in the winter, which in 1963 was very bad. In 1964 the hut on the Surrey side was vandalised, and not rebuilt.

That year the ferry was bought by David Hastings, a former Admiralty diver. At first he used a glass-fibre boat but then commissioned Gibbs, the Trowlock Island boatbuilder who had built a previous ferry boat, to build a wherry to the old specifications. It was 'a good solid honest job in mahogany and elm, held together with three hundredweights of copper fastenings'. In this he had the privilege of conveying Glenda Jackson as the Queen in the television production of *Elizabeth R*.
Declining trade and a long dispute about the right of way over the slipway on the Twickenham bank led to the closure of the ferry in the late 1970s.

Nevertheless, Hammerton's Ferry continues to this day, in summer only. After the appeal they were left with a deficit of £300, but with sales of the song and a total number of passengers ferried of about 8,000 a year, this was overcome. A purpose-built clinker skiff designed to carry twelve passengers is now deposited in the Museum of Docklands. When Hammerton retired in 1947, he left the ferry in the hands of Sandy Scott. Francis Spencer became owner and the boat used now is a type of landing craft built at Teddington in 1947 named *Peace of Mind*. The nationally designated Thames Path now provides plenty of passengers, paying £1 per head and 50p for bicycles. Service is from 1 February to 31 October between 10 a.m. and dusk. In winter months the ferry operates at weekends only from the boathouse at the end of Orleans Road across to the grounds of Ham House. As ever, there is no means of summoning the ferryman, except by standing on the jetty and signalling. Although the official name is 'Hammerton's Ferry', ironically the signpost to it says, 'Twickenham Ferry'.

Eel Pie Island. Passengers being punted back to the wharf at Twickenham. A lighter is moored beside the wharf. Postcard posted on 13 August 1914 from Twickenham. (The war, then nine days old, was not mentioned.)

Eel Pie Island. Passengers approaching the island on board the steamer *Diamond c.* 1850. Steel engraving. (Courtesy of www.old-england.com)

EEL PIE ISLAND

Eel Pie Island is an ait used primarily for entertainment since at least the seventeenth century. It is situated a short distance from the Middlesex bank opposite Twickenham church. A bowling alley was marked on a map of 1635, and an inn has been an attraction there continuously. Until 1957 when a bridge was put across, the only means of access was by ferry. Annabel Grant Duff, whose father owned York House, one of the large villas on Riverside, describes the situation in the 1870s. 'The old boatman with a wooden leg who took everyone back and forth was a most dreadful old ruffian, but there was no other means of getting across, therefore it was used by all levels of society'.

Steamers in Victorian times would bring holidaying folks to the island to 'banquet upon eel pies for which the tavern is famed'. So when a large, new hotel was built, it was known as 'Eel Pie Hotel'. In the 1950s it attracted many bands and performers, and is said to be the birthplace of British rhythm and blues. Eventually it became outdated and was facing demolition[12] when it was burnt down in 1971. Originally, the vessel used for the ferry was a pole-propelled punt, replaced in the jazz age by a chain mechanism. 'An old man like Charon would haul you across on a chain. After you got off a little old lady would collect your fee from her little hut ... She would stand up to some real monsters to get her tuppence.' This ferry was also owned by the Earls of Dysart.

BUCCLEUGH FERRY

The next ferry downriver towards Richmond Bridge was Buccleugh House Ferry, about which little is known. It was mentioned in the court case, but Earl Dysart was not perturbed by it. Presumably it operated between Cambridge Park on the left bank across to the grounds of Buccleugh House on the right. In the 1770s Richard Owen Cambridge, the man of letters who knew Frederick Prince of Wales, was asked not to allow unlicensed watermen to land on his property. A report appeared in *The Times* in September 1884 on the difficulty for ferry boats at Twickenham because of the accumulation of mud, passengers had to pass over two punts to get into the ferry boat. And opposite the Duke of Buccleugh's it was impossible to work the boats at all.[13] The ferry was marked on the Ordnance Survey map for 1894 and is thought to have operated occasionally until the mid-twentieth century.

CHAPTER FOUR
Richmond to Kew

RICHMOND FERRY

Richmond Bridge (Exp. 161 178 746) was the last of the eighteenth-century bridges to be built over the Lower Thames. The ferry it replaced was so important the Company of Watermen managed to block any proposal until 1773 when the Act for the bridge was passed. Throughout its existence the ferry belonged to the Crown and changed hands by the issue of Crown leases. In certain leases it is described as 'a parccl of land of the ancient possessions of the Crown called Richmond Lands annexed to the Honour of Hampton Court and consisting only of the ferry or passage over the River Thames and the boats thereto belonging without any other buildings or ground save landing places or part of the wastes of His Majestys Manors of Richmond and Twickenham'.[1]

It is possible the ferry started when the King's Manor of Shene, later to become a palace, was developed in the reign of Edward III, for the exclusive use of the king and his household. The earliest documentary evidence is in the State Papers for 27 January 1443 when Henry VI agreed to make a 'grant for life to John Yong for the keeping of a boat and ferry over the water of Thames at Shene Manor … whenever the king or his household tarry at the said manor … as Thomas Tyler sometimes had'. In 1480 Richard Scopeham, 'one of the yeomen of the Crown', was granted the ferry and toll for life, together with 'boats for conveying men, horses, animals and things from the King's Lordship of Shene to the County of Middlesex … provided that nothing shall be taken for conveyance of the King's household,' which suggests it was then a public ferry.

By 1536 the ferryman's position had become more established when, in addition to the profits of the ferry, John Pate by Letters Patent was given a ferry house on the south side of Ferry Hill, now Bridge Street in Richmond. The name of the town of Shene was changed to Richmond by Henry VII in 1499. John Williams of Carnarvon was given a twenty-year lease in 1594 by virtue of his father Thomas 'of the boyling house' who gave 'long and faithful service' to Queen Elizabeth. Thereafter it seems the lease of the ferry became a sinecure for servants of the Crown and they would sublet to a ferryman.

Sir Joseph Ash, MP for Downton, Wilts, who set up the water meadows on the Avon south of Salisbury, took on the residue of five years on the lease from John Glynne, the Lord Chief Justice, and his wife Anne, formerly the wife of Sir Thomas Lawley, in 1657. He then took the lease in his own right for thirty years in 1661[2] at a rent of 13s 4d a year, with £3 increases, and paid a fine. He was to repair, amend and maintain at his own cost two boats, one for horses, the other for carriages. His under-tenant paid him £12 a year but complained that, as Shene Palace was now demolished, the ferry was 'little worth above the charge of attendance and boats'. Ash was not allowed to raise the charge to the public for crossing. When Sir Joseph died in 1687 his widow and executrix[3] Dame Mary Ashe (née Wilson) was allowed to hold the lease until Lady Day 1692, when it expired. Then she would hold it in her own right at a peppercorn rent during the Queen Dowager's life (Katherine of Braganza, wife of Charles II) and thereafter at £3.13.4d per an. An agreement for a sub-let 'of the premises to Charles Osborne and John Knight dated 1678-9 for 99 years terminable on the life of the Queen' was still in hand. Lady Mary died in 1698 and the Queen in 1705, when a new Crown Lease was prepared. This specified a rent of £20 to be paid to the Exchequer each year, and it was to be invested for the benefit of her Majesty Queen Anne.

In 1607 Sir Thomas Gorges obtained a forty-year lease of the Manor of Shene but it excluded the palace, park and the ferry. Sir Joseph's elder daughter married into the Windham family of Felbrigg, Norfolk. The Richmond Ferry lease then carried on in that family. William Windham, who was a sub-tutor to the King's younger son, was given a twenty-one-year lease by George II in 1756, followed by an extension until 1798 two years later. It becomes apparent that he was interested in the ferry only for its business prospects. He applied to the Treasury in 1760 for permission to build a wooden bridge at the site of the ferry.[4] The Surveyor General made a report but the application was refused because of problems with subleasing. Instead, Windham sublet the remaining thirty-eight years to Henry Holland, who hired Joseph King to run the ferry for him and to collect tolls.

The ferry was becoming something of a liability, being outdated. There were now bridges at Putney, Hampton Court, Kew, and Battersea. Richmond Ferry could not cope with increased trade, especially in bad weather. Horace Walpole, who lived at Strawberry Hill, Twickenham, was related by marriage to the Ashe/Windham family. He describes a journey he made in November 1763 in a letter to George Montague. 'I had dined with Sir Richard Lyttleton at Richmond and was forced to return by Kew Bridge for the Thames was swelled so violently that the ferry could not work.' In the following year when in the company of Lady Browne, he chose to risk the ferry rather than the route via Kew Bridge. 'The night was very dark … the bargemen [*sic*] were drunk, the poles would scarce reach the bottom and in five minutes the rapidity of the current turned the barge round and in an instant we were at Isleworth … with much ado they recovered the barge and turned it; but then we ran against the piles of the new bridge, which startled the horses, who began kicking. My Phillis' terrors increased and I thought every minute she would have begun confession. Thank you, you need not be uneasy; in ten minutes we landed very safely and if we had drowned, I am too exact not to have dated my letter from the bottom of the Thames.'

There had been opposition to the bridge, not only from the watermen, but the residents of Richmond did not wish the profits to go to William Windham. Also Henry Holland, his sub-tenant, had his livelihood threatened and petitioned Parliament to prohibit the bridge until he had received compensation. This was granted and he received £5,350 eventually for his interest in the ferry. Joseph King, his employee who occupied the ferry house which he claimed to have rebuilt at his own expense was given £41 5s. Besides his wage and the house, King had retained the small sums paid to him for the passage of troops. Henry Holland's annual income had been £300, after meeting expenses of £250.

Parliament in 1773 passed the 'Act[5] for building a Bridge across the River of Thames, from Richmond, in the County of Surrey, to the opposite shore, in the county of Middlesex and to enable His Majesty to grant the Inheritance of the Ferry at Richmond to certain persons therein mentioned'. The right to operate the ferry passed to the Commissioners of Richmond Bridge by Letters Patent granted by George III in September 1775. They acted on behalf of the inhabitants of Richmond, who had a say on the exact location for the bridge. They favoured Water Lane,[6] the continuation of Red Lion Street which is where the Waterman's Arms, a favourite haunt of watermen since at least 1660, was situated. This was not to be. If Water Lane was used on the Surrey side, it meant a new approach road would be needed on the Middlesex side over land belonging to Twickenham Park House, owned by the Duchess of Newcastle, widow of the Prime Minister. She refused, so the bridge was built more or less on the line of the ferry from the end of Twickenham Road by Cambridge Park to Ferry Hill, renamed Bridge Street, where The King's Head stood on the site of the old Ferry Inn.

Apart from difficulties with land acquisition, the Commissioners had controversy with the Treasury, who on behalf of the Crown demanded a rent of £400, as opposed to the former rent for the ferry crossing of £3 13s 4d. When contested, the Lords of the Treasury agreed to accept the original amount. The Commissioners were empowered to charge tolls on the bridge until the money they had borrowed, plus the interest, was repaid, and a further £5,000 invested for funds with which to repair the bridge. Then it was to become toll free. Actually the bridge was financed by two tontines, and when the last shareholder, an old lady, died in 1859, the tolls were lifted entirely. Previous to that, for a few years, the only charge had been a halfpenny for foot passengers on a Sunday.

While the bridge was being built, the ferry was busier than ever. Richard Prince was employed to run it on contract for one year for £250, out of which he had to pay three men, and one extra for Sundays in summer, and give them board and lodging. The ferry closed in January 1777 when the bridge opened, with tolls charged being the same as the ferry, that is, from one halfpenny for foot passengers to half a crown for a coach and six horses. The largest horse boat and a wherry were then put up for sale.

Even after the much-needed bridge was built, some people regretted the passing of the ferry. George Colman (1732-94), theatre manager and friend of Garrick, had built Northumberland House in 1766, just a few yards above where the bridge was subsequently built. It was said that 'it rises most magnificently to the ferry passengers'. His son, also George, writing of his father in *Random Records*, 1830, said, 'There was a horse ferry across the Thames, and the boat in motion, wafting over passengers, carriages and cattle, was a particularly picturesque object when viewed from his grounds; this was at last superseded by a bridge, and if any friend condoled with him on the loss of the ferry boat he was sure to say "Sir, you could not put a higgler's cart into it, that it did not become beautiful".'

ST MARGARETS FERRY

Twickenham became a large borough and expanded eastwards to cover Twickenham Park, planned as a garden suburb in 1852 becoming known as St Margarets. Dickens lived there and got to know the river well, so did J. M. W. Turner, who built Solus Lodge in Sandycombe Road close by for his father. A ferry was established, presumably as a horse ferry where the horse towing path would cross over. In 1884 it was described as a waterman's ferry,[7] something along the lines of a taxi rank, and up to sixteen ferry boats were plying for hire from here. This practice had been carried on in London for centuries whereby passengers could travel between riverside stairs. As the only reason to cross the river directly would be to reach Richmond Park, this seems to be a more likely reason for the ferry's existence.

Originally, St Margarets Ferry (Exp. 161 171 748) was at a point where the Twickenham Road Bridge, A316, now crosses the river. In 1888 one Mr Percy applied to the Board of Trade to build a causeway at his premises at St Margarets Ferry, Isleworth.[8] It was a substantial construction extending down from high-water mark by steps to the foreshore and then running along just above low-water stilts into the river. The Board gave permission under powers vested in them by the Thames Conservancy

St Margarets, Twickenham, is connected to Richmond now by a bridge carrying the A316 road, seen in the far distance of this photograph. A tank landing craft left over from the D-Day landings is trying to reach Richmond in 1946. The craft was purchased by Richmond Canoe Club, who sailed it from Lowestoft, taking sixty hours. Masts had to be cut away in order to clear some Thames bridges but it was still too big for Richmond Bridge. Here the craft is being turned to return downriver to Isleworth where it was then moored. The Southern Railway Bridge is just before the road bridge.

Act 1857. On the plan are some disused steps and the existing landing stage, which is shown to be further back and smaller than its replacement. The road bridge was opened in 1933, primarily for motor traffic. The ferry continued to run, presumably for visitors to the leisure facilities of Richmond, from a point just a little downriver from the bridge. It is marked on a large-scale London Street Atlas dated 1991.

RAILSHEAD FERRY

There were two cross-river ferries at Isleworth, both still marked on the same atlas and separated by Isleworth Ait in the western bend of the river. Railshead Ferry (Exp. 161 167 754) was upriver, nearer to Richmond at the southern extremity of Isleworth. It was reputed to be an ancient landing place, but the derivation of its name is obscure. It could have something to do with boatbuilding, but not railways, as it existed before they were built. Some authorities believe it was so named because of a weir built there with renewable stakes in the riverbed at the upper end.[9] Charles II in 1670 gave £50 to 'Baker, Justice of the Peace for Middlesex' towards the cost of erecting a brick bridge 'at a place called the Rails Head, Thistleworth, [*sic*] on the way to Richmond ferry'.

Railshead Ferry, Isleworth. Lithograph by J. M. W. Turner entitled *Watercress Gatherers* from his *Liber Studiorum*, 1819. The River Crane is in the foreground, with the Thames beyond.

Railshead Ferry was described as picturesque by Mr and Mrs Hall in *The Book of the Thames*, 1859.

The bridge can be seen in the lithograph by Turner, it would have spanned the River Crane which joins the Thames at this point (by Maria Grey College). George III established the ferry possibly for his own use as he was very fond of his properties at Richmond and Kew on the Surrey side.

Thacker quotes that, up to 1773-74, 'the towing path on the Surrey side ended exactly opposite the Railshead Ferry; here the men who had towed from Barnes or Putney were taken off, and returned to the place they had started from, while others on the opposite bank drew the barges up as far as the Ait at Twickenham. Here the path again commenced on the Surrey side'. When the horse towing path was made, it would have used the same principle, making the ferry an important link in the chain. After Richmond Bridge opened in 1780, the towing path was constructed on the right bank instead.

Rails Head Ferry was mentioned in a case brought at the Old Bailey in July 1807.[10] Three felons were accused of stealing fifteen sacks of malt from a barge moored opposite the owner's house at Richmond. He and a lighterman took a boat and went downstream to Rails Head Ferry where they landed and found cart and horseshoe marks and even forty grains of malt on the ground in the Shoulder of Mutton field. After making enquiries of watchmen, they went to the houses of the men and found the sacks in one of them. The three were found guilty.

Despite being shown on a modern map, some say the ferry stopped about 1945, but Railshead Road still leads to the river from Richmond Road.

Railshead Ferry by H. W. Taunt, *c.* 1890. A passenger is waiting on the Surrey bank. Isleworth Ait is to the right. On the opposite bank is an elaborate boathouse in the grounds of Isleworth House. (Reproduced by Permission of English Heritage)

ISLEWORTH CHURCH FERRY

There was a lane running from Richmond Green through the Old Deer Park to the landing place for Isleworth Ferry opposite, but it was closed in 1774. The ferry (Exp. 161 168 761) is sometimes called Church Ferry, from All Saints church on the corner where Park Road joins Church Street, Isleworth or Syon Ferry, as it borders Syon Park. The first written record[11] for the ferry was in the reign of Henry VIII when it was for pedestrians only, although a horse ferry was operating nearby, and possibly in conjunction with it later.

Although no documentary evidence for the ferry still exists, archaeological finds indicate the crossing was established in prehistoric times. Some artefacts and coins suggest Isleworth was a trading centre of some importance, particularly when a gold Bronze Age torc was found in the river in 1467. Roman coins have also been found. The manor was held by Syon Abbey, founded in 1415, one of the largest and richest in the country. The core of the village of Old Isleworth was within the precincts of the monastery, a House of Brigittine nuns.[12] The cellaress had charge of paying servants and supervising the heavy work to be done; also her responsibility were the boats serving the ferry crossing. There was a Charterhouse establishment across the river at what is now Kew Observatory. As it was usual in this country for ferries to be started by and under the jurisdiction of monastic houses at least until the Reformation, it is fair to assume this ferry had the same origins.

Carl Philipp Moritz, a German pastor, disembarked at Dartford in 1782 for a tour of England on foot. He was delighted with the Thames, comparing it very favourably

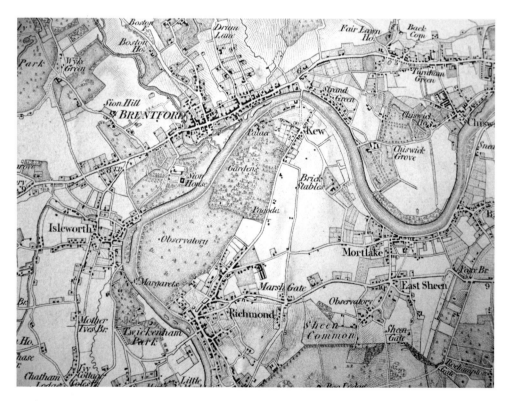

Ordnance Survey First Edition map 1828 showing the stretch of the River Thames between Richmond and Kew. Ferries were not marked.

The Ferry   Isleworth.

Church Ferry, Isleworth. The landing place was at the wharf; the ferry crossed to the Old
Deer Park. The tip of Isleworth Ait is seen on the left by a marker post. Postcard.

with his own river, the Elbe. Finding himself at Richmond, he took a walk over the
bridge, paying one penny each way, and then along the riverside. He was so charmed
by the place, he called it 'Elysium'. The next day, 22 June, he set off for Oxford with
his host's little son to show him the way. They 'walked along a very pleasant footway
by the side of the Thames; where close to my right lay the king's garden. On the
opposite bank of the Thames was Isleworth, a spot that seemed to be distinguished by
some elegant gentlemen's country-seats and gardens. Here I was obliged to ferry the
river, in order to get into the Oxford road, which also leads to Windsor.'

Some other travellers had arrived in Isleworth in September 1717 from Richmond
in less happy circumstances.[13] Six gentlemen had been drinking together in a friendly
manner at the Red Lion Tavern in Richmond. When it grew late, they became worried
they would not be able to get passage over the river, for three of them to get back to
Isleworth, but one Samuel Cook said that was no problem because he was known to
the ferryman at Richmond. So they stayed until 11 p.m. before going down to the
ferry. However, the ferryman had gone to bed, and although Cook gave his name, they
were kept waiting half an hour. When the ferryman came, he denied he knew Mr Cook
but permitted his boy to take them over for a shilling. After they landed and were
walking towards Istleworth [*sic*], William Rutton remarked he was 'glad they had
gotten over the ferry although they had so much trouble about it'. Thomas Heath, the
other man, agreed, but added, 'those ferrymen were surly fellows, and knew no body
at that time of night without money.' At that, Mr Cook, who was feeling aggrieved at
the lack of respect he had been given, said the fellow deserved a shilling, and Heath
agreed but stated they should not have had to wait so long on the shore to make the
bargain. At this, Cook got very angry and tried to draw his sword, but was stopped by
Rutton, who then went on in front. When he heard the clashing of swords he turned
back to find Cook lying injured. Heath had drawn his sword to defend himself against
his friend, who was obviously drunk. Meanwhile, some watermen who were night
fishing heard the conversation and the clashing and came over to help. The injured
man was put in the boat and taken to the Coffee House at Istleworth where he was

laid on the watermen's tilts and cushions. A surgeon was sent for, then another, but they could do nothing about the wound to the abdomen. Heath tended his friend tenderly and was duly sorry. While he was dying, Cook said he forgave Heath and entreated that he should not be prosecuted, but he died the next day. The case was heard at the Old Bailey when Heath was found part guilty of manslaughter, and punished with branding.

Some deeds for the Ferry House at Isleworth exist among the papers of the Cooper family of Isleworth House, now renamed Nazareth House.[14] Ferry House is large and prestigious close to the river but apparently was not connected with the actual ferry. J. M. W. Turner[15] took a short lease on Syon Ferry House while he was waiting for his Twickenham house to be finished. He knew the area well, having spent much of his boyhood with relatives at Brentford one mile downstream. 'He was a child of the Thames.' Turner's boat that he bought was like a Thames wherry used by watermen. It was clinker-built, with a raking stem and a broad stern with a sail, perhaps orange, and was called *The Owner's Delight* or perhaps *Argo*. From it he sketched scenery, boats and sometimes people. His *Isleworth Sketchbooks* are deposited in the British Museum and include one delicate sketch of a horse ferry.

The ferry closed when war broke out in 1939 and reopened for weekends when it ended in 1945, closing finally in 1970. Visitors are still attracted to the waterside where vestiges of the ferry can still be seen. The stone embankment for the wharf is in place and the old ferry slipway is popular with fishermen and boaters. Nearby, The London Apprentice in Church Street overlooking the river remains a Mecca. It dates from Tudor times, deriving its name from the City of London apprentices who would row out here to celebrate achieving journeyman status. Whether they were just from the Company of Watermen is not known. There are other explanations. A major renovation in 1905 gave the inn an extension[16] at first floor level, a glazed veranda said to have come from an eighteenth-century building. It looks remarkably like one which was part of a tavern by Gravesend Ferry, shown in a Tissot painting. For the benefit of river travellers, the inn used to stay open all night.

As part of a Thames Landscape Strategy, a firm of landscape architects made a survey of a twelve-mile stretch of the river from Hampton to Kew. A report was published in 1994 giving brief details of the history of the area, a landscape character study and a vision for the future. Some of their proposals have been implemented but not this one: 'If the ferry was re-instated, it would provide a popular connection across to the Surrey bank and Kew Gardens.' The next week, following publication of the report, *The Independent*[17] announced 'Ancient ferry rights up for auction'. It was being offered for sale by receivers acting for the property group Speyhawk, which had obtained the rights when building an office block at Old Isleworth ten years before. Included in the sale was the right to use steps at landing places on both sides of the river and a small piece of land on the Isleworth bank but no boats. The property title refers only to a conveyance dated 6 January 1887 signed by a Commissioner of HM Woods, Forests & Land Revenues. To promote the sale, the auctioneer said, 'There aren't many of these crossings on the market. The scarcity makes them more appealing and there might be a commercial element.' No, crossings do not come on the market at all.

BRENTFORD FERRY

Brentford grew up where there was a ford over the River Brent, which enters the Thames at this point (Exp. 161 182 774). There might also have been a Thames ford, as many historians believe this is where Julius Caesar came in pursuit of

Cassivellannus. Saxon spearheads have been found in the riverbed, and close by, in what are now grounds of Syon Park, King Edmund fought one of his battles with Canute in 1016. The town was known as Oldebrayneford in the sixteenth century. The site was later covered by Brentford Dock and the Brentford Cut, which formed the entrance to the Grand Junction Canal from the Thames. The waterfront has been cut into by water channels for centuries, with docks, wharves and industrial buildings all making it difficult to determine the exact location of the ferry or ferries. In fact, the present-day Thames Path (north) has to divert along the High Street to avoid all the inlets.

In living memory, and indeed on the first edition Ordnance Survey map of 1867, the ferry ran from a point just below where the Brent/Grand Union Canal enters the Thames to the Brentford Gate entrance to Kew Gardens where the car park is now. Ferry Road and Ferry Square are both in the vicinity. The Crown always held the ferry as a monopoly and granted leases to the royal servants and favourites. Inhabitants of Brentford[18] claimed they and strangers had enjoyed free passage over the river in their own boats since 'time out of mind'. They complained when one John Hale tried to charge them in December 1536, claiming he had a life grant of the monopoly of Cao (Kew) Ferry from Henry VIII. He said, 'I will suffer no man to passe with any manner of boote but only in his boote, exactyng a certain some for every passage for every horse and man a halfpenny and for every man woman and chylde one farthing.' Hale imprisoned Richard Cockyng for using a ferry boat 'to the great unquyetnes vexacon and troble of your beseechers'. The inhabitants asked the Duke of Norfolk to intervene, 'onles your beseechers shulde resyste the said John whereby manslaughter and other damiges and inconvenyences myght insue.' Hale stuck to his ground, maintaining that the King and his progenitors had habitually granted the ferry to their subjects. He had been granted it by Letters Patent and was working it according to old custom and was the only one left to carry horses and vehicles. No charge of manslaughter is yet found.

Another ferry was started sometime a little further downstream, possibly near where Ealing Road joins the High Street, opposite Lot's Ait. Whether this was a rival, cheaper ferry or a horse ferry working in conjunction with the original is not known. In 1605 James I[19] granted Kew Ferry, also known as King's Ferry, to George Hickman, this was later superseded by Kew Bridge. Therefore there were three ferries in a short distance and documents are confusing on the whereabouts of each one.

The press-gang was in force in 1689 when Henry and Joseph Parker and Marmaduke Greenaway were given a protection order against impressment because of 'their service being absolutely necessary for working the ferry boats between Brentford and Kew'. This was renewed by William III in 1694 when the recipients were William Rose and Greenaway.

Frederick Prince of Wales, father of George III, lived at the White House at Kew, very close to the ferry landing place. He and his household used the ferry to Brentford almost every day thus providing the ferryman with a sizeable income. An account book labelled 'Waft book', for the years 1734-37, exists and shows detailed entries. Waft (pronounced woft) is an old word with many meanings, one of which is 'to convey safely by water, to carry over or across a river or sea.' Usually applied to matters relating to the sea, it was used in the eighteenth and nineteenth centuries to describe ferrying, possibly by sail.

By 1751 Brentford Ferry was getting too busy and perhaps not very safe, situated as it was on a bend of the river where the narrow old channel on the Middlesex side of Brentford Ait rejoined the main river. One mishap is recorded. A coach and four belonging to Mr Latwood of Brentford Butts was being taken across by the coachman when the horses took fright and leapt into the water with the coach. The coachman

Brentford Ferry Waft Book shows entries on account for a week in July 1737, including those for the Prince of Wales. (Courtesy the Thomas Layton Museum Trust (Hounslow Library))

jumped free, there were no passengers, but two horses drowned. Often accidents happened, especially when the ferrymen were drunk. The ferry was not the only hazard because the inn at Brentford was a favourite place for highwaymen to shelter. If necessary, they could escape quickly by ferry.

Despite competition from another ferry just downstream, Brentford Ferry continued until 1939, long after Kew Bridge opened and took away income. There was a substantial Ferry Hotel at the landing with steps and mooring on the steep slope to the river. Hansard, for 26 July 1939, records a written answer from the Minister of Transport to an MP who had asked about the 'proposed closing of the Brentford-Kew ferry; will he consult with the local authorities in the area and take such steps as will preserve this historic and useful facility for crossing the river; and will he make a grant for this purpose?' The Minister replied, 'I understand the ferry ... is a row-boat ferry, operated under private ownership, and that it is unlicensed by the Port of London Authority ... I will make inquiries'. The last ferryman, Charlie Humphries, rowed across shortly afterwards. It was uneconomic.

The Thames Landscape Strategy, in a draft report issued in May 2009, draws attention to the potential for enhancement of Brentford's waterside. Considering it is opposite Kew Gardens, a World Heritage site, there should be scope to further develop 'Arcadian Thames – the countryside in the city'. The ferry should be restored or a footbridge provided at Ferry Quay to Brentford Gate, which was specially constructed about 1847 to give a pleasant access to the gardens, now the car park. From there a 'figure of eight' walk could be established through the Old Deer Park and linked to the gardens.

The Tunstalls was a family to be reckoned with in Brentford and Kew for several generations. Tunstall Walk near the Brentford waterside commemorates them. By 1659, during the time of the Commonwealth, Henry and Robert Tunstall had set up a rival horse ferry to that at Kew. There were some limekilns on the Middlesex side and initially they obtained permission to transport lime from a new kiln along the river. Gradually they took on other business as well, including taking passengers, and they advertised accordingly. A lease for a year dated 16 March 1703 gives three parties, Robert Tunstall, a cooper, and Thomas, his son, being two of them. The lease referred to a freehold messuage lately in the tenure of Tunstall senior with three cottages, 6 acres of land and 1 acre of pasture, called the Hallowes (The Hollows), Old Brentford. Also included was a limekiln, barn, stable, wharfs, ferry and ferry house, gardens, yards and other buildings. When the Tunstalls were brought to court[20] they pleaded through witnesses that the old ferry was very dangerous at the time of high water or in a south-west gale There had been two drownings and a ferryman with a load of wheat had also drowned. Sometimes, they said, passengers had to wait an hour at the old ferry. One deponent said whenever he wanted to return home from the Surrey bank, the ferryman refused to take a single passenger, and he was forced to sleep in the open air at Kew all night! Furthermore, the old ferry charged 18d for wafting over a laden brewer's dray with two horses, whereas their ferry (presumably the lime-kiln ferry) would charge only 8d, and bring the dray back over free of charge.

KEW OR KING'S FERRY

Kew or King's Ferry worked more or less where the present Kew Bridge stands (Exp. 161 190 779). It was granted in 1605 by James I to Walter Hickman. Charles I issued a perpetual patent to Basill Nicoll[21] and John Sampson for Kew ferry. They were likely the immediate predecessors of John Churchman Esq., the man who brought the order against the Tunstalls and Henry Dible, their servant, an old man who had previously worked for Churchman[22] as ferryman. The depositions were written on a very long roll of parchment. The reason for the charge was that it was believed the annual value of what was now known as Powell's Ferry would be reduced from £50 to less than £30 (with an annual fee-farm rent of 13s 4d paid to the King) if the rival ferry was allowed to continue, but continue it did. In the edict about ferries not working between sunrise and sunset issued the same year, 1659, Lymekilne in Brentford was included.

Thacker notes the names of two men who gave evidence, one Messenger, a waterman, and Robert Cromwell, a yeoman of Ealing, aged sixty-four. He goes on to say he believed the Tunstalls bought out Churchman because 130 years later he noted the father of a Robert Tunstall as being the proprietor of the old ferry 'known of old time as Powell's ferry' (this name had died out of local memory by 1911 when he was writing his book). So the Tunstalls owned two ferries and sought to replace them with a bridge, not intending to offer compensation to other ferry owners.

An Act was passed for raising a bridge on the line of the Limekiln Ferry in June 1757 and was built in wood and stone soon after by a tontine. It opened in 1759, slightly early because the future George III and his mother wished to pass over instead of taking the ferry. For this concession Robert Tunstall as proprietor received £200 and the workmen 20 guineas. Not being of good construction, the bridge needed major repairs in 1774, lasting two years. The bargemen and inhabitants desired a new bridge to be erected on the site of the King's Ferry. An Act was obtained quickly and the second bridge, of stone, was built by another Robert Tunstall in 1789. It was a toll bridge, which meant that some people preferred the ferry, and watermen continued to ply their 'immemorial custom' in the area for some time, possibly from The Hollows, an area of land against the northern abutments, although the regular ferries had closed. The Tunstalls owned the bridge until it was sold to T. Robinson in 1819. A new bridge was built for Middlesex and Surrey Councils in 1903.

Strand-on-the-Green, a hamlet on the downriver side of Kew Bridge. The Bull's Head was frequented by bargemen and watermen. It is said the song 'Rule Britannia' was written here. Photo S. W. Rawlings, from an album. (Reproduced by Permission of English Heritage)

STRAND-ON-THE-GREEN/OLIVERS ISLAND

Strand-on-the-Green is a small settlement just below the northern abutment of Kew Bridge on the downriver side. Actually it is part of Chiswick (Exp. 161 192 778). The picturesque houses and cottages along the waterfront were built for watermen and fishermen. In times past there was a ferry to the Surrey bank, possibly to reach the towpath, but the only evidence for it left, according to Thacker, is a dug-out canoe which was dredged up on the right bank and thought to be a ferry boat.

Olivers Island, in the river close to Strand-on-the-Green, was used by the City for collecting tolls from 1778 when they bought it for 60 guineas. Repairs to weir tackle were also carried out here. The Lord Mayor's state barge house was in the vicinity, but was pulled down about 1916. The barge was used annually in the Lord Mayor's Procession on the Thames until the Thames Conservators took over jurisdiction of the river in 1857 and the procession took to the streets.

CHAPTER FIVE
Watermen of the Thames

Along the course of the River Thames through the City of London and its immediate outskirts and ever-growing suburbs, there were few designated ferry crossing places. Instead, a unique system of ferrying by private watermen in their own boats was in operation for centuries. The river was a highway. Like today's taxis, boats could be called at any point from either bank, although watermen had to be registered for particular plying places, like taxi ranks. As their numbers grew, the watermen became more aggressive and unruly. A governing body was needed.

The Company of Watermen of the River Thames was incorporated by an Act of Parliament[1] in 1555 during the reign of Philip and Mary, the only City of London Guild extant to have been formed thus. It is not a livery guild. However, the Act was to both confirm old and to introduce new rules and regulations for the better governing of the disparate body of watermen on the river, which was for centuries the main highway for the city. In 1197, when the Lord Mayor and Corporation of the City of London first became Conservators of the river, they introduced a form of licensing for passenger boats. Henry VIII in 1514 gave licences to watermen which allowed them exclusive rights to carry passengers on the river. From this it seems the first Royal Navy was formed, for in time of war the watermen were the first able-bodied men to be impressed. They tried to shake off this yoke, with the aid of the Company, for hundreds of years.

Humphrey Humpherus, who was a Clerk to the Company from 1849 to 1882, wrote their definitive history, beginning with the licence of 1514. *The History of the Origin and Progress of the Company of Watermen and Lightermen of the River Thames, with numerous historical notes, 1514-1859* was published in three volumes in 1887. Some records were burnt in the Great Fire of London; only three record books survived. Humpherus goes through the surviving records year by year, noting significant events, notably alterations to the constitution of the Company, new rules for watermen, and short entries about ferries, usually giving the first date they were documented.

By the Act of 1555 it was laid down that only licensed watermen could ply on the Thames between Windsor and Gravesend. In order to curb the large number of accidents, only qualified watermen were allowed to be in charge of a boat. They had to serve a seven-year apprenticeship and gain complete knowledge of all the complex currents and tides of the river. Like today's taxi drivers, they had to teach themselves the 'knowledge' of all the plying places, creeks and stairs and how they were navigated. After apprenticeship the watermen became freemen and were required to pay quarterly contributions to the Company. The Lord Mayor and Aldermen had jurisdiction over the watermen and each year they chose eight of the 'best sort' to act as Rulers to enforce regulations.

At various times the Watermen's Company exercised considerable influence over different affairs of the river. In the time of Shakespeare, when playhouses on the south

The Coat of Arms of the Company of Watermen and Lightermen emblazoned on a silver arm badge worn by Nick Beasley, a Thames Free Waterman.

bank were very popular, the watermen derived most of their trade from ferrying playgoers over the river, London Bridge being the only alternative way of crossing. Proposals were made to open playhouses elsewhere, and in 1586 the Company violently opposed the measure as being against their interests. Many times when plans for bridges were projected, they would be thwarted by the watermen, who eventually, when the bridge was built, would gain considerable compensation.

On 18 September 1585 the Watermen's Company received their coat of arms. It was granted by patent of Robert Cooke Clarenceaux with crest and supporters to 'the overseers and rulers of watermen'. To quote from Humpherus,[2] the 'Arms are barry wavy of six argent and azure, a boat, or, on a chief of the second pair of oars saltire ways of the third between two cushions of the first the crest on hand proper holding an oar as the former, the supporters two dolphins proper, the motto "At Command of our Superiors"'. The ordinances performed the function of a charter, which was not granted until 1827. The coat of arms was adapted as an armband badge for the Free Watermen, incorporating their individual licence number, to put on their sleeve. One on display in the London Transport Museum is 110 mm wide and 122 mm in height.

If the watermen wanted a patron saint they would choose the Blessed John Roche. He was a waterman of Irish descent who in Queen Elizabeth's reign was befriended by one Margaret Ward. She, like John, was a Catholic, and when she heard of a priest, Father William Watson, being tormented in Bridewell prison, hatched a plot to free him. First she became friendly with the gaoler's wife and managed to smuggle a rope to the prisoner. Bridewell was on the banks of the River Fleet before it was canalised underground; Bridewell Place off Bridge Street, leading to Blackfriars Bridge from the north, marks the precinct in which the prison stood. It is just before the Fleet enters the Thames. John Roche waited in his boat below the prison wall and when the priest descended on the rope they both exchanged clothes. It happened that the priest escaped but John and Margaret were arrested. Margaret was flogged, then she and John were hanged on 30 August 1588 at Tyburn. John had refused to become a Protestant and ask for Queen Elizabeth's pardon.

The Blessed John Roche and the Blessed Margaret Ward were beatified in 1929 by Pope Pius XI. She was made a saint in 1970. John became a patron of sailors, mariners and boatmen. They are both commemorated by being included in the group of almost life-size statues of English martyrs erected in 1962-64 in the nave of the church of St Etheldreda in Ely Place, Holborn, and stand opposite each other. (A pilgrimage is recommended.)

Major changes to the constitution were made in 1642, when after much deliberation the watermen achieved more democracy by shaking off the influence of the Mayor and Aldermen. Now watermen from the fifty-five 'leading towns and stairs' would choose each year their own representatives, who in turn proposed candidates to become Company Rulers. They all sat in Company Hall to make regulations 'for the better government of the Company'. One rule made for watermen at this time was that none of them were to 'bring over in their boats any such vagrants or beggars into this City or adjacent parts on this side the water'.

Samuel Pepys, in his capacity as secretary to the Navy Board frequently 'took oars' to Greenwich, Deptford, Woolwich and Gravesend on business. On 13 July 1665 he had to go by night, 'There being no oares to carry me, I was fain to call a Sculler that had a gentleman already in it; and he proved a man of love to Musique and he and I sung together the way down – with great pleasure'. Not long afterwards, on 14 September, when the plague was raging all round the city, Pepys was not so happy. He heard that Payne, his waterman, had buried a child, and was dying himself and 'one of my own watermen, that carried me daily, fell sick as soon as he had landed me on Friday morning last … is now dead of the plague'. A year later, in 1666, London was

Waterman taking passengers on board his wherry at the Sunday ferry at the Red House, Battersea. Detail from print by W. J. Callcott. *c.* 1840.

struck by the Great Fire, which although a disaster for many, proved to be profitable to the watermen.[3] 'The fire was the wherrymen's harvest time.' Humpherus gives a graphic description of the events of three days and three nights at the beginning of September. 'Everyone was endeavouring to remove their goods and furniture and those having property on the riverbanks, flinging it into boats and barges, or in their frenzy into the river. Watermen's boats, barges and craft of all descriptions was afloat and of great service during the terrible conflagration in receiving property from burning houses and picking up all kinds of property drifting away with the tide and conveying it to Bankside.' King Charles II came down river to watch the sight from the river. When he saw Watermen's Hall at Coldharbour, Upper Thames Street, was about to be totally destroyed, he gave instructions to the Lord Mayor to pull down some buildings in the path of the fire. As the fire progressed, the watermen were charging more and more for their services, against the rules of their Company.

Contrary to expectations, the watermen also did quite well during the great frosts. During that of 1608, paths across the frozen river were established by ferrymen. The ebb of the tide caused the ice to move when the water was sucked from under it, so each day a new path would be established. For some reason, the path at the Lambeth Horse Ferry remained very firm and that passage was free. In another great frost which lasted between December 1683 and 5 February 1684, the watermen decorated large tilt boats with flags and streamers and used them as sledges, drawn by horses. Other boats were mounted on wheels and drawn across.

A Public Act was passed in 1677[4] which affected any boatmen, not just Thames Watermen. It was described as 'An Act for the better observation of the Lord's day' and enacted that 'no person should use, employ or travel upon the Lord's day with any boate, wherry, lighter or barge, except it be an extraordinary occasion, allowed by the Justices of the Peace'. If anyone was found guilty, the fine was 5*s*.

More measures were introduced in 1696 to foster health and safety. Boats as well as their owners now had to display a number and operate from a designated and approved plying place. In deference to passengers with a delicate nature, steps were taken to prevent the rudeness of watermen to other people on the river. As well as requiring the boats to be marked with a number, the boats had to display the owner's name and plying place, thus making it easy to identify the culprits and report them. Despite heavy fines, this practice did not stop. It was a sort of water dialect or 'mob language', often referred to in literature, as by Henry Fielding in *Voyage to Lisbon*. Edward Ward speaking of this language in about 1699, quoted William Wycherly, the playwright (*c.* 1640-1715), 'many ladies will take a broad jest cheerfully from the waterman.' Writing home in 1725, a young Frenchman, César de Saussure said 'Nothing is more attractive than the Thames on a fine summer evening: the conversations you hear are most entertaining, for I must tell you that the custom for anyone on the water to call out whatever he pleases to other occupants of boats, even were I the king himself, and no one has the right to be shocked ... Most bargemen are very skilful in this mode of warfare using singular and quite extraordinary terms, generally very coarse and dirty and I cannot possibly explain them to you.' (Nor me neither.) Dr Samuel Johnson was able to match such attacks of abuse. James Boswell records an incident in about 1780,[5] when Johnson replied, 'Sir, your wife, under pretence of keeping a bawdy-house, is a receiver of stolen goods.' Being guilty of such behaviour did not deter watermen from aspiring to be buried on the southern side of the churchyard at St Martin-in-the-Fields, where a flat pavement was called the 'Waterman's Burying Ground'. They would be brought to their final resting place by boat to Hungerford, York or Whitehall Stairs.

Watermen on the Thames used a type of rowing boat designed by common practice to suit their needs, called a wherry.[6] It was wooden, clinker-built (overlapping planks bent round), usually painted red or green and was light and easy to row. It had 'a raking stem, hollow lines with a pronounced flare, and a broad rounded stern. It was wide at the centre and could carry at least eight passengers comfortably.' The backrest developed into an ornamental feature after the injunction to watermen to display their name. 'When the boat was beached the raked stem could be brought on to dry land for the convenience of passengers; when they moved aft, the shift of weight would lift the boat off the bottom and the waterman could push the wherry afloat.' Usually the wherry was rowed by a single free waterman, but sometimes an apprentice would assist. They could go very fast. A foreign visitor in 1618 commented, 'the wherries shoot along so lightly as to surprise everyone ... They row like galley oarsmen, with extremely long oars, and are very dextrous at steering clear of each other.' Watermen would vie with each other for customers, calling out "oars, oars" or "sculler, sculler" if they had the smaller and cheaper boat. John Stapleton in the Chiswick to Chelsea section of his long poem *The Thames*, 1878, illustrates the scene: 'Or hear the watermen his prowess vaunt.' When the customer had made his choice, the winning boatman would be treated to some mob language from his losing colleagues.

Tilt boats were a more sophisticated type of wherry used mostly on the Long Ferry from Gravesend to London. The tilt was an awning, usually red or green, to protect passengers from the weather. The Chamberlain's accounts[7] for 1585-86 include payments to the water-bailiff for 18 yards of tilt for a wherry at 9*d* a yard = 13*s* 6*d*, and hoops for the same wherry = 2*s* 6*d*. Total = 16*s*. Shallops were a better type of barge fitted out with canopies and cushions for when important people took to the water. They were similar to the City Company barges and would be used in processions as in 1717 when Handel's *Water Music* was played all the way from Lambeth. On these occasions the watermen taking part would be dressed in livery, as the Queen's Bargemen still are (they no longer have a royal barge to row).

Normally the watermen did not wear a uniform, except sometimes 'a peculiar kind of cap made of velvet or black plush and sometimes of cloth the same colour as their waistcoats'. However, if they were lucky, watermen could win a Doggett's coat and badge in the annual race inaugurated in 1715 by Thomas Doggett (*c.* 1640-1721).

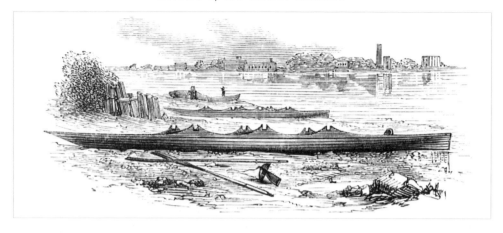

Waterman's wherry, generally used above London Bridge. This particular example is a randan wherry which three persons could row and was used for fast journeys and racing. (From Halls' *The Book of the Thames*, 1859)

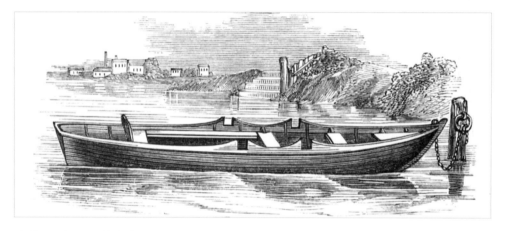

Skiff, used generally below London Bridge in rougher waters and sometimes used with a sail. (From Halls' *The Book of the Thames*)

Shallop. A sophisticated form of wherry used for special occasions by important people. (From Halls' *The Book of the Thames*)

Doggett was a famous Irish actor in comedy and a Whig. He strongly supported the Hanoverian cause and set up the race to celebrate the coronation of George I. It was contested by six young watermen within a year of the completion of their apprenticeships. Small four-seater wherries were used for the race but not carrying passengers. The course is from London Bridge to the Swan at Chelsea, almost five miles, and at first was rowed against the tide, but this is no longer stipulated. To ensure there was no cheating, beadles were appointed to check on 'tickling', which was the practice of sanding down the planks to lighten the boat. In his will Doggett listed the cost of providing the scarlet coat and silver badge for the winner. 'Five pounds for a badge of silver weighing about 12 ounces and representing Liberty to be given to be rowed for by six young Watermen according to my Custom, eighteen shillings for cloth for a livery whereon the said badge is to be put, one pound one shilling for making up the said Livery and Buttons and Appurtenances to it'. On the badge is depicted the white horse of Hanover and Brunswick, and their motto 'Liberty'.

On his death Doggett entrusted the administration of the legacy to the Worshipful Company of Fishmongers who still control it at present, although the Company of Watermen and Lightermen have an interest. The race takes place usually in July each year, according to the state of the tides. Thomas Doggett is buried in the churchyard of St Johns at Eltham and a plaque records him as a pauper, but he lives on in the race and in the following verse found scratched on a Lambeth windowpane[8] in 1737.

> Tom Doggett, the greatest sly droll in his parts
> In acting was certain a master of arts;
> A monument left – no herald is fuller –
> His praise is sung yearly by many a sculler.
> Ten thousand years hence if the world last so long
> Tom Doggett will still be the theme of their song.

There were other wagers to test the skill and prowess of the watermen at rowing but Doggett's is the only one remaining, and is said to be the oldest sporting contest in the world in continuation. Other sports were played out on the river by watermen[9]

Game of quintain played on the river. (Engraving from Joseph Strutt's *Sports and Pastimes of the People of England*, 2nd edn, 1810)

Justs or tilting upon the water. Taken by Strutt from a fourteenth-century manuscript.
(Engraving from *Sports and Pastimes of the People of England*, 1810)

in their spare time, like in the Easter holidays, when they fought sham battles. In 1253 it is recorded 'the king's servants came to the City to play a game of quintain on the river'. They jeered the citizens who then turned on them and beat them. The King was displeased and punished the Corporation of London by fining them 1,000 marks. Tilting and jousting also took place on the river from at least the fourteenth century. Humpherus transcribes it. 'A shield is hung on a pole fixed in the middle of the stream, a boat is prepared without oars, to be carried by the violence of the water and in the forepart of it a young man stands ready to give charge upon the shield with his lance. If he breaks his lance against the shield and does not fall, he is thought to have performed a worthy deed; if so be without breaking his lance he runneth strongly against the shield down he falleth into the water, for the boat is violently forced with the tide; but on each side of the shield ride two boats, furnished with young men which recover him that falleth as soon as they may.'

Great fun was derived from this type of sport as outlined by Stow and quoted by Humpherus. 'I have seen, in the summer season, upon the river of Thames, some (two competitors) rowed in wherries, with staves in their hands flat at the fore end, running one against another, and for the most part one or both of them were overthrown and well ducked.' Similar pastimes also took place on the ice. Watermen were delighted when water processions were held. The first one was in 1453 when John Norman[10] became Lord Mayor and progressed to Westminster by barge, 'for which he was commended by the watermen'. Boxing too was practised, but in remote open spaces like Battersea Fields. Jack Broughton was a waterman who in 1743 drew up the written rules which governed prize fighters for the next hundred years or so.

In 1700, as the Port of London was becoming more prosperous and expanding, more lightermen were employed. Their work was to unload cargo from ships moored in the river and take it into their lighters, which were long, narrow open barges propelled by one or two sweeps, or very long oars. The cargo was taken into the port. In other words, they were making the ship's cargo lighter. Previously, members of the Woodmongers' Company, the Lightermen now joined in with the Watermen's Company, which became the Company of Watermen and Lightermen, and so it continues today. They use Watermen's Hall in St Mary-at-Hill close to the Old Billingsgate, off Lower Thames Street. The first hall destroyed in the Great Fire

Thames Lighterman working in Greenhithe Reach with Greenwich Power Station as background. S. W. Rawlings, from an album *c.* 1950. (Reproduced by Permission of English Heritage)

was rebuilt in 1670 but in 1778-80 the present hall was built to the design of William Blackburn, on a new site. It is the only eighteenth-century Company hall in the City and has a remarkable Court Room where apprentices are examined before being made freemen, five years now being the norm for apprenticeships.

An Act was passed in 1698[11] which was supposedly to explain and bring into line former Acts, although it did include clauses specifically in preparation for lightermen joining the Company. Contrary to previous Acts, Sunday trading was now to be allowed but only to a chosen few. The rulers of the Company on their Court days were to appoint not more than forty watermen to ply and work on every Lord's Day between Vauxhall and Limehouse at such stairs or places of plying as the rulers should specify. Only one penny must be charged to each passenger. Every Monday morning those watermen must pay in to the rulers all their Sunday takings. Then the rulers would pay back to them an agreed amount, or percentage, as their wages, and the rest or 'overplus shall from time to time be applied to the use of the poor, aged, decayed and maimed watermen and lightermen ... and their widows'. Failure to do this or if short payment was made would result in a fine of 40s. Detailed accounts of these transactions are among the Company records deposited in the Guildhall Library in London. An exception was made for the watermen of the parish of St Margaret at Westminster who had been used to working like this on a Sunday but for the poor of only their own parish, under the supervision of two Justices of the Peace. In future the watermen would appoint their own supervisors.

There were a lot of watermen, an unconfirmed figure for the eighteenth century gives 5,962 registered wherries and 1,730 lighters with a possibility of another thousand unregistered. The work was long and arduous and the river water became more foul, causing disease. To care for retired and indisposed watermen and their families was a major concern of the Company. Even before it was incorporated, Henry VIII built an almshouse in 1545 in the Woolstaple (now Bridge Street) in New Palace Yard, Westminster. Named the Hospital of St Stephen, there were eight houses, seven for poor watermen, and one for a matron. As the wool warehouses were close by, it is likely the watermen had been engaged in the wool staple. The almshouses were demolished to make way for the building of Westminster Bridge and the charity moved elsewhere. Another set of watermen's almshouses were in Queen's Arms Court,[12] Upper Ground Street, Southwark, but perhaps were reserved for the poor watermen of that parish.

Alterations to the circumstances of working the Sunday ferries were made by an Act of 1859. Apart from the repeal of the law requiring watermen to serve in the Royal Navy compulsorily, the limits for Sunday ferry working were extended to between Chelsea and Bow Creek at places where the Company court saw fit, provided 'so as not to interfere with any established private ferry'. The number allowed to ply and work was also increased, no limit being specified. Not more than tuppence could be charged for crossing the river or for being taken to or from any vessel moored in the river; if more was charged the fine now was £5. A percentage of the takings was still to be given for the 'poor, aged, decayed and maimed watermen and widows at the discretion of the court'. The special provisions for the watermen of the Parishes of St Margaret's and St. John's at Westminster were continued as before. But this time, with regard to Vauxhall Bridge, it was stipulated that no Sunday ferry was to operate within two hundred yards of either side of it, so as not to affect the collection of tolls on the bridge.

New powers were given to the JPs of Greenwich and Milton in that they could grant licences to freemen of the Company to carry goods and passengers from Gravesend across the river on a Sunday. Profits would also be applied to the poor. Widows were allowed to use and work their husband's boat. To try and foster better relations with their passengers yet again, watermen were to pay a fine every time they avoided or refused to take a fare, or did not answer when called. Furthermore, if he did not 'proceed with due diligence and exertion to the place where the passenger directs – he would incur a penalty'. (That is, he should not dilly-dally on the way.) Likewise, if he should use abusive language to the passenger.

The Company built an enormous range of almshouses in 1840-41 in the High Road at Penge, five miles south of the Thames. Although not an architectural masterpiece by George Porter, great care was taken in the design by the founding father, John Dudin Brown, who gave 2 acres of land for the site and who was Master of the Company in 1845. It has a magnificent gate-tower with turrets and extensive ornamental gardens with stone creatures mounted on pedestals. Subscribers paid for the building which consisted of forty almshouses They were converted to private dwellings in 1973 and the almspeople moved to Hastings.

Almshouses for lightermen were founded on the outskirts of Ditchling, Sussex, by a gift of William Vokins, a Master Lighterman, in 1888 and became a registered charity. They consist of a two-storey block of twelve houses, each one with a small backyard. Now known as the Royal Cottage Homes for Watermen, they are within a conservation area. The schedule for that describes the almshouses as 'institutional in scale and appearance'. In 2007 the Company made a loss on these almshouses, which then housed private tenants paying rent on several properties besides the needy watermen. On 1 July 2008 the Company declared its intention of disposing of the property.[13] The Royal Cottage Homes for Watermen also owns a complex of small bungalows at Watermen's Close in Hastings.

Education has played a part in the affairs of the Company and its watermen and continues its interest to the present day. But it was the Drapers' Company who had the direction of the Green Coat School in Church Fields, Greenwich. It was endowed in 1672 by Sir William Boreman[14] for the support and education of twenty boys, being sons of watermen, seamen and fishermen of Greenwich. Twenty sons of watermen[15] at Putney were provided for by an endowment founded in 1684 by Thomas Martyn after he had been rescued from the river. The school, situated in Southfield House in

Temple Stairs. Johnson and Boswell took water at this popular landing place for a jaunt to Greenwich in 1763. (From James Boswell, *The Life of Samuel Johnson*, ed. Roger Ingpen, 1925)

Putney, opened in June 1718. When the house was demolished in 1887 to make way for the District Underground line, the school moved to other premises, but closed in 1911. Today the Thomas Martyn Charity provides grants for the sons and daughters of watermen.

Dr Johnson took an interest in the education of a young waterman when he and Boswell hired a sculler at Temple Stairs to visit Greenwich on Saturday 30 July 1763. Boswell asked Johnson if he really thought a knowledge of Greek and Latin was an essential requisite to a good education. He replied, 'Most certainly, Sir, for those who know them have a very great advantage over those who do not. Nay, Sir, it is wonderful what a difference learning makes upon people even in the common intercourse of life, which does not appear to be much connected with it.' Boswell went on, 'And yet people go through the world very well and carry on the business of life to good advantage without learning.' To which Johnson's retort was 'Why, Sir, that may be true in cases where learning cannot possibly be of any use; for instance, this boy rows us as well without learning, as if he could sing the song of Orpheus to the Argonauts, who were the first sailors'. Johnson then called to the boy, 'What would you give, my lad, to know about the Argonauts?' The boy said, 'Sir, I would give what I have.' 'Johnson was much pleased with his answer and we gave him a double fare. Then Dr. Johnson turning to me and said, "Sir, a desire of knowledge is the natural feeling of mankind, and every human being, whose mind is not debauched, will be willing to give all that he has to get knowledge". This quotation is one of the more famous of Johnson's truisms.

The Company administer the Philip Henman Foundation,[16] founded in 1961 with a gift of shares from Dr Henman. It is intended to help with the education of young people who want to make a career working on or in connection with the Thames. Most beneficiaries come from families who have had associations with the river for generations.

The Company of Watermen & Lightermen continues to act on behalf of the 600 or so licensed watermen whom it represents, but changes have been made because of a new EU licensing regime. A new national licence system[17] came into force on 1 January 2007 which does away with the old apprenticeship scheme of five years, and instead a waterman can become a master after only two years and can work on any inland waterway and limited coastal areas. However, it will still be necessary to spend six months training on local knowledge before being allowed to work on the Lower Thames. Watermen do not consider this long enough to ensure complete safety for passengers. Local knowledge involves little details, like how to judge the height of the tide by a particular line on a bridge and how many steps it can cover before there is insufficient air space to clear a bridge. On some parts of the Thames a master can command a commercial vessel with no previous experience on the river. The British Government maintain the system will be safer because licences, including the local knowledge, will be endorsed every five years. Other countries have had their rivers, like the Rhine, exempted from the ruling.

Before the new ruling was brought in, several hundred people[18] accompanied watermen wearing their uniform of Doggett's coat and badge to present a petition to Parliament. They were concerned that safety issues would be compromised and their jobs might be cut if companies employed cheaper manpower. Watermen would need to exchange their old licence for a new one on payment of £28 to the Maritime & Coastguard Agency. The Act was passed.

CHAPTER SIX
Chiswick to Westminster

Unlike most other bridges on the Thames, Chiswick Bridge,[1] which carries the Great Chertsey Road over the river (A316) from the Hogarth Roundabout, did not begin life as a ferry. The road bisects the left peninsula formed by the river making like an S-bend lying on its side; Barnes is on the right bank and forms the other peninsula. The old village of Chiswick remained as a fairly isolated fishing and transhipment settlement clustered round St Nicholas' church until the mid-nineteenth century. As transport became easier, Chiswick and its neighbour Mortlake grew. By the beginning of the twentieth century, a new road became necessary. The Great Chertsey Road was proposed in 1909 but proved too expensive and controversies over the route led to its abandonment. The scheme was revived in the 1920s and the road finally opened in 1933. It is not certain there was not a ferry at that crossing but no evidence has come to light, and as neither bank was hardly populated, it is unlikely.

CHISWICK-BARNES

Chiswick (Exp. 161 217 778) itself did have a ferry across to Barnes on the other side of the river where it was named Barnes Ferry. Thought to have started in medieval times, the first written mention of the ferry is in a document of 1659,[2] and nothing else. Reputedly it ceased operation in the mid-seventeenth century, but had started again by the 1820s. Normally it went from close by Chiswick church where Church Street now meets Chiswick Mall on a corner. Sometimes in the nineteenth century the landing stage was further downstream on Chiswick Mall opposite where Chiswick Lane joins it and is shown thus on a panorama of the Thames of about 1830. Charles Dickens Jr also describes the ferry in 1887 at this place. One authority suggests it was moved back to the church site at Chiswick wharf when the draw dock became busy in the late Victorian age. A draw dock is a gently sloping bank on a tidal river where vessels can be drawn, or run up. Barges would be bringing hops and malt to Chiswick for the renowned breweries in the vicinity. Finally, in the early 1930s, the ferry came to an end.

On the Surrey side the landing stage was reached by Ferry Lane, which actually is directly opposite the Chiswick Lane landing place. On 2 February 1851 a waterman, James Meathing,[3] aged thirty-five, was drowned attempting to cross the ferry in his own boat late at night. His wife Elizabeth gave evidence at the inquest held at the Crab Tree Inn at Chiswick Ferry. She said the family and relatives had been visiting friends in Barnes and at 1 a.m. James brought her and their younger daughter back to Chiswick. As it was dark and foggy she begged him not to return for the other people, but he kissed her and set off. When he did not come back she went several times to call his name at the ferry but got no answer. She then went to cross the nearest bridge and met the other people coming. They feared he might be drowned because they

Chiswick Bridge under construction. Photo taken 16 July 1931. Bridge opened 3 July 1933. (Taken from commemorative brochure published by the county councils of Middlesex and Surrey)

Chiswick Ferry. Showing the ferry landing and the draw-dock. Engraved print from Dr David Hughson's *New Description of London*, 1807. (Courtesy Heatons of Tisbury)

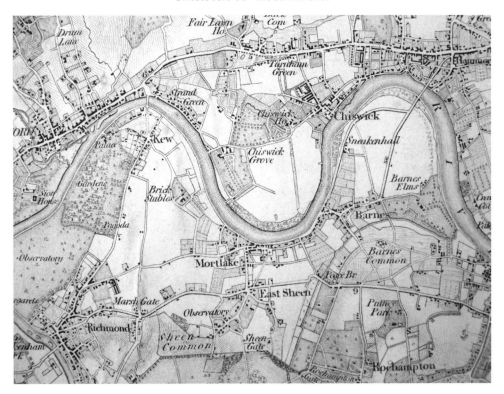

Ordnance Survey First Edition, 1828, showing the stretch of river between Kew Bridge and Hammersmith.

had heard splashing in the water. The next morning his boat was found upturned near his cottage, his body was not recovered until three weeks later floating near the same spot. James had been perfectly sober on the night. Although he had 20s in his pocket when he left his wife, when he was found there was only 18d. The jury were apparently satisfied with this explanation and recorded a verdict of 'Accidental Death'. Whether it was a unanimous decision is not known. James may not have been the official ferryman.

HAMMERSMITH BRIDGE

The nearest bridge to the old Chiswick Ferry downstream is Hammersmith. It is unlikely to have replaced a ferry, but was commissioned by gentlemen of Hammersmith obviously to relieve a bottleneck in their town, taking traffic from north to south London (now A306). A suspension bridge built by the Hammersmith Bridge Company opened in 1827. Subsequently it was found not strong enough to take all the traffic, including the thousands who watched the University Boat Race from it each year. A new bridge designed by Sir Joseph Bazalgette and erected on the old superstructure opened in 1887.

Hammersmith. Showing suspension bridge and draw-dock. The public house is the Red Lion, proprietor W. Murphy. Vessel in foreground is a small lighter, with a wherry just behind it. Entrance to Hammersmith Creek is to the left. Photo Taunt, 1870s. From an album. (Reproduced by Permission of English Heritage)

PUTNEY-FULHAM

Domesday Book records that in 1085 a ferry between Putney and Fulham (Exp. 161 242 756) was yielding 20s p.a. to the owner of the southern half, the Manor of Wimbledon. The northern half at Fulham was owned by the Bishop of London, whose palace and grounds occupied a large area bordering the Thames. This point in the river appears to be a natural crossing place, especially as it carried two main routes out of London and Westminster to the west and south-west. One was the road following the river on the north, or left bank, then over by ferry; the other by water to a landing place possibly by the end of Brewhouse Street behind Putney church. Putney High Street and riverside was lined with inns and taverns, which suggests this was an important place for travellers, possibly dating back to pre-Roman times. The King had his own private route to the ferry, through Chelsea and Fulham, the King's Road!

Important ferries throughout England had chapels on either bank where travellers could pray for a safe crossing, then give thanks afterwards. Notably they occur by the Lower Severn and the River Wye, but here in London are large churches, denoting the relevant importance of the crossing. St Mary's on the riverbank at Putney has thirteenth-century foundations. All Saints at Fulham, now much altered, was fourteenth century. Both are described in a tour book of 1834 as similar 'bride churches'.[4] The tourist explains their origin is due to the piety of twin sisters in Saxon times. They lived on opposite sides of the Thames to each other and when they paid visits would call the ferryman to take them over. One would call 'Full home, waterman', and her sister 'Put nigh'. And that is how Fulham and Putney got their names!

Most of the history of this ferry is gathered from *Fulham Old and New*, Vol. I, 1900, by C. J. Feret. The first written reference to it is in the time of King John when in 1210 Thomas Marescall claimed his expenses. When he went over the river with two carters and seven horses of the wardrobe, the payment for carriage of the harnesses alone was one penny. Harness again was carried by itself in 1253 when Eleanor of Provence, Queen of Henry III, hired ferry boats at Fulham to take harness of her horses and those of her ladies, possibly to Lambeth. There were two types of ferry operating at Fulham/Putney, the standard straight across, from one landing to the corresponding one on the other side, and a long ferry by which passengers were ferried to London or Westminster along the river. Feret does not always distinguish between the two.

During the reign of Edward I (1272-1307), the Treasury records a payment of 4s to Robert the ferryman of Putney for conveying the household and servants of the King's hospice with two barges across the Thames during two days in March. The specific date is not known. At the end of Henry V's reign in 1422 two men, Bartholomew East and John Wassingham, held a partnership in the ferry. When a new boat was needed, they quarrelled about sharing the expense of building a new one, so they went to arbitration. Their neighbours decided that East should order the new boat before Holy Trinity Day and pay for it. Then Wassingham should pay half the cost. If he should back out, then East would keep the boat to himself and Wassingham may keep the old boat if he paid 13s 4d for his share of it.

The Bishop of London had leased his half (moiety) of the ferry to East with certain messuages and then it passed through a succession of lessees until in 1606 it was taken by Edmund Powell, in whose family it remained for several generations. The other moiety had a more chequered history. It was leased with a messuage known as 'Passors' and remained in the tenure of the Thurston family for a long time, until 1494. Then the lease was compulsorily surrendered, probably because they had allowed the property to become ruinous. However, if Thurstons would pay £24 into the court, plus the costs of 'all repairs and other necessaries there made and imposed by the Lord on the tenement, passage and wharf', the surrender would become null and void. Perhaps the Thurstons never complied with this, as in 1513 the lease was in the hands of John Moreton and John Young.

By 1518 John Moreton had died and his wife Petronella 'enjoyed' the moiety in his stead. At a court baron held in 1520 as she had died, John's nephew William Moreton of Moreton Hall, Asbury, Cheshire took over the moiety. But in 1532 William signed a lease for thirty years to Sir Ralph Warren to include the ferry, two boats, a tenement and a close. The rent was £5 8s p.a. with quit rent of 12s which was payable to the Bishop. For the lease Warren paid £21 12s plus a peppercorn for the first four years if demanded. In 1567 Lady Johanna Warren, Sir Ralph's widow was admitted to half of the passage of Fulham Ferry. She was succeeded in 1572 by her daughter, Joan Cromwell.

Various regulations for ferries appear in Court Rolls. One for the Manor of Wimbledon, dated 42 Eliz I (1600) and endorsed 1606, states that each passenger living in the parish was to pay the ferryman one farthing, and if the passenger was a stranger, he should pay one halfpenny, but if he had a horse with him, the charge was one penny. If the ferryman did not pass the money to the Lord of the Manor, he should forfeit 2s 6d himself. By 1629 the Lord was receiving 15s p.a. from this source.

Joan Cromwell's son, Sir Philip Cromwell, was admitted to the moiety in 1604 but disposed of his right to Edmund Doubleday, who then included it in a marriage settlement. In 1618 Thomas Hill bought the moiety and passed it to his son, also

Thomas Hill, whose widow Judith is recorded in the minutes of a Court General in 1650. 'She was granted half the passage of the ferry and allowed by the Lord of the manor of Fulham, and now used in and from Berestreet across the Thames to the village of Putney in Surrey – for life'. The rent was 6s 8d payable at Michaelmas and to carry the Lord, his chattels and cattle by day or night free of charge. After Judith's death in 1651 the family surrendered their interest to Benet Hamon at the same rent and terms.

The ferry played a significant part in the Civil Wars. The State papers for 1639 contain a warrant for payment to be made to the ferrymen of Fulham, Richmond, Hampton Court, and Shepperton for ferrying King Charles I and his household over a period of three years. Payment amounted to £93 13s. A noted character called John Fludd held the ferry during the reigns of James I and his son Charles I. The Earl of Essex, who lived at Putney, threw a bridge of boats across the river a little below the ferry in November 1642 in order to pursue the king when he withdrew to Kingston following the Battle of Brentford when many Parliamentarians had drowned in the Thames while attempting to escape. A contemporary newspaper report describes the circumstances. 'The Lord Generall hath caused a bridge to be built upon Barges and Lighters over the River of Thames, between Fulham and Putney, to convey his Army and Artillery, over into Surrey to follow the Kings Forces, and he hath ordered that Forts shall be erected at each end thereof to guard it, but for the present, the seamen with long Boates and Shallops full of Ordinance, and musketiers lie there upon the River to secure it.' Nevertheless, Charles managed to reach Oxford; it was the end of the campaign season. Later the bridge and earthworks were dismantled, as navigation would have been blocked, and the commandeered boats were returned to their owners.

Protection of ferries and bridges was of great concern during the Civil Wars. A proclamation was issued from Derby House on 7 July 1648, addressed to the horse ferries of Lambeth, Chelsea, Putney, Braintford (*sic*), Richmond, Hampton Court, Hampton and Shepperton, 'The better to prevent the confluence of people to those that have taken arms against the Parliament and are now in and about Surrey. We do desire you to take care That the Horse Ferry Boat be fixed on the Middlesex side at Sun setting and not let loose till sun rising and that there be good and sufficient guards set upon that place that none be suffered to pass in the day tyme but onely markett people and such as have business from the state and passes to warrant their going over'.

Perhaps because of the bridge of boats, people began to think there ought to be a better crossing. The approach to the ferry at Fulham was on the site of a draw dock to the west of where the abutments of Fulham Bridge were later built. The Swan Inn was at the landing place. On the Putney side the approach was by an opening to Putney Hythe at the end of Brewhouse Lane. The ferry was busy and fraught with danger. Sometimes, with the river running high, boats were driven downstream as far as Wandsworth before reaching the Surrey shore. A Bill was introduced to Parliament in 1671 to build a wooden bridge. There was much opposition because it would be an obstruction in the river; encourage London to grow too big; would harm the watermen's trade; lead to other bridges being built (possibly of iron); and furthermore it would affect the interests of the nation! One of the main reasons given by the promoters was it could be used when the King went hunting. The Bill was lost by thirteen votes. Another attempt to obtain a Bill was made in 1687-88 but again it was thrown out largely because of opposition from the City of London.

Some significant changes of lessees were made in the early part of the eighteenth century. The Bishop of London, whose moiety was divided into two shares, sold one to Thomas Symonds in 1719, who then sold it on to Daniel Pettiward of Putney. He, or maybe his son, another Daniel, also held one of the two shares on the Putney side. William Skelton held the other Putney share in 1726. A descendant of Benet Hamon, Bennett Hamon Gotobed, still held the other Fulham share but had sublet, the yield of £50 p.a. being his entire income. Therefore, the four shareholders were the joint tenants of the horse ferry. A foot ferry was also provided by local watermen, who were allowed to keep the fares they charged, except they had to pay part to the ferry owners at Fulham. A statement made to the Commissioners of the Fulham Bridge in 1726 revealed that the watermen had claimed equal rights to the Sunday foot ferry. Their basic income was paid to the owners, but any excess was given for the relief of watermen's families in the two places. After this system had been abandoned at this ferry, it continued under the jurisdiction of the Watermen's Company at other London ferries for centuries. Mr Pettiward in evidence given to a Parliamentary Committee earlier declared his average income from one share was about £100. Increased profit had followed increased building in the area.

As with many enterprises embarked upon for the common good, several factors conspire to bring them to fruition. This was the case with the first bridge to replace the ferry, Fulham Bridge. Sir Robert Walpole was not a popular Prime Minister in the reign of George I. The story goes that one day in the early 1720s he was returning from Kingston with a servant after attending the King. Being in a hurry to get back to the House of Commons, he arrived at Putney to take the ferry, but found the boat was hauled up on the other bank. Seeing no sign of a waterman, they shouted, to no avail. The ferrymen, 'Tories to a man' Feret said, 'were carousing at The Swan and in secret were enjoying the discomfiture of the would-be passengers.' Walpole had to take another route and swore to abolish the ferry and replace it with a bridge. Reputedly, it was to Walpole that the Prince of Wales (later George II) turned when he was often inconvenienced by the ferry when returning from hunting in Richmond Park and preferred a bridge. At the same time petitions were presented to Parliament for bridges at Vauxhall and Westminster/Lambeth, but the Bill was dropped partly because of opposition to Walpole over his involvement with the South Sea Bubble Affair. One positive decision made in 1722 was that a bridge should be built at a suitable place between Chelsea and Kingston.

Putney Pier, close to Putney-Fulham Bridge. Paddle steamer named *Fuchsia* is moored alongside. Postcard sent by Lillian from Fulham in 1904.

66   *THE COUNTRY DANCE BOOK.*

PUTNEY FERRY.
Round for six ; in three parts (4th Ed., 1670).

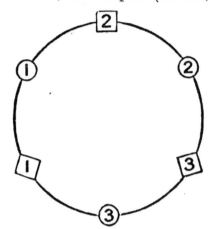

MUSIC.		MOVEMENTS.
		FIRST PART.
A	1—4	Hands-six, eight slips, clockwise.
	5—8	The same back again, counter-clockwise, to places.
B1	1—4	Men meet and hands-three once round clockwise, facing outward ; while women turn single twice round, clockwise and counter-clockwise.
	5—8	Men turn their partners.
B2	1—4	Women meet and hands-three once round clockwise, facing outward ; while men turn single twice round, clockwise and counter-clockwise.
	5—8	Men turn their partners.
C1	1—2	Each man sets to the woman on his left.
	3—4	Each man sets to the woman opposite him.
	5—6	Each man honours his partner.

Putney Ferry. Country dance as set out by Cecil Sharp. The other two parts are repeats. At the end the 'dancers were wiping their eyes with their handkerchiefs as they set'.

Surveys were made at three places and Fulham/Putney was chosen. A Bill was presented to Parliament in March 1726. The usual petitions against the proposal were heard, including one on behalf of a hundred or so watermen who claimed their right to the Sunday foot ferry which brought an income of £100 a year. Walpole was a member of a committee set up to consider amendments and 'the Act for building a bridge across the river of Thames from the town of Fulham ... to the Town of Putney' was passed on 24 May 1726. Two years later a further Act gave the Commissioners more financial flexibility to raise money.

Walpole subscribed £1,000 and together with a number of his political and financial friends became proprietors of the bridge, a timber structure which opened in 1729 and known as Fulham Bridge. Built at a cost of £23,975 it was described as a black structure with twenty-six openings called locks, one named after Walpole, and lighted by oil lamps. Compensation for the loss of the ferry was paid to owners. Sarah, Duchess of Marlborough, Lady of the Manor of Wimbledon, had £346 10s; but the Lord Bishop of London received only £23 together with free passage over the bridge for himself, his horses, household, etc. Daniel Pettiward, William Skelton and Mr Bennett Hamon Gotobed had compensation of £8,000 between them. At the time the annual total income of the ferry was an average £400. The Act specified that an annual payment of £62 was to be paid in perpetuity to the Churchwardens of Fulham and Putney. The money was to be divided among the watermen, their widows and children of the two towns in recompense for the loss of proceeds of the Sunday ferry. Sunday was their busiest day; the weekday ferry was not taken into account.

Putney Ferry was discontinued, but an unusual remembrance of it is left in the form of a country dance called 'Putney Ferry' included in Cecil J. Sharp, *The Country Dance Book, Part II*, first published in 1911. It is a circle dance for three couples and first appeared in John Playford *The Dancing Master*, 4th edition, 1670. The delightful little tune can be heard on line.[5]

Mention must be made of a much more recent ferry operated independently[6] by Mr O'Dell, 'a large barrell-chested man', now a legendary character. He would carry up to eight adults or nine children in his skiff, which he rowed between the end of Rotherwood Road on the Putney Embankment to the river steps at Bishop's Park. The park was an attraction, but his main business came from ferrying people across on Saturday afternoons to see Fulham play at Craven Cottage, just down the road. After the Second World War his service became intermittent and ended about 1949 through lack of demand. This was the days before life jackets; fortunately, it is said, he never lost a single passenger!

BATTERSEA-CHELSEA

Battersea and Chelsea (Exp. 161 270 774) both developed early in the expansion of Metropolitan London westward, communication between them, probably by ford at first, then by ferry, dating from prehistoric times. A large quantity of human bones and weapons from various ages has been found in the Thames at the site of the crossing. Very famous is the Battersea Shield discovered in 1857.[7] Now deposited in the British Museum, it is described as made of highly polished bronze with twenty-seven studs of red glass or enamel, measuring 77.7 cm and dating from the Iron Age, 350-50 BC. Its size suggests it was not used in warfare, being too small and ornate, and was actually just bronze sheets riveted to a wooden backing. All the rivets were cleverly hidden by overlaps in the design, a unique example of Celtic art. A recent article in *The Antiquaries Journal* describes the primary plan of the design, 'its schema'. 'The essential form is a deliberately constructed configuration, crafted specifically

The famous Battersea Shield found at the bridge site in 1857, now in the British Museum. (Reproduced via Wikimedia Commons)

by a constructional geometry, within a tradition which persisted and later pervaded insular art'. The shape and longitudinal layout of the design, incorporating one central roundel between two smaller ones is constructed using dividers and a straight edge. Overall, the design, being slightly irregular, is based on 'ordered geometric structures'. The article goes on to show how readers may make their own drawing. Experts suggest the shield was a votive offering to the river.

As early as 1292 a passage over the Thames at 'Cenlee' was mentioned.[8] This could be interpreted as Chelsea. The earliest positive reference to a passage at Chelsea was in the time of Elizabeth in 1550 when the owners were William Wylkyns and his wife Alice. It was named Chelsea Ferry, with the same owners in 1564, and was included in the edict concerning horse ferries in 1592. The ferry was held freely of the Manor of Chelsea to which the heirs of Francis Bowes owed a quit rent of 10s a year in 1587.

It was usual for ferries particularly around London to be owned by the Crown as Lord of the Manor and Chelsea ferry was either escheated (surrendered to the King) or bought by the Crown before 1618. Then 'Chelchehith Ferry' was granted by Royal Letters Patent for payment of £40 with its landing place, and Thames Mead, being 9 acres of meadow and 47 acres in Kensington. The recipient was King James I's 'dear relation' Thomas Fiennes, 3rd Earl of Lincoln, together with John Eldred and Robert Henley. Those three were given a licence in 1618 to alienate all that property to William Blake, owner of Chelsea Park. In 1623 Blake and his wife Mary sold the ferry with its appurtenances to Oliver St John (1559-1630), the second son of Nicholas St John of Lydiard Tregoze, Wiltshire, who later became first Viscount Grandison of Limerick. Besides holding the Manor of Wandsworth with the ferry, St John also held the Manor of Battersea, with its ferry, through his marriage in about 1592 to Joan, daughter and heir of Henry Roydon of Battersea. After Sir Oliver's death the lands, including the ferry but not the title, descended through the St John family until 1763 when they were sold to John Spencer, Viscount Spencer, who became Earl Spencer two years later.

Owners of the ferry would let out the ferry rights to individual operators, most of whose names are not recorded. Thomasina Cootes, widow of a waterman, left Chelsea Ferry and the boats to her father Laurence Chase when she died in 1665. In 1668 the lessee was Samuel Chase (see below). Bartholomew Nutt was listed as paying rates for the ferry in 1696 and again in 1704. By 1735 John Medley was working the ferry and George Ludlow was ferryman in 1750. Parish rate books list the ferry at £8 p.a. in 1710.

In 1668 the owner, Sir Walter St John, and the lessee, Samuel Chase, brought a suit against the City of London's appointees for the jurisdiction of the river and against thirty-four watermen of Chelsea who were claiming that the plaintiff's rights to operate their own ferry from the 'Ferry Place' opposite the end of Danvers Street to Battersea applied only to the horse boat, and not to the passenger boats. The objectors also claimed that the ancient ferry was near the Crown Inn at Chelsea and that the ferry had superseded a public draw dock used by watermen at the east end of Cheyne Walk, which now cut across the end of Danvers Street and Lawrence Street a little to the east. The ferry charges at the time were one penny for every horse or beast and horseman in the horse boat and one halfpenny for persons on foot. The verdict on the suit is not known, but the watermen were presumably appeased, for in 1808 and 1812 there were more plying places for them. One was a stretch under the trees opposite the Yorkshire Grey by Manor Street, where there were wooden stairs and a good causeway; another opposite Lawrence Street where there were small stairs and the original ferry landing opposite Danvers Street and the White Hart where the brick stairs were 8 feet wide alongside a brick wall and a dock.

The text of a Coroner's Deposition[9] taken at the Old Bailey on 22 November 1753 mentions the Chelsea horse ferry in the account of the mysterious death of Elizabeth Webb. She was found four days previously lying dead on the shore near the limekiln in Hammersmith by James Gould, a Chiswick waterman, with her arms tied together. Her husband John Webb told how he met his wife in the afternoon of 15 July in Fleet Street and took her for a drink at the Star near Parliament Stairs in the Strand. She wanted to go to Wandsworth and asked a person which was the best place to take water. The reply was to go to the horse ferry at Chelsea. Webb accompanied her there and hailed a boat, but the waterman refused to go to Wandsworth. However, standing by was George Cooper who agreed to take her for sixpence and return her to London. Betty got into the boat and sat at the bottom. Webb never saw her again and believed she had drowned from the 'copper boat'. It was often said, without proof, that watermen would tip passengers into the river if they could not or would not pay the fare. It may be remarked that in *Our Mutual Friend* by Charles Dickens Lizzie is against her father's business of combing the Thames looking for bodies.

John Spencer, the 1st Earl Spencer of Althorp (1734-73), had inherited the Manor of Wimbledon from Sarah, Dowager Duchess of Marlborough. An immensely rich man, he realised the value of a bridge which could be built between Chelsea and Battersea instead of his ferry there. He obtained an Act in 1766 which empowered him to erect a bridge at his own expense and to buy land for the approaches. The tolls charged were to be the same as the ferry, and the Act stipulated that if the bridge should become 'dangerous or impracticable', then the Earl should provide a convenient ferry again, at the same charges.

Despite this concession the ferry kept in operation, giving a good return on investment of an average £42 each year between 1765 and 1771. Meanwhile, the Earl set up the Company of Proprietors of Chelsea Ferry & Battersea Bridge. Fifteen shares of nominally £100 each were issued, some being owned by more than one person. In a file for bankruptcy made in August 1772 by William James, Henry Neale, Alexander Fordyce and Richard Down a 1/15 share was for a 'free passage or ferry over the River Thames called Chelsea Ferry and all grounds, wharfs, landing places, rights etc with it and also all rights etc granted to John, Earl Spencer by virtue of an Act of Parliament'. Although 'the bridge now finished and open for passage' was included, in fact it was only ready for people on foot, and not available for carriage traffic until 1773, having begun building in 1771. By that time the total expenditure was £15,662, which included a further payment of £900 on each share.

That particular 1/15 share was granted to Thomas Rhodes, who paid £1,015 to P. Cust, George Ward and William Matthews. Rhodes bequeathed the share to his daughter Ann when he died in 1789 and it became part of her marriage settlement when she married Timothy Cobb in 1795. They both covenanted to convey it to Joseph Hodgetts of Dudley, nail merchant, and James Cobb of Kettering, ironmonger.

An indenture dated 25 March 1773 concerns the sale of the ferry house[11] situated near the late ferry and the bridge at Battersea, then in the occupation of Jane Munday, a widow. The premises included an osier ground measuring 7 acres 36 perches; abutting the river on the north, previously occupied by James Field; a yard, garden, outhouse and buildings, other lands and roads leading to the Common Field (later Battersea Fields). The purchasers were Sir Timothy Waldo of Clapham and Thomas Tritton, a brewer of Battersea who paid £1,155 to Earl Spencer. Previously, Waldo and Tritton had rented the property for a peppercorn. In 1795 Tritton bought another share from Henry Holland, for which he paid £800.

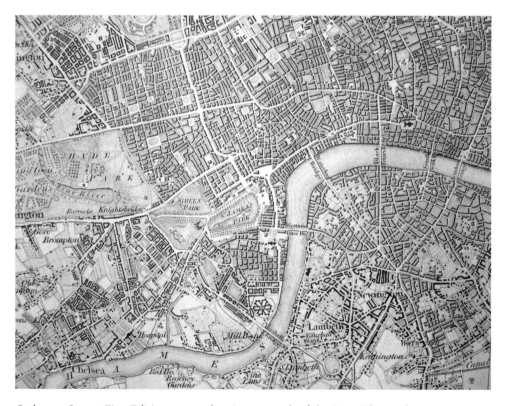

Ordnance Survey First Edition, 1828, showing a stretch of the River Thames between Chelsea/Battersea Bridge and London Bridge.

Before the timber bridge was completed, the proprietors frequently used the white ferry house for their meetings. When a Bill was put before Parliament for improvements at Chelsea, including construction of an embankment and roadway and a suspension bridge to replace the Old Battersea Bridge in the mid-nineteenth century it included a proviso that the White Ferry House[11] should be surrendered to the Marquis of Westminster. The new bridge opened in 1858. A White Ferry House was listed as a public house in Commercial Road, Pimlico, in 1839 and another of the same name is listed at present at 1a Sutherland Street, Victoria. Neither can be the original house, merely perpetuating the name. We have in the public domain a superb watercolour by Thomas Girtin (1775-1802) called *The White House at Chelsea*, now in Tate Britain. Ferry houses or cottages were often painted white so they could be distinguished from afar by travellers. This one has a reflection in the water, although the artist is facing upstream at sunset. In fact, the ferry house was on the right bank and was in Battersea, not Chelsea.

Other late-eighteenth and early-nineteenth-century artists also drew inspiration from the Chelsea/Battersea locality with its wide vistas and continually changing sky and shipping. Ferries themselves offer a focus and purpose to a painting. J. M. W. Turner, when too old to take out his own boat, would hire one with a boatman from Charles Greaves' boatyard at Chelsea, just by Battersea Bridge. A delicate ink and chalk drawing of the boat workshop by the son, Walter Greaves,[12] is in the Museum of London. A coloured landscape view of the riverside at Battersea was engraved by Francis Jukes in 1784. Wandsworth Museum has a small watercolour by an unknown artist of the Swan Inn and horizontal windmill at Battersea. The windmill had its sails inside. David Cox (1783-1859) resorted often to Battersea Fields for painting expeditions. His *Battersea Fields*,[13] a watercolour over pencil on wove paper is a panorama of the Battersea bank from Chelsea, made in the 1830s. He shows the windmill with no sails, and the Red House with the ubiquitous poplar tree behind, which usually denotes a ferry is close by.

THE RED HOUSE, BATTERSEA

W. J. Callcott produced an oil and a watercolour painting of The Red House, Battersea, a place beloved of watermen who would ferry crowds of people to it, particularly on Sundays. The inn stood on the riverbank about 500 yards below where the suspension bridge was later built and opposite the Royal Hospital at Chelsea and Ranelagh Gardens. It was at the edge of Battersea Fields, 'a flat unbroken wilderness of some three hundred acres' where unmentionable activities went on, much to the consternation of the Victorian middle class. By 1858 they had managed to turn it into a respectable public park. A writer in *Old and New London*, Vol. 6, published in 1876, describes what the place used to be like. 'It was the resort of costermongers and "roughs" and those prowling vagabonds who call themselves "gipsies". The week-day scenes here were bad enough; but on Sundays they were positively disgraceful, and to a great extent the police were powerless, for the place was a sort of "no man's land" on which ruffianism claimed to riot uncontrolled by any other authority than its own will. Pugilistic encounters, dog-fights and the rabble coarseness of a country fair in the worst aspect were "as common as blackberries in the autumn".'

The leisured classes also came to partake of asses' milk,[14] considered to be a panacea for many complaints, particularly pulmonary diseases, gout, scurvy, nervous diseases, and 'even the decay of old age'. Mary Heideggar, a stout lady who kept asses, was landlady in 1768 and charged 3s a pint for the milk. Her clients would engage in rowing as their main pastime along with gambling, swearing, shooting for nuts, dicing, card playing, boxing, skittles and cocking. Worse still was thimblerig, also known as the shell game, played with three shells and a pea, or originally with thimbles instead of shells. In the army it is supposedly a gambling game, but actually it is a carefully contrived con, achieved by sleight of hand and played in this country since the Middle Ages.

Duels also were fought here, one of the most notable being that of the Duke of Wellington in 1829. He had to defend his honour in the Catholic Relief Bill and called out the young Earl of Winchilsea, one of the leaders of the anti-Catholic party. No harm was done and an apology was made. Pigeon shooting took place in the grounds of the tavern, known as the 'Red-'us' (*Sketches by Boz*), when the cream of society took part. Many boat races would finish here with prestigious prizes, like in 1825 when a new wherry was offered by actor Edmund Kean to the winner of a race of seven pairs of oars rowed down river and back to the Red House.

Before the ferry began there was a ford from the vicinity of the Red House to the Chelsea bank. A shoal of gravel showed at ordinary low water wide enough for ten men to walk abreast. Ballast was added to it on the Surrey side to strengthen it. Mention is made of the causeway in a tour guide of 1820. Paths leading to the tavern were intricate and winding because of all the reed pools in the marshy ground. The proprietor would cover the paths with slag for the benefit of his pigeon-shooting clients.

The Watermen's Company fought for compensation when the Act was passed in 1846 for the new suspension bridge and the ferry was finally to be closed. They were awarded a substantial amount, particularly for the Sunday Red House ferry, a percentage of the profits of which went to their charities. When foundations for the bridge were laid in 1856, two skulls were found besides iron and bronze weapons, some Celtic, some Roman. Most interesting was the sole of a shoe – the caliga – worn by Roman soldiers.

The Act for making Battersea Fields into a park was passed in 1846, and amended in 1851. At that time the Old Red House, which had become the headquarters of the Gun Club, was bought for £11,000 by the Government and demolished.

LAMBETH HORSE FERRY

Horseferry Road in the City of Westminster is known to many people, especially for the Channel 4 building. Few will realise its name is the last vestige of a very important and lucrative ferry that plied between the two top places of government, the Palace of Westminster and Lambeth Palace, the seat of the Archbishop of Canterbury for centuries. The crossing is thought to have begun as a ford; the date when the ferry rights were granted to the Archbishop is not known but certainly before 1189 (time immemorial). It remained in his possession until it finally closed when Lambeth Suspension Bridge (Exp. 161 306 790) opened in 1862. The ferry took all the main London vehicle traffic upstream of London Bridge and was the only horse ferry allowed in London. The Company of Watermen had a stranglehold on its operation.

As early as 1281 there is a reference about the ferry when the Archbishop complained to the monks of St Peter's Abbey at Westminster that some of their tenants were defrauding his men of Lambeth at the ferry. Another reference[15] to the crossing occurs in 1367 when £16 was paid to the Clerks of Chancery for the barge 'for the passage to and fro across the Thames to the Manor of Lambheth [*sic*] of Simon Archbishop of Canterbury, the Chancellor, where the Inn of Chancery is now held and for the wages of the keepers of the said barge'. Because ownership of the ferry did not change hands, records of it through the ages are sparse in the public domain. All records remain in Lambeth Palace.

Lambeth Horse Ferry, with Lambeth Palace on the south bank of the Thames, showing numerous craft, but not the horse ferry itself. A waterman with his wherry is in the foreground. View by Tombleson, engraved H. Winkles. (From *Bridges of London*, 1830s)

The Archbishop leased Lambeth Horse Ferry in 1513 to Humphrey Trevilyan at 16*d* a year, with the proviso that the Archbishop, his servants, goods and chattels were to be carried free of charge. Thomas Cromwell's accounts for 1538 have an entry for ferrying his horses and in 1546 a bill from ferryman Edmonds Lewes was paid for horses taken 'over the water at Lambyth Ferry'.

When Archbishop William Laud moved into Lambeth Palace on his appointment in 1633, the ferry carrying his servants and horses being overloaded sank to the bottom of the Thames. There was no loss of life, but the accident was regarded as a bad omen. Laud was beheaded in January 1645. Likewise, a similar occurrence happened to Oliver Cromwell in 1656 with his coach and horses. Three horses were drowned.

During the Civil Wars Lambeth Ferry, together with the rest of the Archbishop's property, was confiscated. A petition from wharfingers, brewers, woodmongers and inhabitants beyond 'The Chayne'[16] in the Old Palace (of Westminster) was presented to the House of Lords on 7 October 1644 saying they had been stopped from coming with their carts through the Old Palace by the chain. On 26 October, the same day as the Battle of Newbury,[17] the House of Commons Journal refers to the petition but also includes lightermen and carmen as petitioners. They claimed that their way through the Old Palace Yard to the Lambeth Horse Ferry was stopped by the chain which was set up by order of the Lords and requested it may be laid open. The Commons ordered that a message be sent to the Lords 'to desire them to join with this house in putting down the chain and laying open the way to Lambeth Horse Ferry'. Men's livelihoods were at stake here and ancient ways and rights were not to be tampered with.

An order was given to Captain Brookes,[18] who was in charge of a 'hulk lying over-against Lambeth be required and hereby authorized to stop and seize all horses that pass the ferry, and likewise to stop, search and seize all boats laden with ammunition or warlike provisions.'

In December 1648 the ferry was sold to Christopher Wormeall,[19] but it reverted to the Archbishop at the Restoration. A Mrs Leventhorp was given a lease of it in 1664. She may be the Lady Dorothy Leventhorpe who was the subject of a petition brought to the House of Lords in May 1643. The petitioner was widow Dorothy Brograve, sister of Thomas Leventhorpe, who had died intestate. She made reference to a Statute made in 1530 which enacted that in any case where the deceased has died intestate the judge shall grant administration of the goods to his widow or the next of kin. In this case the judge had granted administration to Lady Dorothy Leventhorpe, who was not kin to Thomas, and to Edward Leventhorpe, who was only of remote kin. Edward was a servant to the Archbishop of Canterbury and 'endeavoureth to possess himself of a Lease of great Value, which belonged to the said Thomas'. Mrs Brograve petitioned the House to call the judge and the two beneficiaries before them to administer proper justice. The House then adjourned. The 'Lease of great Value' was probably the ferry because even forty years later a Mr Leventhorpe was accused by the Churchwardens of St Margaret's, Westminster, of 'usurping the whole profits of the horse ferry and neglecting to repair the roads leading thereto'.

Frost Fairs were held on the Thames when the river froze over during extreme cold weather. One such year was 1676 when it first froze over in November.[20] Then it came again on Christmas Eve and lasted until 3 January 1677. Obviously watermen lost their trade because passengers could walk over the water with torches, even carts and coaches could be driven on the ice between the horse ferry and Lambeth. Some coaches went as far as Chelsea. Huts were made of snow from which brandy and wine were sold. To combat their losses some resourceful watermen were able to fix up boats on runners to act like sleighs and would charge the same fare as if they went by water.

One dramatic event in English history[21] took place at the horse ferry. On the night of 9 December 1688 Mary of Modena, the Queen Consort of James II, escaped from Whitehall with her baby son, pending the arrival of William of Orange to take over the English throne. From the Palace of Whitehall she went through the Privy Gardens into the street with two nursemaids and two attendants, St Victor and the Count de Lauzun. There a coach was waiting to take them through the abbey precincts to the ferry, where a boat was waiting. Later St Vincent described their experience in his *Narrative of the Escape of the Queen of England*. 'The night was wet and stormy, and so dark that when we got into the boat we could not see each other, though we were closely seated, for the boat was very small.' St Victor confessed he was terrified at the peril to which they were exposed and he relied on the mercy of God. 'Our passage was rendered very difficult and dangerous by the violence of the wind and the heavy and incessant rain.' When they reached the Lambeth shore, the coach was not waiting, so St Vincent ran to fetch it, leaving the Queen and her company to shelter under the walls of Lambeth Old Church. The coach took them to Gravesend from where they sailed to the French coast and safety. The baby, six-month-old James Francis Edward Stuart, slept through the whole adventure. He was to become the father of 'Bonnie Prince Charlie'.

Meanwhile, James II's hold on the throne became more tenuous and two evenings later he attempted to escape too. He took a small boat with only a single pair of oars at the ferry, carrying with him the Great Seal of England, possibly with the intention of setting up court in France. However, halfway across he threw it in the river. When he got to Faversham in Kent, he was discovered and returned to Whitehall. Soon afterwards William arrived and deposed James, who took to the water in his barge to Gravesend and thence to France. The Great Seal was found in their net by some poor fishermen and returned to the Lords of the Council.

On the Lambeth side the public ferry did not go to Lambeth stairs, but to the door of St Mary's Church a little to the south, and approximately where the pier is now built. Traffic would then turn left for a few yards along the northern end of Fore (or Ferry) Street (swept away when the Albert Embankment, stretching now from Lambeth Bridge to Westminster Bridge was made). Lambeth Road was Church Street, leading to the ferry on Rocque's and other eighteenth-century maps. A late-fifteenth-century rental document reveals that the Abbot of Westminster paid one noble a year for a landing place at Lambeth because 'the Thames from Westminster to Tutthill is the common royal way from Greenwich through Lambeth to Windsor, and from Windsor to Greenwich'.

Horseferry Road which now leads straight to Lambeth Bridge was named Market Street for a short distance approaching the ferry. The street formed the eastern boundary of the extensive grounds of Peterborough House, part of the Grosvenor estate. An inn was recorded at the ferry place in 1692 when it was stated, 'Jane Wadsworth had lived at The Beare Inn at the Horse Ferry for six years.' Close by was a wooden house built for a small guard during the Commonwealth. It was still there in 1850 when Dickens wrote in *David Copperfield*, 'There was, and is when I write, at the end of that low-lying street, a dilapidated little wooden building, probably an obsolete old ferry-house. Its position is just at that point where the street ceases and the road begins to lie between a row of houses and the river'. The scene was depicted in watercolour by I. J. Smith[22] in 1778 and by John Varley[23] in 1800.

Several attempts were made to replace the ferry by a bridge at Westminster and this was achieved finally in 1750. Evidence has shown there was a ford at the site in Roman times when Watling Street, coming from the south-east skirted the Thames, crossed and continued up what became Edgware Road and on to Chester. Later the crossing became

The same horse ferry at Millbank on the north bank of the river. Engraving from *Old & New London*, 1891, after the watercolour, *c.* 1800, by John Varley, which shows less activity. (Courtesy www.old-england.com)

a ferry. In medieval legend St Peter himself consecrated the predecessor of Westminster Abbey. On his arrival incognito on the South Bank he asked fisherman Edricus to take him across the swollen river. In gratitude, on his return journey after the ceremony, St Peter told Edricus to cast his net, whereupon it filled with salmon and the fisherman realised the identity of his passenger. Large catches were guaranteed henceforth to Edricus provided that one tenth of the bounty was given to the abbey. This story explains the significance of the images of salmon in the floor of the Chapter House.

In 1664 strong opposition from the Company of Watermen and the Archbishop caused Parliament to turn down an application to bring in a Bill for a bridge at Westminster. Both parties had vested interests. Promoters argued that the ferry was dangerous, citing boats carrying coaches which had capsized. Another attempt was made in the reign of James II, to no avail. A Private Bill was introduced in the early 1730s which prompted a printed broadsheet outlining the 'Reasons against Building a Bridge over the Thames at Westminster'.[24] The opposition claimed the new bridge would prejudice the navigation of the river; retard the flux of the tide; increase shallows and sandbanks and create new ones and cause danger and delay to the conveyance of goods and passengers more especially in and about the new bridge. It would become a danger not only to wherries or smaller boats but to larger barges in particular, which are unwieldy when heavy loaded and not governed easily either by sail, rudder or poles. The bridge would cause danger by the fall of water there, both on the flux or reflux of the tide, also by eddies which would be created, and by shallows and sandbanks which would be cast up. Delay would be caused to wherries and small boats but more especially to larger vessels which could no longer pass that way by night, nor in daytime except at high water, and not even then without the danger of falling upon the piers of the bridge, especially in high winds. 'All which suggestions are verified by experience in the like case.'

They claimed certain results would follow, firstly the rise of labour and wages; the price of all commodities, whether of such necessary provisions as grain, meal, malt and fuel, etc., or other goods and merchandise brought here from western parts; as of commodities sent from here as coals, merchandise, etc., there would be danger of the loss of valuable cargoes valued at £2,000 or more. Of particular significance would be a decrease in the number of watermen 'so useful to the Sea Service whether private or public service' (a reference to the press-gangs which targeted watermen for centuries). Danger would be caused to houses and lands adjoining, especially between the bridges (London and Westminster). Also by overflowings and breaches made in the banks, 'which may neither be prevented nor retrieved'.

Other clauses were added regarding the expense of the undertaking, and its injury to the City of London. Income from rents, tolls and profits of markets would be lessened because of maintenance costs of the bridge. 'The revenue of the City of London will in many respects be injured and trade thereof ruined', and especially the orphans would suffer, part of the security for their debt being lost. Although the City may be able to pay £8,000 per annum now to the orphans, it will be impossible to pay £14,000 in a few years, 'as the City stands obliged to do'. The trade of the City will be transferred to the west end of the suburbs resulting in the City being no longer able to pay the annual Land Tax of £60,000 plus, besides all other public taxes, ward taxes, and parish taxes, which are all very large. Moreover, the bridge will be injurious to the property of the city, namely the soil of the River Thames and its Conservancy, 'which reaches from above Stanes [Staines] Bridge down to Yenland [Yantlet] in the county of Kent'. They note that all these reasons have been put forward before when proposals for a bridge have been rejected.

The broadsheet was followed by another entitled, 'Conjectures as to the most proper place between Scotland Yard and Vauxhall for erecting a bridge across the river

Thames from Westminster to the opposite Surrey Shore'. The only place suggested was from the horse ferry to Lambeth because the river there is a third narrower and will cost a third less to bridge. Eventually Lambeth Bridge was built on that line, but not until 1862.

Meanwhile, despite repeated opposition, the Westminster Bridge Act was passed in 1736 and provided for compensation to be paid to the Archbishop of £3,780 when the bridge opened and the ferry closed. Enquiries then revealed that the ferry had made a profit of £928 during the previous seven years, and this would have been more if two new boats had not been built, 'the ferry being in a very bad condition at the commencement of these seven years'. The Act was amended in 1737 to give a choice of location for the bridge, either from New Palace Yard or the site of the horse ferry. The former was chosen, and the bridge opened in 1750, but as it took mostly vehicular traffic, the ferry seems to have continued, taking foot passengers.

Lambeth continued to grow as a suburb and another bridge was being considered. A private company obtained an Act in 1809 but failed to get the necessary finance. Following a petition received in the Commons[25] on 23 February 1830 from freeholders, occupiers of houses and inhabitants of the parishes of St John the Evangelist in the City and Liberty of Westminster and St Mary at Lambeth in Surrey, leave was given for them to bring in a Bill to build a bridge from Horseferry Road to near Fore Street and Church Street on the opposite shore, and to make convenient roads leading to it. There were other Bills brought to the House which came to nothing until in 1861 the Lambeth Bridge Act incorporated a company and in 1862 a suspension bridge was opened. The Lambeth Horse Ferry then closed for good.

REGENT BRIDGE

Regent Bridge was built between 1809 and 1816 as part of a scheme to redevelop the south bank of the Thames at Vauxhall, upstream of Lambeth Bridge. When the Bridge Company obtained their Act they were obliged to pay compensation to the watermen who operated Huntley Ferry, a Sunday service to Vauxhall Gardens. The amount paid was to be decided by a jury of twenty-four 'honest, sufficient and indifferent men'. The best way to get to the gardens, which opened about 1659 and lasted until 1859, was by boat. An evening would begin about seven o'clock when parties arrived at Whitehall or Westminster Stairs to be ferried across to Vauxhall, just south of Lambeth Palace from where it was a few yards walk to the entrance of the gardens. Supposedly this ferry was also known as Millbank Ferry, which ran from a place where the Tate Gallery now stands. Sometimes landing places with large jetties were called bridges rather than stairs. Soon after it opened the bridge was renamed Vauxhall Bridge.

CHAPTER SEVEN

The London Stairs

London Bridge is the stuff nursery rhymes and legends are made of. The identity of 'My fair lady' is not known but the nursery rhyme could refer to this legend which has been handed down for a millennium. In the tenth century the ferry which crossed the Thames between Southwark and Church Yard Alley (the site of St Magnus the Martyr) and carried the main highway between Middlesex and Surrey was rented from the City of London by one John Audery or Over, a waterman.[1] He and his wife willed the ferry to their daughter Mary. On hearing of this windfall her lover made haste to London but fell and broke his neck. Whereupon Mary founded a House of Sisters known as St Mary Overy's.[2] Later it was taken by a College of Priests who built a wooden bridge and were responsible for its upkeep. By 1163 the bridge had been destroyed by fire or swept away by flood. A stone bridge was erected in 1209 and despite being damaged by fire several times, it lasted until 1831, thus fulfilling the prediction of the nursery rhyme's last verse, 'Build it up with stone so strong, Dance o'er my lady lee ...'twill last for ages long.'

The narrow bridge, with its twenty pointed arches, top-heavy with houses of three and four storeys high built along its length, remained the only means of crossing the river for centuries, other than by boat. Between the City and the sea no other way was possible. Few, if any public ferries existed in the stretch of river through London and the Pool of London. Instead, watermen would ply for trade from stairs or steps down to the water on both the left and right banks. Apart from some private ones attached to large houses or establishments, all the rest of the stairs, about a hundred, were recognised as places where by 'custom and practice' it was safe to be picked up or put down by a specified boat, usually a wherry operated by a licensed waterman. Each waterman was allotted a particular place from where he could work by the Company of Watermen, who also determined the fares to be charged. These regulations were strictly enforced.

'Fare' is a word meaning the expense of a journey or passage across water and derives from the Anglo-Saxon 'fare'[3] or 'foer' – a journey, also the verb 'faran' – to travel. The term 'feriage' is an archaic term meaning the fare for crossing a ferry. Charges were set out for watermen long before their Company was inaugurated. The set charge in 1293 on the Long Ferry from Gravesend to London was one halfpenny but watermen were charging double and were fined. In 1313, when the case came up again, the fare was the same. By 1370 the cost of river travel from Billingsgate to Gravesend was 2d. Fares were altered in 1559 and again in 1671 when the cost of travel from London to Limehouse was 1s by oars and sixpence by sculler. All journeys from stairs between London Bridge and Westminster were to be sixpence or threepence according to the type of boat. Fares were much the same in 1770 when passengers could be ferried directly over the water from stairs situated between Vauxhall and Limehouse for 4d. Longer journeys could be undertaken from both Queenhithe and

Old London Bridge. Looking towards the city. Billingsgate Wharf is just downstream to the right. The tall ships could not get through the bridge. Engraving published 1710. (via Wikimedia Commons)

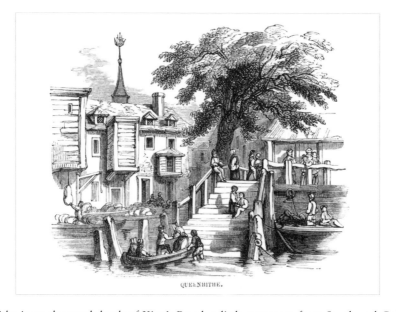

Queenhithe is on the north bank of King's Reach a little upstream from Southwark Bridge. To Mr and Mrs S. C. Hall it was reminiscent of the Thames bank in the eighteenth century but it dated from Saxon times. (From Halls' *Book of the Thames*)

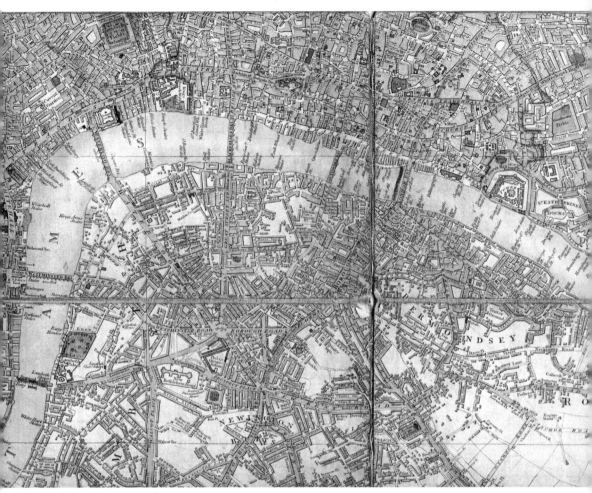

Cary's 'New Plan of London', 1828, marks many stairs and docks existing at that time. Scale 1 mile to 1 inch. (The thick lines show where the sections of the map are pasted to the linen backing.)

Hungerford stairs to Walton on Tuesdays, Thursdays and Saturdays in summer, and Tuesdays and Saturdays in winter. A barge went to Staines from Queenhithe stairs on Tuesdays and Fridays.

Each set of stairs had a name, sometimes taken from that of the neighbouring inn, or an important place like Whitehall, or an obscure derivation as with Pickle Herring.[4] Watermen were required to memorise the names and places and the fares before they were given a licence. The taxi-drivers' 'knowledge' works in the same way today, taking three years to obtain. Stairs were often timber built, but the busier ones were of stone for use at high tide. To access the littoral zone (the shore between high and low water levels), causeways would be provided. These were constructed into the water, like bridges, which explains why they were referred to as such.

Landowners who had access to stairs through their property would try to gain benefit from it. A letter book of April 1417 under Henry V records an 'Ordinance forbidding the exclusive of the common people from certain wharves and stairs

on the banks of the Thames'. 'Certain persons who hold wharves and stairs have been making profit by charging one penny or tuppence or more for them to wash their clothes, taken their water which they have done time out of mind, whereas those persons pay nothing for the land they occupy. The common good has been supplanted. It is ordained that they shall not disturb or molest any one fetching, drawing and taking water or beating and washing their clothes. On pain of imprisonment.'

Henry VIII was very concerned about the governance of the river and in order to control it he set up the Company of Watermen in 1514. To make the river safer for navigation, he ordered that extraneous structures like water-wheels and weirs should be removed from the river. He was alarmed by how skill, dexterity and brute force were needed by the Royal Watermen to 'shoot' the rapids caused by the narrow arches of London Bridge where it became a blockage. Specialist watermen called 'bridge shooters' were engaged to navigate the bridge. Cardinal Wolsey[5] was not alone in refusing to risk this dangerous undertaking when making his weekly

The Custom House overlooking the Upper Pool of London. Just downstream from
Billingsgate, it had its own sets of stairs for the benefit of visitors. The scene shows Thames
barges, a lighter and wherries. The present structure is a replica of the one shown here which
was bombed in the Second World War. Print undated.

visit to the King at Greenwich. Instead he would take to his barge at his own stairs
at York House (renamed Whitehall in 1530 when it was taken by the King) with
his yeomen and his gentlemen. They landed again at Three Cranes in the Vintry,
and with all his paraphernalia and the broad seal carried in front, the Cardinal
would ride on a mule through Thames Street to Billingsgate, where his barge
was waiting, to be rowed to Greenwich. Other noblemen's houses were situated
between the Strand and the left bank, each with their own stairs, often very
elaborate. They included Somerset House, Arundel House, Essex House, Salisbury
House and Northumberland House. Somerset House had alterations and its stairs
removed in 1776, but all the rest have been demolished, remembered only by
street names. The York Water Gate preserved in Embankment Gardens by Temple
Underground Station was built in 1626-27 for the first Duke of Buckingham at
another York House, not Wolsey's, but a different house bought by the Archbishop
of York in 1557.

People were still being oppressed over their right of access to the river in 1690,
as recorded in the House of Commons Journal.[6] A petition was presented from

landowners and tenants bordering the River Thames within the jurisdiction of the City of London. They claimed the Water Bailiff 'under such pretended powers hath very unduly and oppressively exacted great sums from the inhabitants living on the banks of the river, for letting down stairs on their own freeholds and taking compositions for the same.' He has taken some who refuse to pay to court but many have not been able to defend their suits and have lost their rights. Petitioners have been charged tolls and taxes illegally by the City officers. The House referred the matter to the committee who kept the markets of the City of London.

However, stairs and access to them continued to be free. An indenture of 1656 for the Star Tavern[7] in East Smithfield mentions the messuage and wharf, also the liberty of ingress and egress and the passage unto and from the River of Thames (obviously an entry leading to stairs). Some stairs were situated at the corners of wharves, but as the river became more and more hemmed in by buildings, the alleyways leading to it were protected. Old photographs show archways to covered ways through warehouse buildings made to preserve the rights of way which were so important. Up until the 1850s new bridges were being built with stairs at both ends and often on both sides too. Nevertheless, when Sir Joseph Bazalgette engineered the Thames Embankment in the 1860s, many stairs were obliterated.

We note some of the more well-known stairs, beginning with Blackfriars Stairs (a list of names is published in the appendix). On Thursday 23 July 1795 Rev. William MacRitchie wrote in his *Diary of a Tour through Great Britain*, 'About 10 o'clock walk to Blackfriars Bridge on purpose to take a boat up the river to Westminster, but find it impracticable on account of the high west wind and the want of the tide'. Instead he walked along the Strand. Blackfriars Stairs were in existence in 1294 when a lane was noted which led to the 'Comon Staires of the Thames'. A bridge was built at Blackfriars in 1766, replacing a ferry which had been very popular, as it conveyed theatre-goers to the theatres on the South Bank. The Bridge Management Committee agreed to pay the Company of Watermen for the loss of their Sunday charity ferry. As an average of £409,000 had been taken in fares over the previous fourteen years, the recompense was considerable. It was a sum of £13,650 in consolidated 3 per cent annuities. Blackfriars Stairs feature in a typical[8] English folk song, first recorded in 1595, which tells of a love match between a young waterman who 'sang so sweet, he sang so merry' and a young goose girl who wanted to go to Faringdon Fair and had no money for the fare. Consequently, 'And now they have waterman one, two, three, four.'

Stangate Stairs at Lambeth were built for his own convenience by John de Shipley (or Sheppey), Bishop of Rochester, in 1356. There might have been an ancient crossing here, which went out of use when the Horseferry and then Westminster Bridge made it unviable.

Temple Stairs was the scene of a dramatic event in 1440. Eleanor Cobham, the Duchess of Gloucester, was convicted of witchcraft and high treason and sentenced to perform public penance at three open places. On 13 November she landed at Temple Stairs and walked to St Paul's carrying a large wax taper which she offered at the high altar. The next day she landed at Old Swan Stairs and took another to Cree-Church near Aldgate. Two days later, from Queenhithe she went to St Michael's Cornhill and completed her penance.

Traitor's Gate at the end of Water Lane was one of three sets of stairs at the Tower of London and was for prisoners. The Queen's Stairs were beneath the Byward Gate and the belfry, with a passage by bridge and postern through the Byward Tower into Water Lane and were used for royalty only. Galleyman Stairs were seldom used and lay under the Cradle Tower from where there was a private entrance to the royal quarters. A wharf was on the riverfront.

Limehouse Hole Stairs shown on the left. A regular ferry across to the Surrey shore also worked from here. Postcard. (Courtesy of www.eastlondonpostcard.co.uk)

Wapping Old Stairs next door to the Town of Ramsgate on Wapping High Street is a rare survival of the passages down to the river. (Courtesy www.eastlondonpostcard.co.uk)

One edition of Izaak Walton's *The Compleat Angler* edited by Sir John Hawkins tells the story of waterman John Reeves, who plied from Essex Stairs. Most of his customers were anglers in the Thames. Reeves would watch for a shoal of roach coming downstream from the country, then go round his customers to alert them. Usually the fish would settle at Blackfriars or Queenhithe or most often about the chalk hills (rubble) near London Bridge. He charged 2s per tide. Some of his regular people were so grateful they raised enough money between them to buy him a waterman's coat and silver badge which had an impression of himself in his boat with an angler. A new coat was given to him each year until he died in about 1730!

Dowgate Stairs in the Dowgate Ward encountered problems. In 1677 the chamberlain was admonished for not rebuilding the stairs and not paving the wharf at the bottom of Ebgate Lane, 'which are now in a bad condition and dangerous to all passengers'. The inhabitants complained about the City water bailiff in 1698. He had 'greatly vexed and molested for years' those tradesmen who had stairs and piles, saying they were nuisances. The tradesmen maintained the piles, etc. were actually beneficial to the Ward and to the City and the bailiff was harassing them 'for private lucre and gain'.

Limehouse Hole Stairs date from the end of the seventeenth century when a substantial malt distillery was built on the riverside.[9] Nearby was a public house known as the Chequers, later the Horns & Chequers. Watermen plied from two sets of stairs there but one was stopped, leaving those at the end of Thames Place. When steamboats were threatening their livelihoods in 1843, watermen erected a floating pier at the stairs. The Thames Conservancy built new stairs onto the foreshore in 1860, followed by a floating pier in 1870. This was replaced in 1901 by a LCC pier, a walkway onto a pontoon to serve the 'Penny Steamer' service but removed by the PLA in 1948. Although the stairs and Thames Place were closed off in 1967, they survived until redevelopment took place in 1990.

Sabbs' Stairs were at Sabbs' Dock opposite number 75 Lower Thames Street on the west side of Bear Quay near the Custom House.[10] Probably the stairs date from 1516 when a licence was given to John Sabbe to make a bridge (landing stage) 24 feet long and 6 feet wide into the Thames at the south end of his wharf, 'Sabbes' Key'. There was to be a stair at the end of 16 feet down.

Wapping Old Stairs are the best known and still exist, looking steep and dangerous. Once known as a hideout for smugglers and notorious criminals who frequented the Prospect of Whitby and Town of Ramsgate taverns, it is now a perfectly respectable area. Still, it will always be associated with Execution Dock close by, although the exact site is not known. Crimes committed at sea had to be dealt with at sea, so this is where pirates were hung for the tide to wash over them three times, the so-called 'Grace of Wapping'. Captain Kidd in 1701 deserved worse treatment; he was hung over the water in a cage for twenty years. An execution here was first mentioned in 1440. The pub has erected a gallows for its customers to be reminded of this. Originally the pub was known as Devil's Tavern and dates from the time of Henry VIII. It was renamed after a fire to become the Prospect of Whitby after a square-rigged collier which frequently moored there.

In another old song, 'Wapping Old Stairs', which was incorporated in *A Song for the Lord Mayor's Table* by William Walton (1902-83), Molly laments the roving eye of her waterman. She implores him to be true and if he is she sings 'Still your trousers I'll wash and your grog too I'll make'. A slightly different version has been attributed to Charles Dibdin (1745-1841), composer of *Tom Bowling*.

Your Molly has never been false, she declares,
Since last time we parted at Wapping Old Stairs.

There was so much thieving, looting and corruption in the docklands in the eighteenth and nineteenth centuries that a magistrate, Patrick Colquhoun, decided to form a special police force in 1798. Together with John Harriot, a master mariner, they set up the Marine Police Force at Wapping. The site by Wapping Old Stairs is still the headquarters of the Marine Support Unit[11] of the Metropolitan Police, which operates for 54 miles between Staines Bridge and Deptford Creek. The Force cost £5,000 to run annually and this was shared between the Exchequer and the West India Merchants & Planters Company. Both would stand to benefit by increased surveillance on the river. Five of their surveyors were watermen engaged to patrol the river by day and night in open rowboats. It is the oldest police force in Britain. Robert Peel formed the Metropolitan Police Force in 1829.

Wapping was said to have eight public stairs. Pelican Stairs were next to The Prospect, reputedly London's oldest riverside inn, at 57 Wapping Wall, and were approached along a narrow alleyway. The name may also derive from a ship. Sir Francis Drake's flagship *The Golden Hinde* was first named the *Pelican*.

The Custom House is situated to the west of the Tower between Lower Thames Street and a terrace beside the river. It began as a wool wharf a little to the east and in order to regularise the wool trade the Sheriff of the City of London in 1383 started the Custom House. King Richard II was so grateful he gave the sheriff 40s a year for the rest of his life. The building was burnt down in the Great Fire and rebuilt by Wren. It was destroyed by fire again in 1714 and rebuilt. This happened again in 1814 when it was rebuilt by architect David Laing. Robert Smirke took down the centre and erected a new front in 1828. Throughout its existence the Custom House quays have been very busy. There were a number of wharves, with stairs to them, and also stairs for people going about their business. Bear Quay and Bear Key Stairs were particularly well known.

Pickle Herring Stairs at Southwark are known because of the quaint name. It probably refers to the pottery making tin-glazed earthenware, or English Delft, which stood on the site now occupied by City Hall (the Dutch are fond of pickled herrings). Flemish potters had brought the craft of tin-glazed pottery to England in the late sixteenth century and Southwark dominated production from 1615 to around 1685. Pickle Herring Street ran in front of the present-day Potters Fields Park. Vine Lane on the east side of the Unicorn Theatre ran directly to Pickle Herring Stairs.

Bargehouse Stairs were on the South Bank, where Bargehouse Street now reaches the river. They were used as the landing place for the King's old bargehouse where the great barge of state and other lesser river craft were kept by the Crown. Trade tokens inscribed 'Bargehouse Alley' have been found. The alley branched off from Upper Ground. A pub called The Old Bargehouse, which stood at the corner of the alley and Upper Ground was marked on an OS map of 1857. It was demolished in about 1908 for the new Post Office Electric Works.

In the face of new riverside developments in the Pool of London (from London Bridge to just beyond Tower Bridge) and further downstream, many of the stairs together with the rights of way to them have been eradicated. Some groups of people, like amateur rowers, walkers and archaeologists, have campaigned to save them, with little success: only about eleven remain to give free access to the river. This, as has been shown, is a common right, inherited since time immemorial. The City of London in 2002 recommended that river and foreshore access (the stairs and steps) should be opened up where there is an 'historical precedent and a practical need'. When has a practical need given us a humanised, interesting and safe environment in which to live? Organisations such as the Pool of London Partnership and its offshoot, the

Cross River Partnership, are concerned with the big issues, but it is the little nooks and crannies in London which lift the heart. Those that survive are indicated in The Thames Path by David Sharp. The book is a National Trail Guide which follows the Thames for 184 miles and through London to the tip of the Isle of Dogs on the left bank and to the Thames.

CHAPTER EIGHT
Wapping, Ratcliff and Rotherhithe

The Thames where it passes Wapping on the left bank and Rotherhithe (Exp. 173 350 802) on the right is somewhat narrower than elsewhere, and provides a convenient crossing point. The hamlet or district of Ratcliff is half a mile further downstream nearer to Limehouse, but now called Shadwell in the Borough of Tower Hamlets. Ratcliff used to figure quite strongly in the history of the river, where ships were built and embarkations were made. It was here that a red cliff, the end of a fold in the underlying tertiary rock of the Thames Basin that was met by the river, provided shelter from the winds. A ford lay between Ratcliff and Rotherhithe but was superseded by ancient ferries from both Wapping and Ratcliff to the Surrey shore when Wapping Marsh was reclaimed and the river deepened. Daniel Defoe in his journey round Britain in 1722 visited 'Redriff (or Rotherhithe as they write it)' and explains how the place is so built up it merges into Deptford, but he meant only on the landward side.

WAPPING-ROTHERHITHE FERRY

Trinity House of Deptford Transactions records a site meeting,[1] thought to be at Ratcliff, on 24 March 1619, of Trinity Masters with two men, Coytmore and Rogers, an anvil maker, concerning a wharf Coytmore wanted to build out into the river. They decided that the wharf would not be prejudicial to the river or to the trade of Rogers. Also 'if Rogers was licensed to build out his wharf only as far as the wharf of Cotymore', it would not be prejudicial to the river, provided that Rogers 'carry out his wharf only fifty feet adjoining to the wharf of Cotymore, and then to fall off by a right line fifteen feet and then again to go right out keeping equal distance from the wharf of Coytmore'. If built like that, Rogers' wharf would 'leave a way of seven feet on it for the ferry place and for people to have free recourse to the waterside. The falling of fifteen feet is to leave space for a ferry and boats to land, as hitherto.'

Volume Four of the Victoria County History of Surrey describes a grant made in 1684 to Christopher Monck, Duke of Albemarle. The grant concerned a right to hold a market at Rotherhithe every Thursday and Saturday and two fairs lasting two days each in April and October every year. Besides this he was given a ferry 'for the transport of men, beasts, wheels, carts, goods and merchandise across the Thames with profits correspondent to those of the ferry at Greenwich.' Monck died without issue in 1688, but in 1700 the markets, fairs and ferry were held by another Christopher Monck. After making this statement the historian in 1914 declared no more references to those rights had been found. Nor has any more documentary evidence been found for this ferry ever since.

The conclusion is made that the ferry lapsed, because in 1755 a petition[2] was sent from inhabitants of Ratcliff and Rotherhithe for a ferry to be established between the two places with new roads for the convenience of the public. A further petition from the inhabitants of Blackwall asked for an extension of the ferry to Duke Shore, the cost of which would be £1,500, with annual running costs of £146 4s. The Act, entitled[3] 'An Act for Establishing and Maintaining a ferry across the River Thames in the hamlet of Ratcliffe [sic] in the County of Middlesex and the Parish of Rotherhithe in the County of Surrey', was passed the same year. In 1761 a plan was drawn by George Dance for a new road to the ferry in Narrow Street, Ratcliff. A piece of garden ground was to be taken to widen the original road. Queen Street also was a new road constructed to the ferry.

A 'headfast' (rope) about six fathoms long was stolen from a barge at Rotherhithe ferry in 1769. Joseph Booth and Michael Hagen were accused at the Old Bailey of the theft from James Burrows of Lambeth, a lighterman. They passed it to one Nicholls of Deptford, who received the headfast knowing it to be stolen.

It was a horse ferry,[4] described in 1775 as 'that ferry from Narrow Street, Ratcliff is accounted as a safe, easy and short communication for horses and carriages of any sort, between roads on the north side of the Thames and east of London and the counties of Surrey and Kent. But with all its inconveniences this ferry is but little frequented and the lease of the adjoining Ratcliff estate to Mr. Beesley is mortgaged and foreclosed.'

Notwithstanding, there was still a need for a crossing, especially as the docks were getting busier. It was thought that a tunnel would be the best solution. The Thames Archway Company was formed in 1805 to provide a tunnel as a substitute for the ferry, using the same line and approaches. Under the supervision of Richard Trevithick a pilot scheme began in 1801 but soon ran into trouble from quicksands which became suspended in water. Another attempt was made in 1807 using proven tunnelling methods but they were not satisfactory and the work was abandoned only 200 feet away from the target. New technology was needed. The Thames Archway Company was dissolved in 1809; it was generally thought tunnelling under the Thames was impossible.

THE THAMES TUNNEL

Meanwhile, a brilliant engineer, Marc Isambard Brunel (1769-1849), who already had many important inventions to his name, was working on the problem. His solution proved to be one of the best engineering feats of all time, using a method of tunnelling basically the same, using modern technology, as today. Marc Brunel with Thomas Cochrane patented the tunnelling shield in 1818.[5] It was an apparatus built like a wall at the required height of 22 feet with twelve cast-iron frames which were divided into three working platforms. It was then divided into twenty-four cells (some say thirty-six), each one for a workman. In front of each man was a wooden board placed against the earth to be displaced. The workman would remove the board, excavate the earth to a certain depth, a few inches at a time and replace the board against the new surface. Props would keep the boards in position. Bricklayers would follow behind, and when they had lined the top, sides and bottom of the tunnel, the shield could be propelled forwards into the space created using two screw jacks, one above and one below.

Private investors, including the Duke of Wellington, could see the potential of this new invention and set up the Thames Tunnel Company in 1824. Before tunnelling could begin on a new line, a large shaft had to be constructed at Rotherhithe. This encountered many problems but was ready by 1825 for work to begin underground. Progress was slow, workers, Brunel included, were made ill by the polluted air, and when the resident engineer resigned because of ill health, Brunel's son, Isambard Kingdom Brunel, aged twenty, took over his position. Only about twelve feet a week could be cut and about 600 visitors a day would come to watch, paying one shilling each. The tunnel flooded from above in 1827 but was repaired by Brunel Jr by sealing the breach with bags of clay, which he dropped from a diving bell suspended from a boat. To celebrate his success, a banquet was held in the tunnel.

Marc Brunel's tunnelling shield. Contemporary illustration *c.* 1840, possibly from *The Illustrated London News*. (via Wikimedia Commons)

Thames Tunnel became part of one of the first underground railways in the world. Illustration from *The Illustrated London News* of 8 January 1870. (via Wikimedia Commons)

Unfortunately, another flood came the following year when six men died and Isambard just escaped with his life. Financial problems caused the project to be walled off and abandoned for seven years while Marc Brunel sought to raise more money. This he did, partly with a Treasury loan of £247,000. Work began again in February 1836 with a new shield and after further delays and setbacks the tunnel finally opened to the public on 25 March 1843. It is 1,200 feet long and consists of two parallel vaults, horseshoe shaped, fourteen feet wide and sixteen feet high, which join at intervals by cross arches.

Described by an American traveller as the 'eighth wonder of the world', the tunnel was fitted with lighting, roadways and spiral staircases at each end, accessed through marble halls. An engine house was built at Rotherhithe to house the pumping equipment for drainage. Many thousands of pedestrians passed along after paying one penny each at the turnstiles. Among them were tourists come to see the new wonder and visit the shops and fairground in the underground arcades. Souvenirs were created for them, in particular a peepshow, also a Protean view or transformation, which was a lithograph printed on thin paper with a second view pasted behind. When held to the light the first image would disappear, revealing the hidden second image.

Although popular with pedestrians, the tunnel was not a success financially, partly because the projected spiral ramps for vehicles were never built. It had two bends almost at right angles, to avoid horses being frightened by the light at the end of the tunnel, it is said, so it remained a foot tunnel until sold to the East London Railway Company in 1865 to become one of the first sections of underground railway in the world.

THAMES STEAM FERRY (ABORTED)

An abortive attempt to set up what could have become a monopoly of Thames river crossings was made in 1857. A company was launched on 4 February named the Thames Steam Ferries or Floating Bridge Company Ltd.[6] The objects were for 'building, keeping and maintaining ferries or floating bridges across the Thames with proper chains and landing places for the conveyance and passage of foot passengers, horses, carriages, cattle, goods and merchandise and other portable articles over and across the Thames between such points or places as the company from time to time determine'. Nominal capital was £75,000 divided into 7,500 shares of £10 each. Already there were seven subscribers all from London, who had taken 240 shares between them. Their signatures had been witnessed the day before by Ward Tucker, a solicitor of 25 Clements Lane, Lombard Street.

Hon. Frederick Cadogan, Jonathan Hopkinson and Charles Lennox Peel were the promoters of the Company and were also directors, together with two other persons. In March 1859 George Taylor, registrar of Joint Stocks, London, received a letter from Moores & Sills of Bread Street, London. 'In reply to your letter … we beg to inform you that this company ceased to exist in the month of November 1857'. The matter did not end there; the Company's registration office had a letter, 'we have to call your attention to the failure of the Thames Steam Ferries or Floating Bridge Company Ltd requesting returns as per the Companies Act 1862'. Finally, twenty-four years later, in March 1881, Reeves & Hooper of 17 Warwick Street, wrote to W. H. Cousins, Registrar, Company's office, Somerset House. 'In reply to your letter to the secretary of the Thames Steam Ferries or Floating Bridge Company we inform you that nothing was done beyond registering the Company. No shares were subscribed for and no business was undertaken. Therefore the name of the Company can be struck off the register.' The floating bridge was invented by James Meadows Rendel, Civil Engineer (1799-1856), initially for crossing the Dart at Dartmouth, in 1831. No floating bridges were installed by Rendel on the Thames.

The demise of the Thames Tunnel Company left the field open for another ferry enterprise to become established, using steam as propulsion. Rev. Harry Jones, writing in *East and West London*, published in 1875, describes the project. 'This, if provided, will be able to carry the loaded wagons which are now obliged to go round by London Bridge, some mile and a half off. As it is, I generally like to cross by a wherry, which provides a pleasant change from the usual modes of locomotion in London and in this case, when the place to be reached is Rotherhithe, affords the quickest, most obvious, though sometimes the least conventional means of access'.

THAMES STEAM FERRY COMPANY

Frederic Eliot Duckham, a member of the Institute of Civil Engineers, gives an account of the setting up of the Thames Steam Ferry Company in 1874 in the Proceedings of the Institute for 1879/80. Given certain data, Duckham of Millwall Docks was asked, as project manager, to design 'appliances' to work this new ferry. His brief was not an easy one. The main point to contend with was the tidal river, 320 yards wide with a range of 20 feet 6 inches at spring tides. There was a big difference in the low-water mark at the two landing places. Tunnel Wharf at Wapping had a low-water mark of 170 feet from the quay line, whereas at Church Stairs, Rotherhithe, it was only 70 feet away. His instructions were that the ferry boat should be able to convey twelve two-horse wagons each way, plus foot passengers at quarter-hour intervals. The Thames Conservancy had given a concession allowing for landing stages within certain limits. However, gangways connecting the landing stages with the shore must be fixed at 8 feet above Trinity House high-water level. These requirements had not been precedented.

The Company had been incorporated with a nominal capital of £100,000 and Limited Liability. The site they selected was across the Thames directly over the Thames Tunnel, 1½ miles downriver from London Bridge. This had the advantage that, as no vessels were allowed to moor within a certain distance of the line of the tunnel, the ferry boats could steer a clearer course than in any other part of the river. The landing place on the Middlesex shore was near London Docks, whilst on the Surrey side it was near Commercial Docks, thus providing plenty of custom.

Duckham began his task by designing the vessels. They were to be 82 feet long, 42 feet extreme width, 9 feet deep and draw 5 feet of water when laden. Disconnected low-pressure paddle engines of 30 horsepower were fitted, meaning one paddle wheel could be disconnected while the other was in motion, thus giving valuable manoeuvrability. They were equipped with two funnels of 6 feet placed on the sponson near the paddle boxes. The deck would be a clear rectangle the full length of the hull and 27 feet wide for vehicles. There would be plenty of space at the side for foot passengers. Bulwarks at the ends were hinged so they could be lowered to form a connecting stage between the deck and the lift platform (as in today's ro-ros). They would be counterweighted to allow for varying strains on the hoisting chain.

As to the landing stages, dolphins to support them to be cast-iron cylinders sunk 20 feet into the bed of the river. Dwarf lampposts to show two red lights at night as regulations specify would be set above them. The platforms or stages would be 70 feet long and 35 feet wide. The Wapping platform would have a lift with the tide of 26 feet, and the Rotherhithe 23 feet. A jetty, supported by cast iron screw columns, to connect the lift with the shore, would be needed only at Wapping. It would be 100 feet long by 19 feet 6 inches wide and spread like a fan for the remaining 40 feet. There was to be a unique way of embarking. Passengers would pass on to the raised pathway on top of the side girders, which would be lowered as the boat approached. The time taken to raise the platform by winding drum connected with eight to ten heavy chains and worked by a 120-hp steam engine was two minutes, then another four minutes to actually cross the river. Chains were used to raise the platforms because there was no other possibility at the time. Balance weights were not in the original design.

Working hours were 6 a.m. to 8 p.m., except Sundays. Fares would vary between one shilling and half a crown, but half price if the vehicles were empty. Cabs were charged 8d but free if empty; omnibuses 1s; foot passengers 1d; but cattle 6d a head and in proportion.

Alderman Stone, Lord Mayor of London, arrived to lay the foundation stone at Wapping on board the ill-fated *Princess Alice* on 11 May 1875.[7] The opening ceremony took place in October 1876 when the Lord Mayor was conveyed on the paddle ferry boat *Pearl*. Her sister ship was *Jessy May*. Both these iron vessels were built by Edward & Symes shipbuilders of Cubitt Town. They were steered at both ends by a rudder, and were squarish, like floating boxes. The engines were built by Maudslay & Field of Lambeth, who also built the tunnelling shield to Marc Brunel's design.

The undertaking was not an overall success. Some expected contracts did not materialise and operational difficulties were experienced in bringing the vessels to shore. The Company purchased land at the landing place at Wapping, possibly from the Thames Tunnel Company, and built substantial warehouses, which were fitted with hydraulic cranes. This area is delineated on a plan included with an application to the Board of Trade to build an embankment 102 feet 8 inches long to Tunnel Wharf. On the landward side of the wharf was the shaft of the Thames Tunnel. The Board gave permission, 'In exercise of the powers vested in them by the Thames Conservancy Act of 1857, The Board of Trade approve of the embankment proposed to be constructed at Tunnel Wharf by the Thames Steam Ferry Company ... Dated 23rd July 1857.' It had been approved by the Conservators of the River Thames on 12 July. The base was to be Portland Cement concrete, and the supporting wall of Blue Lias concrete.

Whether the embankment was not built according to the original specification is not known, but in December 1876 the Board granted permission to the Company for 'campshedding' their premises at Wapping. The term was used along the Thames for the process of lining a riverbank for protection, using piles and planks which were called 'campshots'. The term was first recorded in 1691 when they were found under St Magnus Church by London Bridge after the Great Fire. Probably the word is derived from Flemish, and is related to the old English 'wainscot'. Estimated costs of running the ferry were £11,330 per annum, with receipts of about £30,000. In 1878 the ferry was used for shipping supplies from Woolwich Arsenal to East India Dock by the RASC. A few months later the first Official Liquidator,[8] James Waddell, was appointed and service curtailed. The accounts of the Company from the date of his first entry of 9 November 1878 to October 1887 are recorded in a bound account book produced in the High Court of Justice, Chancery Division.

Waddell noted 'balance remaining due on shares £126.11', with a further entry 21 July 1879, 'returned £591 9s 2d, the amount subscribed to a proposed issue of preference shares under order 30.4.1879 including other small payments'. Harrington Evans Broad, of 1 Wallbrook, London, was appointed as the second Official Liquidator on 25 April 1884. He shows a balance at the Bank of England on 13 March 1884 as £1,111 12s 7d from the liquidation of assets, with an additional sum of £342 16s 5d from E. Vickers. A single entry for costs, £346 1s 0d may relate to the campshedding, as in 1886, by which time the balance at the Bank of England was £975 18s 0d. The land at Wapping was recorded as a sale of asset, with £250 as down payment and £750 due, a total of £1,000. The bottom line in 1887 shows £1,975 18s. Further liquidation proceedings took place until 1891.

Dividends were paid out in July 1886, including £12 2s 3d to the engineers Maudslay & Field and £23 3s 8d to East Ferry Road Engineering Works. Frederic Duckham,

Wapping. Illustration by Rigby Graham for *London Pictures and other Poems* by Victor Fenech, 1976. (Courtesy of the artist)

engineer and designer of the ferry boats, was chief engineer of the Millwall Dock Company and set up the East Ferry Road Works on the Isle of Dogs to manufacture the Duckham Weighing Machine. They became the chief manufacturers of hydraulic machinery in London.

Mr J. Handfield applied to the Board of Trade[9] in 1889 for permission to remove the steam ferry jetty and dolphins at Rotherhithe, which indicates the ferry had already ceased trading. Tower Bridge opened nearby in 1894. It is not known if the Steam Ferry Company had received compensation.

ROTHERHITHE TUNNEL

An Act to make another tunnel was passed in 1900. The Thames Tunnel (Rotherhithe and Ratcliff) Act enabled a new horse carriage and foot tunnel to be built at a cost of £1 million. It took four years to build and then took 2,600 vehicles and many foot passengers a day. Now known as the Rotherhithe tunnel, it runs from the Shadwell area of Limehouse to Salter Road in Rotherhithe, with an air shaft on either bank. Although the original pedestrian ways were later blocked, the tunnel still fulfils its purpose today.

LIMEHOUSE FERRY

There had been a ferry at Limehouse since the Middle Ages, being on a pilgrim's route to Canterbury from Waltham Abbey. Later it became a horse ferry.[10] It ran from the Horseferry in Limehouse to the end of Lavender Lane on the Surrey bank, but may have changed its landing place slightly when the entrance to the Regent's Canal Dock, which opened in 1820, was cut through to the river. Greenwoods' map of *c.* 1827 shows the horse ferry.

Very little is known about the ferry except that it is mentioned in several criminal proceedings at the Old Bailey. Limehouse was a notorious area for robbery with violence, and the ferry offered a means of a quick getaway. One case heard on 29 January 1855 did concern the ferry and the ferryman.[11] From evidence given something is learnt of the manner in which the ferry was conducted. After attending their niece's wedding at St Ann's, Limehouse, on Sunday 14 January, Mr and Mrs William Timmins went to Limehouse stairs to take a ferry over to their home on the Surrey side, where Mr Timmins had been a foreman at the Commercial Docks. They were accompanied to the stairs by the bride's father, mother and sister. At the stairs a man, who turned out to be Henry Robinson, the prisoner, said, 'Hallo, Timmins' but Timmins said he did not know him and got into the boat. Then he said to the stranger, 'Hand my mistress in, if you please.' This he did, but they both stumbled and fell in the water. When they reached the other side Robinson got out first, followed by Elizabeth Timmins while William stayed to pay the ferryman for all three of them. On arriving at Timmins' house Robinson kicked Timmins' foot from under him causing him to fall, whereupon he stole his watch and its guard. Robinson ran off, chased by other people, including a policeman who apprehended him.

At the trial the ferryman, Joseph William Campion, who lived at 73 Park Street, Poplar, gave evidence. He said he was regularly employed as a waterman and plied at Limehouse Stairs. Asked if he was the Sunday ferryman, he replied, 'No, they knock-off at 10 o'clock in winter-time and we commence the night work.' He did not see the prisoner, only the man and wife who were both 'in a state of liquor'. He had never seen Robinson before in his life until when he was before the magistrate. 'There was nobody but me and the two persons in the boat'. Asked how many he took over that night, he replied, 'Two – I cannot say how many I took altogether – I did not keep an account – sometimes we take four over – I did not take any threes that night at all – I stopped till 2 o'clock in the morning – I took several parties of two – I might have taken a couple of fours – on my oath, I did not take a party of three – I took three or four twos and two fours – I took no ones – I came there at 10 o'clock – the ferryman was there with me – he knocked off – he left off the ferry – he was on the wharf when Timmins came over – his name is Henry Temple – he was at Limehouse Stairs when I pushed off, and he left to go home – that was my first voyage that night – it was from 10 to half-past 10 o'clock – I did not see Mr. Hurley [bride's father] to my knowledge – he did not come down to the boat with the man.' In fact Mr Hurley had pushed the boat off. Later Campion revealed he had met the prisoner's uncle while walking to Greenwich and had bought him a drink. In answer to a question from the jury, Campion said Timmins had paid him fourpence, 'if I had had three passengers I must have had sixpence – it is tuppence each on a Sunday.' Robinson, aged twenty-one, was found guilty and sentenced to four years penal servitude. Added to the record in brackets is 'the witness Campion was committed to prison' (presumably for perjury).

THAMES CLIPPERS

As part of a programme to utilise the Thames for river transport and to save congestion on the roads, 'Thames Clippers'[12] operate the Rotherhithe ferry between Canary Wharf Pier on the west side of the Isle of Dogs and Hilton Docklands Nelson Dock Pier at Rotherhithe. Known also as the Hilton Docklands-Canary Wharf Shuttle, the service can be used by foot passengers staying at the Hilton Hotel and others and operates about every ten minutes (as at May 2009).

CHAPTER NINE
The Isle of Dogs and Greenwich

The Isle of Dogs is the promontory formed by the River Thames making a large loop southerly between Limehouse and Blackwall in the east. Across the river opposite the apex of it is Greenwich, pronounced 'Grinnidge' (Exp. 162 383 783). It is not strictly an island, but it is thought in ancient times there was a small island with that name off the southern shore. The rest of the land was Stepney Marsh, or Poplar Marsh and used for arable and grazing until it was drained and industrialised from the late seventeenth century. Much speculation has been made about the derivation of the name of the Isle of Dogs.[1] One possibility is that it comes from 'dogge' or 'dogger', originally an Icelandic word given to a vessel fishing for cod, as in Dogger Bank. Although generally the vessel came to be regarded as Dutch, it had been applied also to English craft. It was a two-masted fishing vessel with bluff bows, rather like a ketch, first mentioned in 1356 and again in 1491. In the seventeenth and eighteenth centuries they were used frequently as privateers. Possibly either the vessels were built on the island or were moored up there.

Stepney Marsh was held by the Pontefract family (shortened to Pomfret) from the twelfth century and it became Pomfret Manor. In 1302 the manor was granted to Sir John Abel,[2] a royal servant and guardian of the Queen's lands. Abel acquired all the lands, liberties, freemen and villeins, the advowson of the chapel and all appurtenances of the river ferry, together with rents from properties in East Greenwich. On Sir John's death the manor was split between his three daughters. Eventually one third fell into the hands of the Crown and in 1422 Thomas Appleton held another third when he let the ferry for seven years. Thomas Woodward and his wife Emmote, of East Greenwich, took the lease for a rent of 6s 8d a year. They were to maintain the ferry and the wharf, take sufficient care of men and women crossing and allow Appleton, his household and his horses to cross free of charge. Eight years later new owners let the ferry again, this time for a rent of 26s 8d a year. By 1443 the same portion was granted with the ferry to several feoffees and shortly afterwards it was sold or escheated to the Manor of Stepney after the area had been devastated by floods. The ferry was mentioned in the will of Elizabeth Holden of Durham in 1450. It is thought the manorial estate may have been divided into three by this time; the portion to which the ferry belonged was nearest to Greenwich, with a seawall. Reclamation of land took place in the late fifteenth century.

On the Greenwich side the landing place of the medieval ferry was in the oldest part of Greenwich called 'Weremansacre'[3] in Saxon times. Bordering the river, it stretched from the local Billingsgate (Billingsgate Street still exists, near the Cutty Sark Dock) on the west to the location of Ballast Quay just east of Trinity Hospital where there is a gravel beach. It was owned by the Abbot of Ghent and the ferry was alluded to in deeds to that affect. Not only was Billingsgate the landing place of the ancient ferry to the Isle of Dogs, it was the original port and nucleus for what became the town of Greenwich and its market. Billingsgate in the City of London was closely associated with that in Greenwich. The new London Billingsgate is now situated at Canary Wharf in the Isle of Dogs.

Humpherus mentions a lease of the ferry in 1550, but he says although the ferry was supposed to be in the grant, he could not find it. However, the National Maritime Museum at Greenwich[4] has in its archives a large number of legal documents concerning Potter's Ferry, as this ferry then became known. It includes minute and account books as well as the original charter granted in the reign of Edward VI to Thomas, Lord Wentworth, along with lands in Hackney and Stepney. John Norden (1548-1625) made a reference, 'There are ferreys at Grenwich', on the manuscript version of his 1592 map of Kent.[5]

In 1626 Nowell Warner was given a lease[6] for thirty-one years at 20s a year. It stipulated that he was not to take more than tuppence for a man with horse, or one penny for a person alone, and the carriages belonging to the Lord of the Manor were to be conveyed free of charge to any landing place in Greenwich. Also, he had to repair the nearby banks and wall. The Warner family were Royal Barge Masters for generations from the time of Elizabeth to William III. Nowell's son John bought the ferry outright in 1676 and the rights were held by the Warners until 1762.

A strange occurrence happened off Greenwich, as reported in the *Marine Mercury* of 2 November 1642. 'A perfect mermaid[7] was by the last great wind driven ashore near Greenwich, with her comb in one hand and her looking glass in the other. A most fair and beautiful woman.' Perhaps their readers needed cheering up from the distress caused by the outbreak of Civil War the previous 24 August. A few days later a petition from the inhabitants of the hamlets of Poplar and Blackwall[8] was handed to the House of Commons. As a result an order was issued on 18 November giving them permission to 'cut off and stop the ferry Passage out of Kent, which may prove dangerous to the safety of those parts'. The danger did not stop because on 1 July 1643 the House of Commons Journal records another order. 'Whereas information[9] is this day given, that divers persons that have come from Oxford, or other parts of the King's Army, have passed to and fro with their coaches, horses and arms over the ferry at Greenwich. It is ordered that Captain Willoughby be required to stop the Passage to that ferry on this side of the Thames by cutting a Ditch, that no coach, cart or other carriage, may pass that way: And the Deputy Lieutenants of the Counties of Kent and Middlesex be required to take care, that no Horses, Arms or other Ammunition, or Persons suspected, do pass that way: And that they appoint some to be constantly there, to search such as they should think fit, that endeavour to pass that way.'

POTTER'S FERRY

In 1642 the ferry was valued at £11 per annum but ten years later it had increased by £10. Then described as Potter's Ferry, it ran from the south end of Chapel Lane in Millwall (the southern part of the Isle of Dogs) to East Greenwich. Millwall was so named because at least nine windmills were on the western shore of the island. There is no evidence of when Potter's Ferry first received that name, but a suggestion has been made it was one of several Thames ferries set up by that family. Or it may be a corruption of the place name Poplar.

Samuel Pepys (1633-1703) in his capacity as Secretary to the Navy Board often used the river to go about his business, particularly at Greenwich where he lived for a while when the office was evacuated in 1665 to escape the Plague in London. Early on the morning of Monday 31 July 1665, Pepys in his finery arrived at Deptford to join Sir George Carteret, Treasurer of the Navy, and his Lady to journey to Dagenham for the wedding of their daughter. They went by ferry to the Isle of Dogs, but found on arrival their coach was not there. The tide had ebbed so far the 'horse-boat could not get off on the other side the river to bring away the coach. So we were fain to stay there in the unlucky Isle of Doggs – in a chill place, the morning cool and wind fresh, above two if not three hours, to our great discontent.' They would have had food and shelter at the Ferry House, where John Mather[10] was living at the time. He may not have been the publican or ferryman but gave the House as his address when accused of receiving stolen goods at the Old Bailey.

The ferry house on the Isle of Dogs is shown clearly on all early maps of the area because there were few other buildings then. Now listed by English Heritage as Grade II, it appears to be a late-eighteenth/early-nineteenth three-storey stuccoed building which belies its seventeenth-century origins. It is situated in an area of land which comprised about an acre of what had been marsh and orchard and included part of the marsh wall and the ferry landing. Near the ferry was a building called the Starch House,[11] probably a starch factory rather than a place where starching was done, although a steam laundry was set up later. Simon Lemon, a starch-maker and haberdasher owned land near the ferry. Starch making was likely to have been an offshoot of the flour mills at Millbank in the late seventeenth century. After 1740 when the manufacture of starch was given up, the Starch House was either rebuilt or more likely renamed as the Ferry House. The Hart family had lived at the Starch House and later occupied the Ferry House in the first half of the eighteenth century. Amelia Ingram kept the Ferry House in 1837.[12] She said there were steps up to her kitchen door. Besides Victorian and twentieth century extensions there is a projecting bay on the first floor which may have been a ferry lookout. An ornamental balustrade to a roof garden has been lost.

Celia Fiennes had a happier time[13] when she crossed to get back to Hertfordshire following her 1697 journey to Dover. From Shooter's Hill, 'thence to Greenwitch 2 mile where I ferryd over, and observ'd one little shipp passed by me, which I observ'd was farr behind me in the morning at Gravesend and sailed along in sight all the tyme and was gotten before me; I ferry'd to Popler and Stepney'.

Richard Warner, of the family who owned Potter's Ferry, sold it in 1762 for 15 guineas (£15 15s) to a group of watermen calling themselves the 'Greenwich Watermen & Watermen's Company'. At this time a dispute arose because some 'men do work on the lord's day across the river from Greenwich to the Isle of Dogs, and extract large prices for passengers to pass across the river there'. The Company resolved 'that no more pensioners be admitted from the town of Greenwich, by reason of the watermen of that town laying claim to the Sunday ferry there'. For some unknown reason that Company was disbanded and instead thirteen watermen became trustees of a mutual society they set up in 1776 called the 'Isle of Dogs Ferry Society'. The society was given exclusive rights to ferry from the Isle of Dogs to Greenwich. They were to defend those rights against usurpers for over a hundred years.

At the end of the eighteenth century the ferry was very busy, as shown in a watercolour dated about 1795 by Thomas Rowlandson (1756-1827). It depicts a party landing at low tide from a rowboat (which looks too small) at Garden Stairs, Greenwich, next to the Salutation Inn, with the Royal Hospital for Seamen, now the Old Naval College, in the background. His friend, Henry Angelo, wrote that Rowlandson 'was frequently making his sketches at Greenwich, his favourite resort, both for shipping and scenes relative to the assemblage of sailors'. The assemblage here consisted of plump ladies, some dubious-looking men, two better-class ladies and a mother with two children on the landing stage. Arriving in the ferry boat with the ferryman punting in front are about seven people, two of them standing. The drawing is part of the Paul Mellon Collection. A different version is in the Victoria & Albert Museum.

THE POPLAR & GREENWICH FERRY COMPANY

At some point in the late eighteenth century the ferry seems to have stopped carrying horses, carriages and cattle, the roads across the Isle of Dogs not being suitable for such traffic. Following the opening of the West India Docks in 1799 and increased trade, improvement of the roads became vital, and a horse ferry was necessary for economic growth. After much deliberation an 'Act for establishing a ferry over the Thames from Greenwich ... to the Isle of Dogs in Middlesex and for making and maintaining roads to communicate therewith' was passed on 9 June 1812.[14] It set out to establish a 'Common Ferry for the passage and conveyance of horses, carriages and cattle and goods, wares and merchandise over the Thames in the parish of St. Alphage, Greenwich, Kent to the Isle of Dogs in Poplar Marsh, otherwise Stebonheath Marsh in the parish of St. Dunstan, Stebonheath, otherwise Stepney. It will form a direct communication between Kent and Middlesex and be of great public utility.'

'Persons have entered into a subscription to raise money to form a Company for establishing the ferry, called "The Poplar and Greenwich Ferry Company". It can have perpetual succession and a Common seal. It can alter roads, etc. without incurring any penalties of mortmain. The Company shall have one or more boats or such other vessels sufficient and proper for the passage and conveyance of horses, carriages, cattle etc. And the persons travelling on, in or with the same over and across the Thames from or near a place called the Wood Wharf to the opposite shore at a place called The Ferry House in the hamlet of Poplar and Blackwall. Also to repair a road or carriage way from Wood Wharf to the road leading from Deptford Creek Bridge to Church Street in the parish of St. Alphage. Also a road leading from the north side of the premises of Sir Charles Price Bt. near the bridge at the west end of the canal in the Isle of Dogs and then through Poplar Marsh to the Thames. If necessary they can erect a bridge upon and along the same across the Rope Ground of George Joad and Edward Spencer Curling. Also to keep another road forty-five feet wide from the ditch on the south side of the present road at the south-west corner of a dock yard belonging to Thomas Pitcher & Co. [shipbuilder] near the bridge at the east end of the canal in the Isle of Dogs through Poplar Marsh to the Thames. They can also alter other lanes in the marsh.'

There follows regulations as to when and where the meetings of the Company are to take place and who is allowed to vote at such meetings. Capital can be raised of up to £20,000, divided into 400 shares of £50 each. The Act goes on 'the Company can erect convenient dwelling houses and proper offices for the use of ferrymen or persons having the care and management of the ferry, roads and other works. They can enter any lands etc for making a survey and make good any damages. They may contract to buy lands for toll-houses, etc.

'All persons to be using the ferry shall have free liberty to access it over a road belonging to Deptford Creek Bridge Co. [incorporated by Act of Parliament 1803] ... They shall erect gates and toll-houses on the roads.' The tolls to be, 'for every horse or mule not drawing 1s.0d; Ass 6d; two-wheeled carriages drawn by one horse 6s.0d. plus 6d. for the horse; hearse driven by four horses 11s.0d; wain driven by three or four horses 10s.0d.' Charges were double on Sundays. No charges for foot passengers were stipulated; the reason for this is given later.

Further clauses were inserted regarding tolls. 'A table of tolls is to be erected at every gate and at the ferry. The tolls may be let on lease for up to three years and the lessees to display their name. Persons passing with horses, cattle etc by producing a tickit [sic] shall be exempt from toll.' (This clause is very complicated, according to what is carried – hay, sanfoin, etc. No tolls for Ordnance, barrack stores or HM forces.)

'The Company may not be compelled to ply before 4am or after 10pm between 24 March and 29 September or before 6am and after 8pm' (for the rest of the year). 'There must not be any ferrying within half mile of this ferry. No person shall be employed in navigating any boat is to be employed by the Company who shall not be a Free Waterman of the Thames.'

A special section is included dealing with the Potter's Ferry. 'Thirteen men as Trustees for the Society of Free Watermen of the River Thames, residing at Greenwich in Kent called the Isle of Dogs Ferry Society at Greenwich have or claim to be entitled to the fee simple and inheritance of a ferry for persons, horses and cattle to and from the Isle of Dogs and to and from Greenwich called Potter's Ferry: For several years past that ferry has been used for foot passengers and goods belonging to the foot passengers only, and the Ferry Society are willing to relinquish all claim to any right to carry horses, carriages and cattle across the ferry in order that such ferry may be carried on by the said Society, reserving all such claim or right as they may have to the said ferry in relation to the carrying of foot passengers and such goods across. Nothing in this Act shall give to the said Company any right to carry foot passengers across the Thames at the Ferry or in any way whatever to interfere with the claim or right of the Ferry Society to carry foot passengers and their goods or to use the landing place of the Ferry Society on the Middlesex side without the consent in writing of the Society. But the Society may negotiate to lease their ferry to the Company.'

'Lamps are to be erected on the roads and the ferry, against walls of houses and other buildings if necessary and to be kept burning. The Company may appoint a number of fit and able-bodied men to be armed and clothed in such manner to be employed as watchmen, guards or patrols either on foot or horseback, and appoint superintendents for the roads. They must prevent fires, murders, burglaries, robberies and all outrages etc on the roads. They can arrest, comprehend and detain in the Watch House such malefactors. The Company can charge extra toll for this.'

'Nothing in the Act is to prejudice or derogate from the rights, privileges etc of the Mayor and Commonalty and Citizens of the City of London, or the Lord Mayor or Masters, Wardens and Assistants of Trinity House of Deptford Strond. The Lord Mayor is Conservator of the River Thames. The Company cannot therefore interfere with the bed or banks of the river. Nor shall anything prejudice the Commissioners and Governors of the Royal Hospital for Seamen at Greenwich or the right and privilege of the Society or Company of Watermen, Wherrymen and Lightermen. This is a Public Act.'

So in other words the Potter's Ferry, run by the Society of Watermen crossing along the same or closely parallel line as the Company's new horse ferry managed to establish its sole right to carry foot passengers.

Such a big undertaking was bound to require modifications, particularly to the roads. To rectify some anomalies another Act[15] was necessary in 1814. It was explained in the preliminaries that the Company of Proprietors of the Poplar & Greenwich Ferry Company had already spent considerable sums of money in constructing works and roads 'so that free, easy and more convenient communications are now made to a ferry belonging to or claimed by a society called "The Isle of Dogs Ferry Society" to and from the Isle of Dogs and Greenwich.

'Therefore the Company conceive it reasonable to collect a toll from every person who shall be landed from or embark on board any boat at the ferries on any of the landing places either on the Kent or Middlesex side ... So every person who used the ferry shall pay one penny toll before they are permitted to pass any gate or turnpikes erected by the Company.' This clause is confusing as it suggests that people using both ferries would be required to pay a penny toll, yet only the Potter's Ferry took persons, therefore they were to be penalised. Drovers or drivers using the Company ferry would not pay to use the roads. This anomaly caused several subsequent disputes.

A new road had already been made from Sir Charles Price's premises and this made the former footway on the west side of the Mill Wall obsolete and it should be closed. The Company would provide better ways for the premises in that area to reach the new road, one of them to be a carriage way twenty feet wide. When the roads are completed the Company 'shall ever after keep them in repair'.

HM Customs Officers would have free access on these roads. Also exempt from toll would be two businesses, George Joad and Edward Spencer Curling and their employees because they were so close to the turnpike and toll-house recently erected by the Company. It was reckoned it was only 'just and reasonable they should be exempt when passing the turnpike with cattle or carriages to and from their premises'. These roads ultimately became Westferry Road and East Ferry Road.

Duckham described the ferry boats as rectangular with flat bottoms and capable of taking a two-horse dray or eight head of cattle. They were 'propelled by oars and landed or boarded freight at the sloping foreshores of the river'. Speaking in 1879 he said they were fairly typical of ferry boats[16] on the Thames at that time, ones which were to be seen near Greenwich Pier awaiting the ship breakers. He adds that a small ferry boat like them was still sometimes used between North and South Woolwich. From the ferry landing in the 1850s a one-horse bus ran across the Isle to Limehouse. It was the smallest of the Metropolitan omnibuses.

Obviously there were difficulties caused by the two ferry concerns sharing the same landing place at the Ferry Piece. The Society destroyed the toll-gates twice because, they claimed, prospective passengers for Deptford were using the Wood Wharf Ferry instead of their own Potter's Ferry and so did not have to pay the road toll. (It was illegal, but nearer for the passengers.) Both bodies were involved in litigation several times. The fourth time was in June 1856 when before the Court of Common Pleas[17] the Society as plaintiffs sought to re-establish its exclusive right to ferry passengers and their goods across the Thames at Potter's Ferry. The jury upheld their claim and asserted the defendants had infringed the right. The Society was given a certificate entitling them to costs, including those of a special jury. Expenses for the Company must have been colossal, keeping roads in repair a constant drain, with alterations to be made when new docks opened. An advertisement appeared in *The Times* for 16 July 1821 announcing, 'Poplar and Greenwich Ferry Tolls to be Let'. Tenders were called for a one-year lease for tolls collected at three gates, according to the Act and was for foot passengers, carriages and cattle. A lease for the actual ferry 'for conveying carriages and cattle across the Thames in boats belonging to the Company' was also offered.

A handwritten Statutory Regulation statement concerning the affairs of Joseph Pitt, of Eastcourt, Crudwell, Wiltshire, gives information on the subsequent history of the Company.[18] In 1813, when the share book was first opened, one Robert Robbins, solicitor of Lincoln's Inn, purchased ten £50 shares in the name of Joseph Pitt, MP for Cricklade, of Lincolns Inn. The certificates could not be found. 'The Company appeared to have been a failure and no dividends were paid for upwards of sixty years and the shares appear to have been lost sight of.' The statement, (undated but about 1880) goes on, 'The property of the company has recently been purchased by the Metropolitan Board of Works and shares have therefore become valuable. Enquiries will be made to ascertain to whom the shares belonged.' Although Pitt's address was given as Lincoln's Inn actually he did not reside there, but his son, also Joseph Pitt was admitted in 1818. Pitt the elder died in 1842, and his son in 1869. Robbin's son, George Augustus Robbins of Clayhill, Lechlade, is thought to be the signatory of the document.

Perhaps the ferry boat *Robert Chambers*, recorded as a wreck[19] off Greenwich Pier, (Exp. 161 383 780) found in 1890, was one of the Company's boats, because the horse ferry was discontinued sometime in the 1840s. In 1868 the Poplar & Greenwich Ferry Company assigned its rights to the Isle of Dogs Ferry Society (N.B. not the other way round as provided in the Act). The demise of the Company was not unexpected. It had concentrated on building and maintaining the roads and expended a great deal of money doing so. The island owed much of its prosperity to those roads which were not made toll-free until 1885 when the Metropolitan Board of Works took over.

The Society leased Potter's Ferry to the Thames Steamboat Company, who afterwards conveyed it to the London & Blackwall Railway Company, which ultimately became part of the Great Eastern Railway Company. The foot ferry continued using the *Rifleman*, a small paddle steamer which ran every twenty minutes from a point where *Cutty Sark* now rests. Up until this point the two ferries, horse and foot, had existed side by side from the same or quite close landing places on each shore, from Ferry Piece or Jackson's draw dock on the north and from Wood Wharf or Garden Stairs on the south. From the end of the nineteenth century circumstances would change.

GREENWICH FERRY COMPANY

When the Metropolitan Board of Works took over, according to their Act of 1883, they intended to operate a free steam ferry, but the plan fell through due to heavy claims for compensation.[20] Instead, another company, the Greenwich Ferry Company, obtained an Act and bought the ferry rights for £80,000 from the railway, planning to operate a steam ferry. There was still a need for a vehicular ferry over the Lower Thames, the previous horse ferry was inadequate, the vessels being too small to cope with the potential amount of traffic which could be generated. The Board of Works sought the advice[21] of Sir Frederick Bramwell Bt (1818-1903). He had been apprenticed to John Hague in Cable Street, Wapping, a mechanical engineer, where he learnt about atmospheric propulsion for railways and steam propulsion on roads. On completion of his apprenticeship Bramwell became manager of an engineering works on the Isle of Dogs and after studying law then gained a wide reputation as a consultant mechanical engineer, the management of water being a speciality. In 1874 he became President of the Institute of Mechanical Engineers and ten years later also of the Institute of Civil Engineers. His advice was that a ferry was an urgent necessity and possible. In the USA he had seen a unique system for operating ferries by an ambitious transporter platform which carried persons and vehicles smoothly to a ferry steamer whatever the state of tide. In February 1886 the proposal was accepted and in spite of various setbacks the ferry was officially opened on 13 February 1888.

The following description is taken from a report issued on 15 November 1892[22] following an inspection the day before by a large group of engineers and others interested in cross-river communications: the latest in the process of building being a tunnel near the Tower of London. (This was completed but not a success and now used for storage.) The main concern of ferries in the lower tidal Thames was the problems caused by the large fall of the tide, which was 21 feet. Now at the beginning of the twenty-first century, it is 24 feet.

'Greenwich Ferry has advantages peculiar to itself, which, in a tidal river like the Thames, are of great importance. The arrangements are such that the traffic is always carried on the level at any state of the tide, there being neither inclined gangways nor steep approaches, which are so inconvenient for vehicular traffic, especially that of a heavy character. On the foreshore of the river on either bank is an inclined railway about 350 feet in length by 41 feet wide and reaching down 145 feet into the river at low water. The way is laid with eight steel rails of the bridge section carried by a system of girders on a bed of concrete, the rate of inclination being 1 in 10. This railway carries a movable landing stage and a traversing carriage, which latter conveys the traffic between the landing stage and the shore. When the carriage is at the top of the incline it is level with the roadway, and when freighted, it is lowered to the landing stage with which it is then on the level. The landing stage being also maintained on a level with the deck of the ferry steamer, the carts, wagons, or other vehicles are readily driven from the transport carriages over the landing stage on to the steamer. The vessel having taken in her load, crosses the river to the opposite landing stage, where the vehicles and passengers are quickly transferred to land by the traversing carriage.' In other words the system can operate at all states of the tide.

'There are two ferry boats, the *Countess of Lathom* and the *Countess of Zetland*, each being 120 feet long, 40 feet wide, 6 feet 6 inches draught, and having deck accommodation 60 feet in length by 36 feet in width for vehicles, and room for about 1,300 foot-passengers. The steamers, which are each of 338 tons, are double-ended, that is, both ends are similar, so that the vessel can be worked equally well in either direction. They are propelled by twin screws driven by compound surface-condensing engines of 300 horsepower indicated, using steam at 100-lb pressure. There are two sets of engines, one at each end of the vessel, besides which there are engines for working the hydraulic machinery by which the bulwarks of the steamer are lowered to form a gangway to the landing stage, and afterwards raised.' Again a method similar to the modern ro-ro.

'The landing stages and traversing carriages are lowered and hauled up by machinery situated under the roadway at each terminus, the machinery throughout being in duplicate so as to reduce the chance of stoppage from the failure of any of the parts to a minimum. The traversing carriages are worked by a pair of coupled engines which drive the winding drum, on and off which the steel wire rope attached to the carriages is coiled and uncoiled. The landing stage is moved up or down the inclined railway to follow the tide as it rises or falls, so that the deck is always on a level with that of the steamer. The machinery for this purpose is driven by a pair of engines having cylinders of 6½ inches diameter and 8 inches stroke. The speed of the engines is reduced by worm and other gearing to that necessary for the slow travel of the landing stage up or down the incline, which rate of travel corresponds to the rise or fall of the tide, the piston speed being 75 times that of the landing stage.'

Recently, demolition of numbers 28 and 30 Horseferry Road (now Place) at Greenwich for the building of a block of flats, has[23] allowed access to the large chamber which housed the steam engines which turned gearing supplied to drums which drew the travelling platforms using steel cables 4 inches in diameter. The landing stage and platforms were counterbalanced by 20-ton weights to lessen strain on the steam engines. The weights travelled down three iron-lined shafts or cylinders sunk over 150 feet into the ground under the chamber. Being independently counterbalanced meant the platforms could move as demand dictated. The boiler room was so cramped that holes were made in the walls and earth in order for the rods to be pushed in the fire tubes of the three boilers to clean them. Previously it had been thought there were two or three steam engines used to provide the ingenious moving platforms. However, excavations revealed that only one large engine was used, but it used steam from three locomotive boilers.

Further information is gleaned from the edition of *The Engineer* of 2 December 1892.[24] The landing stages rested on four bogies, with eight steel wheels on each. The travelling platforms were made of steel and weighed 125 tons in total. There were fifteen watertight bulkheads within the structure of each. Their decks (that is, the roadways above) were Memel timbers creosoted and then covered with block paving. Into this were laid tram rails which could take railway wagons. Each carriage ran on twenty-four wheels and was designed to float with 50 tons if it came off the rails.

Despite this ambitious way of operating, this ferry was not trouble-free. At the end of service one night in November 1892, one worker managed to derail the landing stage by drawing it up too fast. The wheels were badly damaged, also the underside of the stage. 'Automatic arrangements' were put in force to prevent a recurrence. Another misfortune is only a rumour, perhaps it was true, but may have contributed to the commercial failure of the enterprise. It is said one of the chains holding a counterweight failed. A diver was sent down in the cylinder to repair it and never returned. Although other divers subsequently were required to go down, his body was never found.

Passengers had a comfortable journey, many features contributing to their well-being. The vessels were technically advanced; being 'spoon-shaped' and having a balance rudder at both ends meant they could work without turning. A captain's bridge, steering wheel and telegraph were also fitted at both ends of the boats. There was plenty of room, as each could carry at least sixteen vehicles plus 200 foot passengers, or 1,300 if foot passengers only. Side-loading was achieved by having trimming tanks which allowed exact alignment with the landing stages. The bulwarks which served as gangways could be lowered hydraulically to meet with the platforms. This method was easier and more desirable than end-loading. Twenty-five tons of coal was carried to fuel the engines.

Although the working of the ferry was reported as being successful and it was fairly well patronised by vehicles, the engineer visitors in 1892 reported it was being worked at a loss. They conclude, 'it is feared that this boon to the dense population on either side of the river will again have to be withheld from them unless steps can be taken to acquire it and make it a free ferry.' Due to financial difficulties the steam ferry had closed between 1890 and 1892 and on its reopening had taken reputedly up to 500 vehicles and 1,000 passengers per week. In its heyday the ferry carried hundreds of football supporters from south of the river to see Millwall play at home. The football club started in the1885/86 season and went professional in 1893. Often they had gates of 5,000 but moved across the river to a permanent site near New Cross in 1910. However, by the 1890s only one steamer was working and the service was reduced to half-hour intervals. Other factors in its demise were the opening of Woolwich Free Ferry in 1889, Blackwall Tunnel opening in 1897 to take road traffic free, and the fact that employers on the Isle of Dogs refused to employ foremen and other key workers who lived over the water and relied on the ferry. It did not run in fog, it cost one shilling a week, which was not cheap, and at the end of the nineteenth century it closed. The London County Council took over the rights and the visiting engineers' prediction had come true.

GREENWICH FOOT TUNNEL

Following their formation in 1889 the LCC were considering how best to organise transport in the capital, especially the river crossings. With Woolwich Free Ferry a success and the first Blackwall tunnel complete, attention was turned to Greenwich. To obviate difficulties caused by the steam ferry not working in fog and not able to keep a regular service, a foot tunnel was planned. A Bill was presented to Parliament in 1896 but it met with strong opposition from Greenwich Hospital,[25] owners of Greenwich Pier; from the London and Blackwall Railway Company, who owned Sir Marc Brunel's original Thames Tunnel; also from the Company of Watermen & Lightermen on behalf of watermen employed in the ferry trade, all of whom claimed compensation. A clause written into the Thames Tunnel (Greenwich to Millwall) Act made provision for this. It said, 'The Licensed ferrymen of the Company of Watermen & Lightermen of the River Thames who now are and have been working from Upper

Watergate, Deptford to Cocoa Nut Stairs, Millwall for three years before the passing of this Act (including any person who was an apprentice to any such ferryman at any time within the said period of three years and shall be a Licensed Ferryman working between the said points at the time of the opening of the subway) shall be entitled after the opening of the subway to such sum by way of compensation as may be determined to be fair and reasonable by an arbitrator to be appointed by the Board of Trade.' However, the Watermen thought arbitration would be expensive and asked if instead LCC would pay £150 to each ferryman for immediate compensation. £100 was settled for each man 'on the commencement of the subway, the agreement being limited to the twenty-four men named in it'. As a result, LCC paid out almost £30,000 in compensation.

Plans submitted by Sir Alexander Binnie (1839-1917),[26] chief engineer to LCC, were accepted for a cast-iron small-bore tunnel to connect Island Gardens in Millwall with Greenwich, close to what was the ferry landing. There were delays in getting the project off the ground but it was spurred on by Will Crooks who was chairman of the Bridges Committee at the time. Finally in February 1899 a tender of £109,500 was accepted from contractors John Cochrane & Co. of Victoria Street, London. Work on the northern shaft started in June the same year. Progress was slow at first because of demand on machinery and materials due to a heavy building programme in London. This 'shaft is a large cylindrical steel caisson sixty feet deep and forty-three feet in external diameter, constructed of two steel skins with four feet of Portland Cement Concrete sandwiched between them. The skins were made of horizontal steel plates rivetted together, with reinforcing plates at the bottom and around the tunnel opening. The steel framework was assembled in stages in the contractor's yard at Island Gardens and sunk gradually as the work progressed. The latter part of the sinking operation was performed in compressed air, with workmen excavating in a small airtight chamber beneath the caisson.'

A small, circular, red-brick rotunda, listed Grade II, caps the shaft. It has square recessed panels and sits on a granite plinth. Over the entrance porch is a bronze tablet to commemorate the opening of the tunnel in 1902. 'The lift shaft was covered by a hemispherical dome consisting of quarter-inch plate glass supported by a framework of steel ribs. … Surmounting the dome is a cast-iron cupola decorated with Corinthian pilasters and details in steel plate and cast metal.' The interior of the round building and the shaft is lined with white glazed bricks or tiles. Pedestrian access was by a steel and cast-iron spiral staircase of 100 steps 6 feet wide around a central well 20 feet in diameter. This allowed space for a lift, which in 1901 LCC decided was necessary. They accepted a tender from Easton & Co. of Erith Iron Works for £7,334 7s to install mahogany-panelled electrically driven lifts in each shaft. However, they were not connected up until 1904, after the tunnel opened because of a lack of a sufficient electricity supply. The shaft on the Greenwich side is identical, but slightly deeper at 68 feet.

Work started on the tunnel itself in August 1900. Progress was quick due to some favourable factors. The subsoil composed mainly of clay and coarse sand was easy to handle, and experience gained in working the Blackwall tunnel was of benefit. Momentum was gained, resulting in an average of 10 feet being cut in every working day by February 1901. The tunnel was cut in only thirty-six weeks. It is 1,217 feet long, held by cast-iron rings each 1 foot 8 inches thick and composed of eight separate segments with a key piece. To complete the lining, a layer of cement 1 foot thick was faced with over 200,000 white ceramic tiles to give off light and make for easier cleaning. Much-needed ventilation is provided by a system of tubes and pipes which exhausts air by a fan and fresh air is brought in. The external diameter of the tunnel is 12 feet 9 inches, giving an internal width for the sloping footway of 9 feet, headroom is 9 feet 4½ inches, reducing to 7 feet 6 inches at the sides. The pedestrian subway was opened without ceremony on Bank Holiday Monday, 4 August 1902.

As it is classed as a public highway,[27] the tunnel by law has to be kept open twenty-four hours a day. When they are working, the lifts are operated by an attendant, who also oversees public behaviour in the tunnel. They are supposed to work between 7 a.m. and 7 p.m. on weekdays and 10 a.m.-5 p.m. on Sundays, There is no charge. Although the highway is part of the National Cycle Route, cycles are not to be ridden in the tunnel for health and safety reasons. However, they can be pushed, and carried in the lifts.

Residents of Millwall had mixed feelings about the tunnel at first. Bert Hiscott did not think much of having to carry his bike all the way down before the lifts were working, especially after he had a girlfriend, whose bike he had to carry too. John Pearson said, 'It did not seem nearly such fun to journey to Greenwich by subway. The ferry boat thrilled but the subway was rather awe-inspiring at first. Until one got used to it there was rather a sense of being "shut-in" in negotiating this five to ten minute walk under the Thames.' An alternative means of crossing is now by the Docklands Light Railway, the stations being close to the tunnel entrances, but no non-folding cycles are allowed on the trains. The Greenwich Foot Tunnel is now semi-closed until March 2011 for refurbishment.

DEPTFORD FERRY

Greenwich was connected to Deptford just upstream by a bridge over Deptford Creek (Creek Road). The name suggests it was originally a ford, and a ferry was established over the Creek in the mid-eighteenth century. In the 1550s a ferry ran from the Isle of Dogs to Deptford, as well as one to Greenwich. Pepys went from Deptford, while his carriage was taken round by Greenwich (*op. cit.*). Watergate Stairs below Trinity House, now Deptford Ferry Road, was the point of arrival and departure (Exp. 162 375 780).

Deptford itself was well known in earlier times. Alexander Pope called it 'a navy-building town'. Here was the Navy Victualling Yard; Henry VIII's shipyard – 'The King's Yard'; the location of the Navy Office for a time and the birthplace of the 'rag and bone' shop. For the existence of all this activity the ferry must have been very busy, yet we have no records of transactions, accounts, changes of lease or accidents. Apart, that is, from the murder of Christopher Marlowe in a pub brawl near the river; he was buried in 1593 in St Nicholas' Churchyard. Pepys visited frequently, though there is only the one reference in the Diaries. His friend, the diarist John Evelyn, lived here but his entries about the Thames refer to long ferries, not crossings. Therefore, it is presumed the ferry was owned and run by independent watermen, like the ones who were allowed £100 each from LCC, and handed down through generations of the same family as is their wont.

CUBITT'S FERRY

William Cubitt (1791-1863) began his working life as a carpenter in partnership with his brother Thomas.[28] They became building contractors in London and were responsible for developments on the Grosvenor and Bedford Estates. In 1827 they split up, and while Thomas continued as developer, William started W. Cubitt & Co. contractors. Covent Garden Market, Euston Station and the National Gallery were some of the buildings they worked on. As civil engineers the firm built docks at Shadwell and became involved with the Blackwall Railway. William acquired land from the Glengall Estate in the east of the Isle of Dogs to build a yard and works for his business. He sublet parts of the river frontage for wharfs and factories. The rest of the land he developed for housing and made Manchester Road to provide access to the rest of the island. Although Cubitts built some of the streets, most were constructed by smaller contractors. Gradually, in the mid-nineteenth century, Cubitt Town, as it came to be known, between the river and the perimeter road became a tight-knit area, with industry and housing side-by-side.

Few facilities were provided; piped water did not become available until the 1860s and then only from stand taps. Apart from some churches and chapels and a few small shops, there was nowhere to go after work. In 1857 Cubitt erected a timber pier about three-quarters of a mile from Potter's Ferry and about a quarter of a mile below his own works and wharf.[29] He then hired a steamboat and established a ferry for the inhabitants of Cubitt Town to travel to Greenwich to enjoy the wide open spaces and shopping and also downstream to Blackwall. There was no intention of taking trade from the ancient Potter's Ferry; it was 'merely to accommodate the occupiers of the new houses'. However, it came about that Cubitt's Ferry was used mainly by dock workers, to the detriment of the other ferry, which reputedly lost more than half its income.

Litigation was sought, the plaintiff being one Newton, on behalf of the Society of Greenwich Watermen before Lord Chief Justice Erle.[30] Yet again the Society asserted their right of ferry granted in 1776 when there were no residents on the island, it was just marsh. The plaintiffs had always exercised a monopoly of that ferry from then onward from the Isle of Dogs to Greenwich. At the first session the jury found that although the defendant's ferry was not intended to injure the plaintiff's, nevertheless it had done so. Cubitt continued to run his ferry but it was unlikely to have used the established landing place at Greenwich after the Court's decision. As Morden Lane, which connected with Marsh Lane to lead into Greenwich, was opposite Cubitt Town Pier, it could have used a landing stage there, where factories including the Thames Steam Soap Works ('Greenwich the world standard in both soap and time') were situated.

The case then went before the Court of Common Pleas in May 1862. By this time William Cubitt was Lord Mayor of the City of London. It involved the question 'whether the conveyance by the Lord Mayor of passengers by a steamer from his new pier in the Isle of Dogs to Greenwich is an invasion of the plaintiff's right of ferry'. Mr Lush, QC on behalf of the defendant, said that 'his client was willing to make the plaintiffs a present of his pier if they would undertake to convey passengers by steamer from Cubitt Town to Greenwich'. After an adjournment for consideration of this offer, the Court met again. The offer was brushed aside and the Court gave the opinion 'that the principle laid down in the old cases applicable to ferries, when districts of the country were thinly populated, and it was of importance to establish one ferry as a highway between opposite shores, was not applicable to the present age and to the requirements of the community. A ferry was now required to many points from opposite shores, and it was an injurious restriction to limit the right.' So Cubitt won this time, but the Society as plaintiffs were not satisfied.

An appeal was heard in[31] February 1863 when the plaintiff's lawyer contended 'that the 1776 grant included the whole marsh called the Isle of Dogs; and that the plaintiff, therefore, had the exclusive right of ferry between the Isle of Dogs and the town of Greenwich'. Although Mr Lush was present, he made no comment and judgement of the first court was affirmed. When Cubitt discontinued his ferry is not known but it was not in operation in 1891 when the Thames Conservancy asked for the dangerous, dilapidated pier to be repaired and it was then demolished.

From this extended court case, Newton v. Cubitt has become an important point of law which can be quoted in any similar future case regarding ferries. To quote

Plan of Greenwich Reach, probably taken from the OS map of 1865. It shows Ferry House and the horse ferry on the extreme left, the beginnings of Cubitt Town and Cubitt Town Pier.

Cubitt's Ferry. Paddle steamer hired by Cubitt. Postcard made from an older print. (Courtesy www.eastlondonpostcard.co.uk)

Willes J, 'A ferry exists in respect of persons using a right of way, where the line of way is across water. There must be a line of way on land, coming to a landing-place on the water's edge (as, in this case, to Potter's Ferry Stairs) or, where the ferry is from or to a vill, from one or more places in the vill.'

BLACKWALL FERRY

Blackwall Stairs are by reputation the oldest on the Lower Thames. A ferry is mentioned in 1568. Most likely it was not public, just a regular service ferrying passengers to and from the large number of ships always moored offshore, this being a major point of embarkation. Boats could be hired at Blackwall (Exp. 162 385 804) for travel to Greenwich and London. In fact, there was little need for a shore-to-shore crossing because on the other side Bugsby's Marsh was barren land with only industrial development of the unpleasant, smelly kind. Iain Sinclair described it as 'a ravished swamp with its history of plague, pestilence and pillage'. Added to this are the exhaust fumes from the Blackwall tunnels which have their entrance and exit here. This was the site chosen for the Millennium Dome opened in 2000, which has the funnel taking the fumes from the tunnels poking through its Teflon roof, at the end of what is sometimes called East Greenwich Peninsula. Actually it is not a peninsula, but an isthmus formed by the Thames making a loop before it reaches New Charlton and the Thames Barrier downstream.

In the 1830s travellers upriver from the ports at Tilbury, Gravesend and Woolwich preferred to disembark at Blackwall Stairs to avoid the long, tedious journey round the Isle of Dogs by water. Instead they would take a horse omnibus to London by the now-improved roads.

Shipbuilding was the main factor in the development of Blackwall through the centuries. Brunswick Wharf was part of the Green's Shipyard estate. The Green family took over the shipyard at the end of the eighteenth century after it had been under the management of John Perry. It became the biggest private yard in the world. In

1835 they sold the Brunswick Wharf part of their estate to the London & Blackwall Railway, who developed it for their terminus. A large, imposing station building reassured passengers on their journey. The Company bought three steamboats for the benefit of their passengers travelling to Woolwich and Gravesend from the wharf. A combined rail and ferry ticket could be bought in advance for the hourly service. When the railway opened in 1840, it was therefore a success until the Woolwich area was given its own railway.

The London & Blackwall Railway was unique. It ran from the Minories, just east of the City, because Parliament, particularly the Duke of Wellington, refused to allow it into the City. It was only 3½ miles long to Brunswick Wharf at Blackwall with a gauge of five feet. For the first nine years of its life propulsion was by cable haulage, big drums being situated by the platforms. This was changed when the Millwall Extension Railway to North Greenwich/Cubitt Town opened in 1872. The station for it was by the Potter's Ferry landing on the east side of Johnson Street (now Ferry Street). The London & Blackwall Railway had acquired the rights to Potter's Ferry, although they did not use them.

Cross-river ferries no longer ply from the Isle of Dogs to Greenwich but it is still a favourite place to visit. Dr Samuel Johnson lodged here in the summer of 1737 when writing his long poem *London*, the work which first brought him fame. Much later he returned for an excursion with James Boswell in a wherry. Boswell pulled the book out of his pocket and read to Johnson.[32]

> While Thales waits the Wherry that contains
> Of dissipated Wealth the small Remains,
> On Thames's Banks, in silent Thought we stood,
> Where GREENWICH smiles upon the silver Flood:
> Struck with the seat that gave Eliza Birth,
> We kneel, and kiss the consecrated earth;

London & Blackwall Railway. Minories Station showing the drums for cable haulage, *c.* 1840. From a contemporary magazine. (via Wikimedia Commons)

CHAPTER TEN
Woolwich

Woolwich (pronounced Woolidge) Ferry is the best known of all the Thames ferries. It is free for all pedestrians, vehicles and animals and has been running now for over 120 years, with trade increasing. It has a long history, sometimes chequered (Exp. 162 433 794).

The town is unique in that it is in two places, both north and south of the river. This made it of strategic importance. An Iron Age hill fort and a Roman fort have been found, which suggests there was a ferry of some sort from an early age. North Woolwich was a strip of land, an outlier of Kent, administered with the main Woolwich until local government reform made it part of the Borough of Newham in 1965. The town of Woolwich itself is now in the Borough of Greenwich, which includes more of the Thames riverside than any other London borough.

Lesnes Abbey, founded in 1178, the remains of which can still be seen to the east of Woolwich towards Erith, acquired parishes over the river in Essex. It had ferry rights and took dues from lessees. William de Wicton was lessee in 1308 when he and his wife Roesia sold the ferry to William atte Hall, a mason, for £10.[1] It was sold again in 1320-21 by Lambert de Tryenham to John and Joan Latimer. By 1340 it was owned by William and Mary Filliol who sold it for a hundred silver marks (about £66) to Thomas Harwold. These frequent changes of ownership reflect the growing importance of the ferry crossing. Two fourteenth-century deeds for North Woolwich indicate the ferry there. Carteris Lane, the street leading to 'Wolwyche Verye' occurs in a document of 1346-47, and in 1348-49 another mentions a croft on the road to 'La Verie'.

Woolwich ferrymen, supported by townspeople, were jealous of their ferry rights and in 1330 petitioned Parliament to have rival ferries at Greenwich and Erith suppressed because their own was 'farmed of the King', the Crown from 1305 owned the Royal Manor of Eltham, just south of Woolwich, and fee-farmed or rented the ferry to the watermen. Both Erith and Greenwich ferries were still working in the nineteenth century. John Pudney comments, 'In guarding his rights the ferryman sometimes carried public opinion with him, where the threat to his ferry was also a threat to local trade or amenities: more often in latter years he was fighting a lone battle against progress.'

However, the ferry continued to flourish along with the town. Henry VIII established a naval dockyard to the west. The ordnance depot to the east became the Royal Arsenal, covering a large area, in 1805. The town in between the two served not only those establishments but the growing river traffic. Few records of the ferry exist after the mid-fourteenth century, apart from a petition from John Blount to King James I asking him to grant a lease or patent in 1622 for a long and a short ferry at Woolwich. It is not known if he was successful. In 1810 the arsenal set up its own ferry from its own landing stage to the Essex shore for the transport of artillery and provisions by the Royal Army Service Corps. The landing place on the north side was at the Old Barge House.

Shepperton. Private ferry to Nelson's Island (a.k.a. Pharaoh's Island). With its bell, boats and enticing view of the other side, we get an idea of what a typical country ferry was like. June 2009.

Laleham. The new house on the Surrey side, taken from the landing place on the left bank. June 2009.

Shepperton-Weybridge Ferry. The unusual craft run by chandlers Nauticalia every fifteen minutes on demand from their headquarters nearby. June 2009.

Teddington. Ferry at Teddington Locks. Amateur watercolour, *c.* 1900. (Courtesy www.old-england.com)

Thames Ditton. Private suspension bridge, which replaced the ferry to Thames Ditton Island. June 2009.

Twickenham Ferry (Hammerton's). Group of ferrymen came to the Ham shore on their unusual craft to pick up two Norwegian lady passengers. June 2009.

Chiswick. Thames barge moored at the wharf. Exact location is not known. Small watercolour by Albert Fleetwood Varley (1804-76), eldest son of John Varley. He was a teacher of drawing who died at Brompton. (Courtesy Abbott & Holder Ltd)

Untitled watercolour by Emily Faithful after a watercolour by John Varley (1778-1842) titled 'Figures on a path by the Thames'. This copy differs from the original only in the stance of the figures and the poultry. A punt-like ferry boat is seen at the water's edge. Location is either Chiswick or Chelsea.

Isleworth. The Horse Ferry. Watercolour by Joshua Cristall (1768-1847), a friend of John Varley. (Courtesy of the Courtauld Institute of Art Gallery)

Battersea. The Red House, *c.* 1840. Aquatint by William James Callcott (fl. 1843-96), a marine artist who lived at Putney. A similar oil painting by him, with less detail, is in the Government Art Collection.

Belvedere. Showing the present-day aspect of the river looking across to the Dagenham works, the gangplank for the ferry on the right. (Courtesy W. N. Tucker)

Belvedere. Gangplank which gave access to Ford's private ferry for their workers. (Courtesy W. N. Tucker)

From the gangplank. Messrs Costain are working with Scapa Triumph at a jetty.
(Courtesy W. N. Tucker)

Belvedere. The ferry gangplank is firmly closed. Ford's Motor Works at Dagenham can be seen
across the river. (Courtesy W. N. Tucker, Sept. 2009)

Regent's Bridge, named after the Prince Regent when it opened in 1816 was later renamed Vauxhall Bridge. Looking upstream with Millbank Penitentiary on the right. A wherry is awaiting passengers. Aquatint 1826. (via Wikimedia Commons)

Woolwich. Showing the Arsenal and a row-boat ferry. From sketchbook of George Whitmore, an army surveyor, late eighteenth century. (Courtesy Gloucestershire Archives)

Nick Beasley on duty at Watermen's Hall. He is of the seventh generation of free watermen in his family. In 2001 he was winner of the Doggett's Coat and Badge Race. July 2009.

North Woolwich. The Royal Pavilion. Demolished in the 2000s to make way for the new terminal. November 1991.

Woolwich. *John Burns*, one of the state-of-the-art diesel-engined craft introduced in 1963, on standby. Passengers ascend the steel walkway to board the in-service vessel, which is berthed end-on, on the level. June 2009.

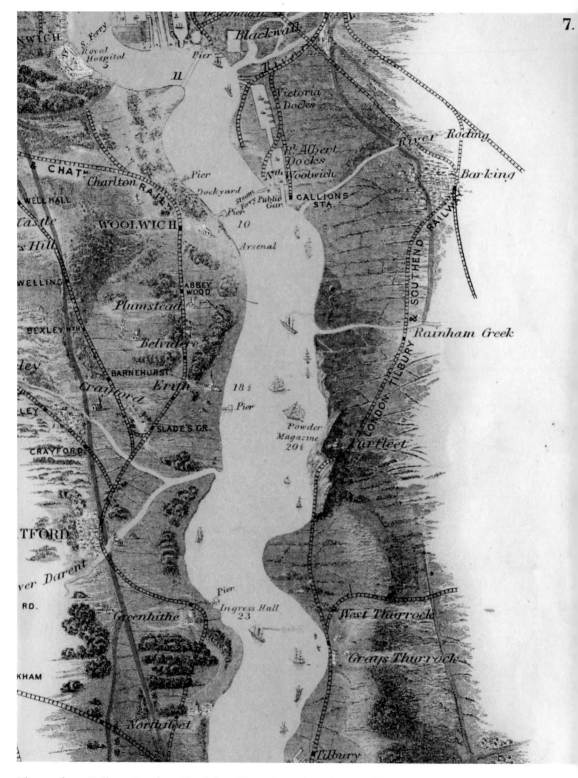

Thames from Gallions Reach to Northfleet Hope. A condensed view of this long stretch, looking upstream. North is to the right. Map from Tombleson's Panoramic Atlas of the River Thames. *c.* 1890.

Dartford Crossing. Age-old crossing point between Essex and Kent which now carries two streams of traffic on the A282, one way through the tunnels, the other over the Queen Elizabeth II Bridge to connect with the M25. Photo taken 1993. (© English Heritage, NMR Aerofilms Collection)

Gravesend. Town Pier looking desolate after its restoration. It should be used as a landing place again.
June 2009.

Tilbury. MV *Duchess* arriving at Tilbury Terminal. Gravesend is seen over the river. September 2007.

Tilbury. Passengers disembarking from MV *Duchess* after a shopping expedition to Gravesend. September 2007.

London Stone at the mouth of Yantlet Creek, Kent. Looking seawards at high tide. June 2009.

To chronicle the history of Woolwich as a ferrying place throughout time is a complicated and somewhat confusing task. The town, by occupying sites on both banks of the river became a target for entrepreneurs, and an obvious place to set up a ferry. Sometimes two ferries were running in opposition at the same time. As elsewhere, ferrymen were always prepared to defend their exclusive rights of ferriage. Little is known of the first recorded ferry, but others of necessity had to be set up by Act of Parliament. Some were successful, others not so. The Woolwich Ferry Company (1811-44), known as the Western Ferry because it was to the west of the town, was preceded by the Arsenal Ferry, for the use of the military, a year before. Known as the Barge House Ferry, the ancient ferry continued as a horse ferry throughout the nineteenth century. The railway ferry operated at the same time, using paddle steamers for which the fare was one penny, hence the nickname Penny Ferry. Finally, the Woolwich Free Ferry was inaugurated and continues to hold the sole right of ferry to this day.

THE WESTERN FERRY

Some landowners and tradesmen of Woolwich formed a Joint Stock or Fund in 1811 called 'the Woolwich Ferry Company' in order to obtain an Act to establish a ferry from the parish of Woolwich to the parish of West Ham in Essex at a place in the marshes which is now Silvertown. The principal shareholders were Dame Jane Wilson, a wealthy widow in her own right, and her son Sir Thomas Maryon Wilson. They held large estates in the area and lived at Charlton House, a fine Jacobean mansion which still stands on the slopes between Woolwich and Greenwich. The family is commemorated by Maryon Park, made out of a sandpit and which was used for the scene of a shooting in the film *Blow-Up*. The capital was £12,000 in £100 shares and Sir Thomas became a director with £1,000 worth. Another was John Lang, who owned the King's Arms at the top of Francis Street. Among the local traders with shares who stood to benefit from the enterprise were builders, carpenters and masons. They were to become bitterly disappointed.

The Act[2] for setting up a ferry was passed on 26 June 1811. The preamble stated it was 'for establishing and the conveyance of persons carriages and cattle and goods, wares and merchandise ... and for making proper roads and approaches to form a direct communication between Kent and Essex and to be of great public utility'. The Company was empowered to do works, purchase land and sell it. It was to be a Common Ferry with one or more boats and to go from The Old Ballast or Sand Wharf to a place on the other side which must be at least 400 feet from the west end of the wharf. They were to alter the highway leading from the Green Gate at Plaistow to the Thames opposite Sand Wharf. Also the highway from the road between Greenwich and Woolwich to Sand Wharf was to be altered. The Company would have full power and authority from the Mayor and Aldermen of the City of London to dig, slope and cut banks of the river near the landing places as necessary and build causeways, but not to obstruct the tide or the navigation and not be more than 50 feet wide. They were allowed to build houses for the ferryman and for offices. A £10 fine was to be paid to the Mayor as Conservator for the liberty of being allowed to do these works. The rent would be £5 a year.

No house or building must be taken for the undertaking which was already in place on 25 March 1811 nor any land which was being used at that date as garden, orchard, yard, path, paddock, planted walk or avenue to a house without the consent in writing of the owners. There followed many clauses concerning the law and forms of agreement for the purchase of lands and the amounts to be paid for them.

A meeting was to be held at the King's Arms between 11 a.m. and 1 p.m. on the Tuesday in the week following the day after the Act was passed. Thereafter the Company must meet on the first Tuesday in June each year at the same hours at a place within 6 miles of the ferry. The quorum must be five persons each holding two or more shares. Proprietors could make by-laws if necessary. They could raise a further £12,000 and were enabled to borrow on mortgage.

Tolls were set out as follows: foot passengers 2d; horse not drawing 1s; two-wheeled chaise 5s; coach with two horses 10s; sheep at 1½d per head. Anyone evading toll could be detained and their goods distrained if the money was not paid within five days. Tolls could be leased out for periods of less than three years, and the name of the lessee to be put on a toll board. The ferry was not to work before 4 a.m. or after 10 p.m. between 24 March and 29 September. For the rest of the year the hours were between 6 a.m. and 8 p.m., but not in times of ice or tempestuous winds or whenever it was dangerous. (Note that fog, the enemy of Lower Thames ferries was not mentioned. It was a phenomenon of the industrial age). Other persons were not allowed to operate a ferry within half a mile of this one (although the original ferry was indeed only a half mile away and was still being operated by licensed watermen).

Nothing in the Act should prevent the free passage of HM Ordnance and Dockyard at Woolwich. They had established the Military ferry, and should it be discontinued, then they should be carried free on this ferry on the boats, with the proviso that they must pay half of the toll on the roads and approach roads. If because of circumstances whereby landing places cannot be used, it shall be lawful to land passengers, etc., elsewhere and the Company to pay for the damage incurred.

Lamps were to be erected where needed. Fit and able-bodied men could be employed as the Company thought fit to act as watchmen, guides or patrols armed and clothed either on foot or on horseback, also a superintendent. These men were to prevent fires, murders, burglars, robbers and other disturbances on the roads, and could arrest and detain offenders in the Watch House. The rights of the City of London and of Trinity House were to be saved.

The half-mile rule was unfair and was amended by a further Act to be two miles instead. So if anyone was to carry over 'any person, carriage, horse or other animal' during the working hours of the new ferry or within two miles of it, they would be fined £5 for every carriage, animal or person if their intention was the avoidance of toll. But this was not the solution the watermen wanted and together with the inhabitants of Woolwich they protested it was 'prejudicial to divers of the watermen working on that part of the river'. Consequently another Act passed 21 May 1816 repealed the previous Act and was 'deemed a Public Act and shall be taken notice of by all Judges and Justices'.

Known locally as the 'Western Ferry' it did not prosper; firstly it was in the wrong place. As FC Elliston-Erwood[3] explains, there was 'no cogent reason for establishing a ferry here, where there were considerable difficulties'. Perhaps the Company felt that with new roads their ferry would bypass the towns. A plan made in 1820 shows the road from Eltham on the hill down to the riverside as 'To the Horse Ferry'. It was situated at the end of Marsh Road, to which the Naval Dockyard had been extended in 1809, nearly on the Woolwich-Charlton parish boundary, beyond which were marshlands. On the other side too the landing place was on marshlands at Plaistow, a completely isolated spot 1½ miles from a road. The only access to the landing was by an accommodation track. To get proper roads, high expenditure and time would be involved as well as a new Bill.

A meeting was held at the King's Arms on 7 July 1811 when Lt Gen. Vaughan Lloyd was made chairman. There was a Company seal on which was depicted Old Father Thames with a ferry boat in front of him. Impressed around the edge was 'Corporate

Seal of the Woolwich Ferry Company'. John Long offered the remainder of his lease on some land belonging to the Bowater estate for an approach road and landing on the south shore. The Company agreed to pay him rent of £43 15s a year, but they were to negotiate with the estate to buy the freehold for £1,200 the following year. Purchase of land on the north side was proving difficult and the clause in the Act permitting compulsory purchase was considered. A call on shares of 10 per cent was made, thus leading to the second reason for failure.

Shareholders did not pay their share instalments. Even Lt Gen. Lloyd never paid a penny, although he had received share certificates – he later forfeited them. Following internal quarrels with shareholders, some directors resigned and Mr John Dorington became a director. An advertisement appeared in *The Times* of 29 December 1815 announcing that five mortgage securities bearing interest of 5 per cent per annum were to be auctioned in five lots. When the last set of minutes was taken in January 1828, Dorington's son, John Edward Dorington, was in the chair. At the winding-up of the Company in June 1842, a letter from the shareholders to the secretary was signed by John Dorington's executors, J. T. Dorington and J. E. Dorington. The latter, in 1847, bought Lypiatt Park, Gloucestershire.

In preparation for the opening of the ferry at the end of 1812, Sir Thomas Maryon Wilson was asked to obtain a plan and estimate for 'a large ferry boat'. Eventually this horse boat was ordered at £200. Meanwhile, two second-hand boats[4] were used, a wherry bought from Gravesend for £35 3s and another from Greenwich costing £25 13s. The appurtenances, ferry oars, sculls, etc., were paid for separately. Two directors were asked to build brickwork piers and arches on the Thames Wall. Thomas Collis of a well-known road-making family, was given a contract to build the road across the marsh from the Cross Road to the ferry at Sand Wharf (also a cause of regret later).

Due to lack of finance and lack of business acumen, the undertaking was rather a hit-and-miss affair. There was only a small building on the south bank for collecting tolls and the toll-house. The way down the steep slopes to the water on each side was a platform made from old ships' timbers to take passengers, goods and horses. On the north bank a temporary licensed house was built of weatherboarding with a tiled roof. This became the Prince Regent. The first licensee was William Jennings from St George's, Bloomsbury. When he moved in there was neither a fireplace nor cooking facilities. Jennings was later dismissed over a matter concerning brewers Barclay Perkins who had delivered a consignment of porter and he could not produce accounts. On the south side the Company built the Marquis of Wellington public house to provide food and shelter for their passengers. It was usually known as 'The Duke' or the 'Ferry House'. Both public houses were very necessary to the Company because both landing places were lonely and exposed to the elements. Although often making a loss, they gradually became the only source of income.

James Bass, a waterman of Greenwich, was appointed the first ferryman with an apprentice in November 1811 at £2 10s per week, including Sundays. He was later replaced by Thomas Bass. By 1828, when the Company was at a low ebb, they agreed that the tenant of the Prince Regent was to provide a new ferry boat at his own expense to offset his arrears in rent. At the same time the Marquis of Wellington was let at £20 a year on a fully repairing lease with the tenant retaining all tolls. Finally, in desperation, the Company offered the licences to their ferrymen, practically free of charge. In about 1842 all the north bank properties were sold, to include ferry rights.

Despite obtaining another Act in 1816[5] which allowed the Company to increase the original tolls by 50 per cent, finances remained precarious. Heavy expenditure was incurred in furnishing the two public houses but expense caused by litigation was unexpected. Thomas Collis, besides making the road on the south was also engaged to do so on the north. His bill was large and unsatisfactory and could not be justified. After court action he was dismissed. Samuel Scarfe, known as the 'Surveyor of Woolwich', took over and completed the roads for much less money. He became leaseholder of the Prince Regent for a time at £250 a year.

The third factor in its demise was the failure of the Company to keep proper records, or have 'a business plan'. They did have meetings at the Marquis of Wellington but fell behind in their payments of the Poor Rate. No records were made of income from the ferry, a suggestion has been made that it all went to pay the ferrymen's wages. No dividends on shares were ever paid. Still it somehow continued in business until the fourth and final deathblow came in 1839-40 after a long period of inactivity when presumably no meetings took place. It transpired that the agreement made in 1811 through John Long over a lease of land in the Bowater estate was invalid; supposedly the Company never did acquire the freehold. The estate claimed considerable arrears in rent, which the Company could not pay. Therefore they were ejected from their access to the riverfront at Sand Wharf and faced bankruptcy in 1842. They were not able to continue the service, and in 1844 the Company was dissolved. 'This was a story of a great failure.' After the ferry closed on the Kent side, Siemens Bros Telegraph Works was built in 1963 to make Transatlantic Cables, and on the north side docks, factories and wharves were built.

BARGE HOUSE FERRY

Throughout this time of competition, the original established ferry from Warren Lane, South Woolwich, to the Barge House had continued, and now found itself with a free run, but only for a short time. In 1839 Mr How, licensee of the Barge House, constructed an esplanade[6] 130 feet wide along the riverbank, and extending for 300 yards. Later

Woolwich ferries. Showing the horse ferry and a paddle steamer on the Penny Ferry. The Barge House is to the right. Engraving *c.* 1850. From a scrapbook compiled by Gerald Cobb. (Reproduced by Permission of English Heritage)

most of it was incorporated into the Royal Victoria Gardens. About the same time, they stationed 'a new ferry boat of larger dimensions than any on the river, with a view to meeting the increase in traffic that has lately taken place between the two counties'. In fact, it was a horse raft. At some point this ferry had floated a Public Company to safeguard its ancient rights dating back to 'time immemorial' to convey persons, cattle and goods from Warren Lane across to North Woolwich. John Bull owned this ferry in about 1810, followed by John Punter. When it was taken by lighterman John Fulford, he also became proprietor of the Barge House.

PENNY FERRY

In 1847 the Great Eastern Railway Company extended its line to North Woolwich and set up its own ferry to capture trade from Kent to their railway. They produced plans in 1849 and in 1850 the ferry started operating.[7] From then on the Prince Regent public house became obsolete and was demolished, and rebuilt further north on Prince Regent Lane, as the Prince of Wales. Paddle steamers were introduced for the new service which became known as the 'Penny Ferry', although the official name was the Eastern Counties Ferry. The steamers were built at Barking and named *Kent* and *Essex,* later joined by *Middlesex*. A pier for landing was built at North Woolwich, while the southern landing stage pier was at Roff's Wharf, Market Hill. South Woolwich received its own railway in 1849 when the South Eastern Railway was extended from Greenwich. However, the Penny Ferry continued to provide a cheap and regular service with train connections to London until 1908. But the steamers did not carry animals and vehicles, so the original horse-raft ferry still functioned.

Paddle steamer *Middlesex* used on the Penny Ferry at Woolwich, *c.* 1850. From a scrapbook.

STEAM PACKET BOATS

This was the age of steam, and steam vessels on the Thames were taking trade away from independent licensed watermen. Excursion traffic on the Thames increased from the 1820s throughout the nineteenth century and steamers would call at North Woolwich Pier en route to Southend, Margate or Clacton. The General Steam Navigation Company in 1824 was the first to be established and along with other companies had a monopoly of the trade until railways started seaside excursions. Other companies included the Woolwich Steam Packet Co.; London Steamboat Co.; Thames & Channel Steamship Co. and the River Thames Steamboat Co. The Victoria Steamboat Association, aimed at the 'classy' market, soon failed; others lasted until the end of the century. The longest-lived, the General Steam Navigation, lasted until 1966.

Some steamboat packets also operated a regular half-hourly service to London and return with calls at, for instance, Greenwich and Rotherhithe, on the way. The fare from London Bridge to Woolwich could be only fourpence, but generally it was about 2s to 3s return as seen in a household accounts book for 1857.[8] It belonged to Thomas James Raikes Barrow RN (1813-63), Lord of the Manor of Randwick, near Stroud, Gloucestershire. It seems the account book was made up by his wife when the family was living in Woolwich with their daughter, Isabella Jane Barrow (Bella), aged about ten.

2nd January, steamer to Greenwich 1s.4d.
4th February, London & back 2s.
12th March, Cab & porterage to boat 3s.1d.
20th March, Fares in steamer 1s.
15th April, Steamer to Charlton 1s.6d.
13th May, Bonnet 1s.10d.
25th May, Steamer to town. 3s. [Same price as she paid for a pineapple]
10th July, Steamboat 4d. [Ferry?]
23rd October, Richmond & back 6s.2d.
11th November, Steamer to town & back 2s. [She bought a teapot and coffee pot]
17th November, Richmond & back 3s.
23rd December, Turkey 16s.

Bella, when she was twenty, married General Sir Hugh Rowlands (1829-1909), who was the first Welshman to win a VC.

THE *PRINCESS ALICE*

According to newspaper reports and marine insurers, accidents involving steam boats were commonplace on the Thames. But an accident which befell the *Princess Alice* in Gallions Reach between Woolwich and Tripcock Ness (Exp. 162 454 810) on the evening of Tuesday 3 September 1878 proved to be the worst disaster ever on the River Thames, with the largest loss of life in peacetime Britain before or since.

The vessel had been in a minor mishap before which was not reported generally. She was built at Greenock on the River Clyde in 1865 some commentators say of iron, some of wood. It is more likely to be the former. A paddle steamer with two cylinder oscillating engines and two haystack boilers, as PS *Bute*[9] she was owned by the Wemyss Bay Company. When that failed *Bute* was sold for service on the Thames and joined the fleet of the London Steamboat Company and her name changed to *Princess*

Alice after the third child of Queen Victoria. As paddle steamers go she was only little, with a gross weight of 251 tons. Her length was almost 220 feet, breadth about 20 feet but with a draught of only 8.4 feet. At the time, her Board of Trade certificate allowed for 336 passengers in winter and 486 in summer, 'for extended river service'. On the Thames more accommodation was needed and a huge fore and aft saloon was built on deck, all above the water line, thus making her into a 'saloon steamer'. The certificate was changed to allow 936 passengers 'for river service in smooth water only or on lakes'. Mr W. Mead Corner FSA of Leadenhall Street, London, writing in *The Times* after the event, gave his opinion that, for the length and shallowness of the boat, she could not carry all that extra weight safely.

That day the *Princess Alice* had taken an excursion to Sheerness on the Kent coast, where the Thames estuary is very wide, almost the sea.[10] Very strict rules for navigation on the seas, being International Law, were already in place then. It was laid down that the rule of the road is that vessels should proceed on the starboard (right) side of the waterway. They specified how a system of lights on vessels should work to signal to other ships which way they were travelling. All vessels must show navigation lights; green lights on the starboard and red lights on the port (left side) directed forwards. There should also be a stern (back) white light and a masthead light (at the top of the highest mast). All lights have well defined angles through which they must be visible. Outside of these angles, the lights cannot or should not be seen.

When two vessels approach each other head to head in the dark or dusk, each should be able to see a high white light at its masthead and two coloured lights, a green light seen on the left, a red light on the right of the approaching vessel. To avoid collision, therefore, ships passing each other should be red to red, or in other words, port to port. If a red light should appear on the starboard side, then it is the master's duty to keep clear! If a vessel is approaching, you should see a red light on the right of it and a green on the left. This will not be the case if the oncoming vessel steers or swings across your path.

The rule was included in the Thames Conservancy by-laws, but was not actually enforced on the Thames, resulting in that some shallow vessels 'punched the tide'. It meant that, instead of hugging the right shore as they were supposed to do when travelling upstream, they would cut corners using a straight line from point to point (or ness as points in the river course are called). The reason was that it was easier to progress upriver in the face of a fast ebbing tide in the lee of a ness where the tide was not so strong. On the other hand, vessels travelling downriver with the tide used the midstream where the tide was fiercest, but safer, 'with the tide up her skirt' as they put it.

Princess Alice left Sheerness on the return journey at 4.15 p.m. with returning passengers and others besides.[11] She arrived at Gravesend at 6.30 p.m. and picked up more passengers, some of whom had missed the steamers they had arrived on, others had been visiting Rosherville Gardens. Other stops possibly were made but there was no record of how many people were on board; it transpired the majority were women and children. The next stop was to be North Woolwich Pier and when rounding Tripcock Point to enter Gallion's Reach, instead of hugging the inside shore and crossing to the north later, at the ferry site, she held her course straight over the river, across the central tidal stream towards the next point on the journey. In fact, this was a short cut to North Woolwich Pier just over a mile away.

Then a large collier was seen coming downriver towards them. It was the *Bywell Castle*, a large Newcastle collier, returning empty with ballast. She was an iron-built screw ship 256 feet in length and of 890 tons and had left Millwall Dock about 6.30 p.m. on the high tide, in the charge of Mr Dicks, the pilot. The master was Thomas Harrison, who was part-owner. There was a light breeze and it was twilight. What happened next is

LOSS OF THE PRINCESS ALICE,
IN THE THAMES, OFF WOOLWICH.

They started that morning so happy and gay,
  With hearts that were light as a feather,
Away from the city to spend a long day,
  Enjoying the fine Autumn weather.
How little they thought, on that beautiful morn,
  As gaily they steamed down the river,
How few of their number would ever return
  To the homes they were leaving for ever.
How swiftly the day passed 'mid scenes of
    delight,
  And health-giving breeze from the ocean
As evening advanced with its quiet twilight,
  They assembled with pleasant commotion ;
On board of the vessel again to return,
  To the homes they had left in the morning,
And renew with fresh vigour the toils of the
    week,
  As soon as next day should be dawning.
They travelled in safety for many a mile,
  So calm lay the waters around them,
While over head brightly the harvest moon
    shone,
  In glory on all things around them.
And many on board that fair vessel that night,
  Sweet songs in the moonlight were singing,
While over the water there came a sweet sound
  Of evening bells that were ringing.
But all in a moment the stillness of death,
  Reigned on board of that ship so ill-fated,

As they saw coming near them so swift on the
    stream,
  A vessel with speed unabated.
Then loudly they shrieked as their fate they
    beheld,
  For the vessel was right down upon them.
Their starboard she strikes and, divided in two,
  She sinks, and the waters close on them.
Oh ! who can describe the wild panic that reigned,
  On that ship as she sank in the river ;
Or the battle they had with the waters so deep.
  The thought of it makes one's heart quiver.
For more than seven hundred were lost on that
    night ;
  And soon the sad news reached the city.
All London was stirred with emotion so great,
  With sympathy, sorrow, and pity.
And many a mother mourned over her child,
  And sisters a kind, loving brother ;
But sadest of all were the orphans that night,
  Who were left without father or mother.
Oh ! sad was the sight the pale moon looked
    upon,
  On that beautiful night in September,
And the dear ones so suddenly snatched from
    our side
  We shall ever with sorrow remember.

VIOLET VALE.

The *Princess Alice* disaster. One of many memorials hastily produced at the time. The name Violet Vale is probably a pseudonym for the poet.

recorded in the ship's log. At 7.45 they were proceeding down Gallion's Reach at half speed and, when about halfway, saw an excursion steamer approaching from Barking Reach. It was showing red and masthead lights, indicating that it was cutting across the *Bywell*'s bows so the *Bywell Castle* was steered over to the right towards Tripcock Point, thinking to pass to the stern of the pleasure craft. However, the *Princess Alice* had seen the oncoming collier and at the same time was trying to steer out of its short cut and back to the south (Kent) bank. She spun round and turned broadsides. A collision was inevitable, so the larger vessel stopped the engines and reversed full speed but inevitably the impetus resulted in the *Bywell Castle* cutting into the *Princess Alice* midships at the starboard sponson (right-hand paddle box), which allegedly is the weakest point.

It seems the collier actually mounted the deck of the steamer and cut it in two, wrapping it round its bows, and when it drew back the two halves fell apart, letting the water in and then both turned end up. Then the boiler burst, scalding some people to death. Within five minutes the whole of the *Princess Alice* had sunk and disappeared, leaving the river a mass of bodies and people struggling to survive. When eventually the wreck was brought up it was found to be in three parts, the engine and boilers being separate from the ends. She was insured for £8,000. From evidence given to the coroner's inquest (no log for the *Princess Alice* was recovered), it seems there was plenty of room for the two vessels to pass, they were coming together at 18 knots (20 mph) and there was no explanation of why the steamer swung back to cross the bows of the collier. John Ayres, the substitute coxswain, who survived, told of being at the helm when the master, Captain Grinstead, shouted from the port paddle, 'mind your helm' on account of the tide and then to 'correct the swing', then at the last moment 'hard over'. Whereupon, he said the vessel 'spun round like a top'. One account revealed the man at the helm was not experienced. He had joined the steamer at Gravesend and, as he was a sailor related to a crew member, asked if he 'could have a go'!

Rescue measures were not satisfactory. Those passengers trapped in cabins stood no chance, but many others should have survived but did not because of a lack of appliances. There were only two lifeboats on the *Princess Alice*, but they were up on davits so difficult to get down in time. No rafts or lifebelts were to hand, only a few rings. Captain Harrison without engines and the fires put out had no power to drive the propellers so could not move. He maintained his crew launched lifeboats, but survivors said that was only after ten minutes. But they did see a lot of ropes hanging over the side of the *Bywell Castle* and crew helping survivors up them. One man escaped by climbing up to the deck of the collier from the wreck of the steamer. One who swam to the north shore, Vernon Hammond, walked home and all his family were saved, but his friend, Frederick Thomas, organist, of Woolwich, drowned.

The collision occurred about 7.45 p.m. and as a result of Captain Harrison blasting his siren continuously, many watermen with small boats came to the rescue. About 8.30 p.m. another London Steamboat Company steamer, the *Duke of Teck*, came alongside. She was even smaller than the *Princess Alice* and by that time no one in the water was still alive, so she took survivors from the *Bywell Castle* to safety instead. Unfortunately, the place where the accident took place was close to the Barking sewer outfall, which was being discharged into the river at the time, as normally the swift tide would carry it out to sea. Therefore, the deaths of some were due to this, others survived, only to die later as a result of diseases incurred. Their deaths were not included in the numbers of those who died in the disaster, which was between six and seven hundred.

Bodies continued to be found for some time; they were washed up a long way both up- and downriver. Many watermen took part in the search and together with members of the Royal Humane Society were paid 5s for every one found. Sadly there was competition among them, leading to fights taking place. At first the Royal Arsenal was used as a mortuary, then the bodies were transferred to the Royal Dockyard. The Thames River Police played a major part in the rescue, and subsequent difficult situations, as when relatives were frantic and desperate to find and identify the bodies. At first Captain Harrison was blamed for the disaster by the crowd and needed protection. PC 56, John Lewis, an ex-Royal Navy diver, was on board the *Princess Alice* with his family and jumped with them into the water. He hung on to his wife, as he thought, but when he got ashore, discovered her to be a total stranger. He obtained a police galley and spent four days searching for them day and night. Watermen were kept busy ferrying people trying to find bodies which could have been taken to several places, like Erith, Gravesend, Barking, etc. William Grinstead, an apprentice waterman, searched for his father, the captain, and his brother, the engineer, for three days. He was not successful but did recover the flag from the mast of the *Princess Alice* and kept it in his family. Four years later, when his apprenticeship was over, he became a river policeman. The flag is now on display in the Police Museum in Wapping. The manager of the Steamship Company, William Towse, lost three generations of his family. One hundred and twenty bodies were never identified.

Mr Carttar was the Coroner for the inquest, which lasted a month at Woolwich. A Board of Trade enquiry took place at the same time on the other side of the river, and to an extent it influenced the coroner's inquest. Some of the same people were called to both. On 13 November 1878 the Coroner commenced his summing-up. He presented the nineteen-man jury with three questions which needed answering:-

1. Which vessel was to blame?
2. Was the cause wilful, criminal, culpable, gross negligence or accident?
3. Did the other vessel contribute to the accident?

The jury were locked into a cold room all night and by 7 a.m. the next morning they had reached a verdict 15 to 4. They had decided the collision was not wilful. The *Bywell Castle* did not take the necessary precaution in time of easing, stopping and reversing her engines. The *Princess Alice* contributed by not stopping and going astern. In future, proper and stringent rules and regulations were to be laid down for all steam navigation on the Thames. Additional findings with regard to the *Princess Alice* were:-

1. She was seaworthy at the time of the collision.
2. She was not properly manned
3. The number of persons on board were more than was prudent.
4. The means of saving life were insufficient.

The Board of Trade enquiry had already concluded that the *Princess Alice* was not properly and efficiently manned and that the numbers were more than feasible, although at the time there were no legal maximums for such a vessel. Their findings were published on 6 November 1878, and a few weeks later Princess Alice, second daughter of Queen Victoria, died of diphtheria.

Following the disaster, Mr Orrell Lever, a director of the London Steamboat Company, wrote to the Lord Mayor of London to say that Captain Grinstead had been in service with his Company for twenty years. In the last ten years they had carried 2 million passengers on their steamers plus they had taken over 300 private excursions every year. In all that time no lives had been lost. He did not mention the previous disaster which befell the *Princess Alice*, although it was not her fault. On 25 October 1873 there was a heavy fog over the river and workmen needed to cross for work. The ferries could not run so some enterprising watermen shouted they would take them across for tuppence. Isaac Digby took more than he should in his boat and pushed off at 5.15 a.m. He headed upstream before striking across the river, hoping to use the strong spring tide to drop him down to the North Woolwich causeway. Suddenly one passenger, John Wright, saw a light from an anchored vessel and called out, 'We're safe! It's the ferry boat at North Woolwich.' But it was not. Digby's boat had been carried downstream and this was the *Princess Alice* moored at South Woolwich. The little boat was swept onto the steamer and sucked under it. Digby was able to save himself, and Wright hung on to the capsized boat until he could haul himself up the paddle box of the steamer. All the rest were drowned.

A *Princess Alice* Survivors Fund was set up in 1878 and the Commissioner of the Metropolitan Police announced each officer would give sixpence of their pay towards it. Many of the dead, including those unidentified, were buried in a mass grave in Woolwich Cemetery at Plumstead. Twenty-six thousand people subscribed to the monument. Captain Harrison had his master's licence suspended and the next year he was more or less exonerated from blame. Sadly, he suffered a breakdown and did not go to sea again. His vessel had its name changed, and it is said went down in the Bay of Biscay. No criminal charges were brought against anyone involved.

Alas, history does sometimes repeat itself. A similar collision[12] occurred in the early hours of 20 August 1989 when a dredger, *Bowbelle*, cut through the side of the *Marchioness*, a pleasure steamer, near Cannon Street Railway Bridge, Southwark. This time fifty-one persons were drowned and the enquiry concluded both vessels had not proper lookouts in place.

As a result of these disasters, the Royal National Lifeboat Institute (RNLI), a voluntary body, has set up stations on the Thames at Gravesend, Tower Pier, Chiswick Pier and Teddington. Above all, proprietors of pleasure craft are governed by onerous strict rules and regulations, requiring them to hold a Master's Licence and have a new boat certificate issued every year.

Inhabitants of North Woolwich, an ever-growing industrial area, had grievances about their administration under South Woolwich. This was exacerbated in 1859 when the Borough of Greenwich[13] was set up to include Woolwich but not the detached North Woolwich. A petition was sent to legislature under the New Reform Bill for enfranchisement. It stated, 'Although in the parish of Woolwich, being on the opposite side of the river, the inhabitants, though called upon to pay all rates and taxes, have not been included in the Parliamentary Borough.' By 1880 they were dissatisfied with the provision of ferries. The Great Eastern Railway's steamboats were still operating and the watermen's ferry was still taking vehicles and animals but the situation was not satisfactory. A public meeting was called in October 1880, followed a year later by one from traders to lobby the local Woolwich Board of Health to provide a steam-driven vehicle ferry. The people felt a free ferry should be provided because already they had paid taxes which went to provide free passage on eleven London bridges in 1880 and they deserved the same. Surveys were made and estimates drawn up, but it proved too expensive to be taken up by the Local Board, who then applied to the Metropolitan Board of Works. After the Free Ferry opened in 1889, local government affairs in North Woolwich were much improved. Four years later a statement was made, 'North Woolwich which has long been in a neglected state is to be better looked after. The Local Board of Health have decided to take advantage of the Free Ferry to administer the operations of road cleansing and dust collecting at North Woolwich direct from Woolwich Town Hall.'

WOOLWICH FREE FERRY

The Metropolitan Board of Works under their chief engineer Sir Joseph Bazalgette in the mid-1880s were contemplating making crossings over or under the Thames to allow increased prosperity and development. Parliament gave authority for plans to be made for the Free Ferry at Woolwich and for Tower Bridge. The Metropolitan Board of Works (Various Powers) Act[14] passed in 1884-85 gave that body powers to acquire land for the approach roads and terminals and to operate the ferry free of all tolls and charges and to pay compensation to the other ferry operators and watermen. The Act was followed in August 1885 by another to establish and regulate the ferry.[15]

In North Woolwich, the landing place was to be on Stanley Road (Pier Road), commencing about 110 yards to the west of the junction of that road and High Street, opposite North Woolwich railway station, and terminating about 170 yards west of that junction. The pontoon in the river was to be opposite the same landing stage, that is, about 80 yards from the bank and connected to it by a bridge. On the south side, the pontoon, with an approach road to it, was to begin in High Street immediately east of Nile Street and terminate on the bank of the river to the east of Bell Water Stairs. The pontoon was to be situated in the river about 80 yards from the bank at the termination of the approach road and was to be connected to it by a landing stage or bridge. The Board were to make all approaches, landing places, dolphins, bridges, etc., connected with the ferry. Other landing places could be built to enable traffic to be raised and lowered between ferry boats and the landing places by means of slipways, hoists or other steam- or hydraulic-powered machinery, which the Board were to provide.

Hours of working were laid down with the proviso they might change, depending on the weather, or if prevented by accident or any other unavoidable interruption. On weekdays they would work between 5 a.m. and 11 p.m. at regular intervals of not more than twenty minutes. Between 11 p.m. and 12.30 a.m. the intervals would be half an hour. On Sundays they would work between 8 a.m. and 11 p.m. at half-hourly intervals.

On the question of compensation, the London & Blackwall and Great Eastern Railway Companies claimed to be the owners of or to have an interest in the rights of ferry and other freehold property. They might be injured by the ferry authorised by this Act and so suffer a loss or damage in respect of their services of steamboats. They should be compensated. The River Thames Steamboat Co. Ltd also claimed to be the owner of or to have interest in rights of ferry and leasehold. If the Company suffered any loss, it was to be compensated.

The Board was to provide and maintain boats and gear and apparatus and employ officers and servants to supply free passage for passengers, animals, vehicles and goods. The Board had permission to dredge and deepen the bed of the Thames to improve the ferry within the limits set out ... and not to alter otherwise without the consent of the Conservators. They could make dams, drive piles, erect coffer dams and temporary staging for ferry improvements, provided they were not more than ten feet beyond the outer line of the pontoons, in which case, the Conservators could ask for them to be removed. Lights were to be put by the works at night for the safe navigation of vessels. Piers were not to be used for any other purposes. The Conservators must have free access to the piers and landing places at all times. The Board could appoint persons to keep order on the piers.

Nothing in the Act was to prejudice or derogate from the charters and grants of the Watermen's and Lightermen's Amendment Act, 1859, or such provisions of the Thames Conservancy Act, 1864. The Board were permitted to alter the lines or levels of the streets described in the plans, and make junctions. They could alter watercourses and pipes or gas pipes or telegraphic wires. Nothing was to interfere with the Electric Lighting Act of 1882 except under section 15 of that Act. The improvements were to be completed within five years. Lands must be purchased within three years. The Act contains a lot of detail about street improvements and how cellars were to be filled in, and what materials pavements were to be made of.

Before work on construction of the ferry could begin, a lot of preparation was necessary. Whole streets were swept away to make room for vehicles, including Hog Lane in South Woolwich. Permission was needed from the Board of Trade for structures affecting the river, and in 1886, assent was granted for the construction of an embankment[16] and a landing stage, among other applications. At their meeting on 30 September 1887, with Lord Magheramore in the chair, the Metropolitan Board of Works considered tenders for this major work.[17] The work comprised 'the formation and paving of approach roads; construction of river walls and other works at both North and South Woolwich; the deepening of parts of the river bed and erecting timber guides, scaffolding and fenders; the construction of two wrought-iron floating pontoons and two pairs of steel and wrought-iron bridges and the execution of other works in connection with the foregoing for the purposes of the intended Woolwich ferry'. The highest tender received was for £69,000 but the Board accepted that of Messrs Mowlem & Co. for £54,900.

Claims for compensation were not settled until 1894 when the ferry was well established. Arbitration was sought from Daniel Watney, who published his report in March 1894.[18] The two steamboat companies, the River Thames Steamboat Company and the Victoria Steamboat Association, were claiming £20,625 from London County Council. It was 'made up as follows:-£10,500 for loss of income already incurred during the claimant's lease of forty-seven years; £2,500 for loss of income sustained during the last five years since the free ferry was opened; £4,445 for prospective further loss of income during the remainder of the claimant's lease; £3,180 for the extension of the pier rendered necessary in consequence of the construction of the free ferry pier, and for interest on the £2,500 during the five years. Experts examined both sides, the difference between some of the valuations being over £16,000. The amount of the award is £4,573'.

There was great rejoicing in Woolwich on the day the Free Ferry opened, Saturday 23 March 1889.[19] Celebrations were marked by a triumphal arch bedecked with flowers and greenery with a plaque displaying the slogans 'Success to the Ferry' on one side and 'Welcome to Plumstead' on the other. Lord Rosebery, chairman of the LCC, performed the opening ceremony. Only two days before, the Metropolitan Board of Works had been disbanded and the London County Council had taken over. Mounted police led the procession through the town, followed by volunteer soldiers and bands and groups from various trade and friendly societies. Mounted police brought up the rear. The civic dignitaries in their forty or so carriages drove straight on to the top deck of the *Gordon*, the vehicle deck. Only three and a half minutes later, they disembarked at North Woolwich to another warm welcome and procession. Then they returned on the *Gordon* and, navigated by Captain Young, returned to the south shore where Lord Rosebery gave a speech to the 600 invited guests. He then had to return to London but all the rest attended a banquet at Freemasons' Hall. The many speeches ended with a toast to the Metropolitan Board of Works officials who had done all the planning and construction over several years. It is not known if Sir Joseph Bazalgette was present, but his obituary, published in *The Times* of 16 March 1891 includes the following remark, 'his responsibility includes ... the Woolwich ferry which has been successfully and gratuitously in operation for now almost two years and has proved an enormous boon to the inhabitants of that thickly populated district'.

Woolwich Free Ferry. Paddle steamer *Gordon*, which began the service in March 1889. Postcard posted from Woolwich in June 1913.

The ferry continued to attract other comments in the press, not all complimentary. A report on the 'Congress of Hygiene' on 13 August 1891 explained, 'The Free Ferry at Woolwich had made the hitherto swampy and useless lands on the north side of the river available for building purposes and a large rental value had been added to the lands of North Woolwich, which previously possessed no rental value to speak of. These increased values were a great deal more than enough to pay for the cost of the ferry'. A letter in reply, published six days later, retorted, 'That ferry is, as I understand, hampered in its usefulness by the crowds of old women who take possession of the ferry boats and fleet the golden hours in a perpetual paradise of knitting and gossip'.

From that first weekend when crowds flocked to ride on the ferry free of charge, the enterprise was a great success, aided by the design of the boats, which allowed for quick and easy loading and unloading. It became a landmark design for vessels used for vehicle and passenger ferries, the top deck for the former, the main deck for the latter. At first *Gordon* worked the ferry on her own. She was named after General Gordon of Khartoum (1833-1885), who was born in Woolwich and attended the Military Academy there. A few weeks later she was replaced by *Duncan* while she was withdrawn to have electric lighting fitted. *Duncan* was named after Colonel Francis Duncan (1836-1888), author of *The History of the Royal Artillery*. He was a soldier and MP, also a director of the St John's Ambulance Brigade and died at Woolwich. Both vessels were steel and iron paddle steamers built by R. H. Green, shipbuilders of Blackwall. They were to all intents and purposes identical, except, according to the Lloyd's certificates,[20] *Gordon* was registered Port number 34 and *Duncan* was 35. There were four diagonal cylinders with a diameter of 33 inches made in 1888 in Greenwich, the length of stroke was 36 inches, with a steam working pressure of 30 pounds. Three days before *Gordon* was put into service, she received her certificate A1 'for Woolwich Ferry purposes'. In the 'Bill of Sale' she is described as having two pairs of engines, one main deck, no masts or rigging, both ends alike, clench-built with steel framework. Registered tonnage 490 tons gross, the vessel was sold by Joseph Fletcher Green of Blackwall Yard, shipowner, to LCC for £13,500 and on 30 April 1889 sixty-four shares in the ship were transferred to LCC.

As Nick Robins points out in *The Evolution of the British Ferry* (1995), what set these vessels aside from other paddle steamers apart from the two-sided loading was the 'cylinders set at right angles on a single crank. There was no coupling between the twin engines, so each paddle wheel could be driven independently. This, together with the prevailing river current, allowed the vessels to crab across the river or to turn in their own length.' In 1893 the *Hutton* was added to the fleet. She was named after Charles Hutton (1737-1823), a professor of mathematics at Woolwich Academy. He had calculated the density of the earth using measurements made by Nevil Maskeleyne, the Astronomer Royal. The new vessel had the same dimensions as the other two, being 164 feet in length, 60 feet in breadth with a draught of four feet. Its speed was 8 knots and tonnage was 490 tons. The carrying capacity was 1,000 passengers plus up to twenty vehicles. However, it was built by a different builder, William Simons & Co. Ltd of Renfrew, Clydebank, at a cost of £15,000.

Each boat had about fourteen or fifteen crew members; usually they kept with one boat, although sometimes they did change to another. They were captain, mate, boatswain, four deckhands, three engineers, two stokers, a greaser and a deckhand/cabin boy. All were employed by LCC, who also appointed them. Thomas Terry Tucker,[21] described variously as an ex-sailor and marine engineer, was chief engineer on the *Hutton*. By about 1900 he was a captain, affectionately known as 'Skipper'. Through working for the Labour Party, he became friendly with Edith Nesbit-Bland, author of many well-known children's books including *The Railway Children*, who lived at Well Hall, a Tudor moated manor house site at Eltham on the heights above Woolwich. After her husband, Hubert Bland, died in 1914, E. Nesbit went to France

Sister ship *Duncan*. Postcard dated Christmas 1917 with the message 'You did not think that we could boast a decent Ferry down at Woolwich in the mud. There are 2 such as these for ever crossing day and night. Horses, wagons, lorries are carried on top, the bridge comes on the road level when let down'.

Woolwich Free Ferry. *Hutton* was added to the fleet in 1893. From an album. Photo taken about that time.

Crew on board *Hutton* with Capt. Thomas Tucker (hands folded), *c.* 1900. (Courtesy Greenwich Heritage Centre)

but returned ill and beset by financial problems. Tucker, a widower, helped out as an unpaid handyman gardener. At the Labour garden party in her grounds in 1916, he rowed customers round the moat at a penny a time. He proposed marriage in his inimitable way, 'it looks to me as if you need a tug round here'.

They married in February 1917 at the RC church in Woolwich. Edith described Thomas to her brother as 'the soul of goodness and kindness', but to a friend he was 'a common little man who never wore a collar and who hadn't an aitch [H] in his head'. Some said he seemed very silent, others thought he was a servant, while Dame Sybil Thorndike regarded him as 'a great yarn teller. He was good for E. Nesbit. He made her laugh again and she was a woman who needed to laugh.' He also encouraged her to write again. Thomas continued to work on the ferry for a time, often on late shifts when Edith would accompany him to cook a meal on board. Soon they decided to move house; Well Hall was no longer a country house – there were shops opposite, and houses being built all around. They went to Dymchurch where she had a holiday home, then settled in two converted military huts at St Mary's Bay, which they called the *Long Boat* and the *Jolly Boat*. Thomas cared for his wife most devotedly until she died of lung cancer (she was a heavy smoker) in 1924, aged sixty-five. He himself carved a simple wooden headboard.

On Saturday afternoon, 9 April 1898, a murder was committed at 19 Kidd Street, Woolwich.[22] The perpetrator was John William Sando, who had shot his landlady, Mrs Harriett Steward. He was sixty-three years old and was the chief engineer on the *Gordon* and had lodged with Mr and Mrs Steward for six and a half years. We learn quite a lot about the working of the ferry from evidence given at the Old Bailey trial[23] in

Woolwich Free Ferry. John William Sando, Chief Engineer on the *Gordon*. Tried for murder,
May 1898. From an album. 1890s.

May 1898. On the day in question, Sando had breakfast at 7.15 a.m. with his landlord, George Steward, who then left to go to Essex for the Easter break. Sando went to work at 7.55 a.m.; it was about a five-minute walk to the pier. Mr Tucker gave evidence that Sando had come to see him at 10 a.m. on board the *Hutton*, but he could not properly find out why he had come, never having been on his boat before. In turn, Tucker had been on the *Gordon* only once and had known Sando for only three months. Sando said he had come to apologise for offending Tucker, who did not know what he was talking about. All the time, Sando was holding him by the collar and shaking his hand. Tucker wanted to read his face to find out the matter, but could not look into his eyes.

William Robinson, the third engineer on the *Gordon*, who lived at Poplar, said he had worked with the prisoner for four years. After work that day, they left the boat at the mooring and went in a small boat to the landing at South Woolwich at 3.45 p.m. They had a quick drink together at Sando's invitation and he then left him in Woolwich High Street, sober, at 3.55 p.m. They had been working for about seven and a half hours. On cross-examination Robinson explained that Sando had gone ashore that morning on private business and would see Mr Tucker. It was Sando's job to be in the engine room where the captain 'would communicate with the engine room by means of what is called a telegraph – there are two dials in the engine room, one for the port and one for the starboard engine, and those orders would be carried out simply by pulling the lever – when the prisoner was at the levers that would be his duty – those were his duties at times, not always – he had to relieve us sometimes to get our meals'. Further, he added, 'besides having to move the levers he has to supervise the whole of the engine room staff, to look after the coal and to see to any repairs which might have to be done – when he went to see Tucker he was away about forty-five minutes, but I cannot be positive – the boiler blows off by itself.'

The captain of the *Gordon*, Charles David Young, said he had to speak to Sando that morning when he was in the officer's cabin, smoking a pipe but with his head down. Young told him he could not have the coals worked down in the bunkers at both ends of the ship at the same time. The reply was 'Don't worry me, captain, my head is so bad'. Young went on to reveal that Sando had been complaining about conspiracies against him, alleging that certain people were trying to get him out of his job as chief engineer. Young doubted this was the case because for that position a man must hold an engineer's certificate, and no other member of his crew had one. The prisoner was always sober on duty and was not a 'butt', the crew treated him with respect. Although he was eccentric and suspicious, he was 'always good for a bit of fun'. Sando had lied about his age, declaring he was fifty-nine because it was a standing rule with LCC they should retire at sixty, but if they were fit to carry on they were not dismissed. With regard to Sando's work, he had two other engineers under him, but they were not always in the engine room at the same time. They had 'what is called a double-engine – if anything went wrong it could be detected immediately in the engine room – not necessarily by him, but by the staff – a most important part of his duty would be to see to the steam pressure in the boiler – we could not have an explosion, we have a safety valve.'

Dr James Scott, the doctor at Holloway prison where Sando was imprisoned awaiting trial, said from his observations there was no sign of insanity but admitted 'it was possible for a man to be sane at one time and insane at other times'. Sando had told him that as a child he had fallen down a ship's hold and had pains at the top of his head ever since. Twenty years previously he had fallen again and had a scar on his head. The jury found Sando guilty of murder, but much to Mr Justice Hawkins' astonishment, they brought in a verdict of insanity at the time he committed the murder. There was no motive. Sando was sentenced to be detained as a lunatic in Holloway pending Her Majesty's pleasure.[24]

Woolwich Free Ferry. Entrance on a pier from the south bank. Postcard posted February 1913.

LCC issued returns for each year, which generally showed improvement.[25] In May 1896 they calculated that the expenditure on setting up the Free Ferry and running and improving it had been £182,775. Total staff employed was eighty-four, which included landing stage staff. In the six and a half years from 2 June 1889 to 31 December 1895, almost 26 million passengers and 1,662,000 vehicles had used the ferry. The greatest number of passengers carried in one day had been 54,484, and vehicles 1,488. The annual working expenses were £18,405,000. Fog had stopped the service only twice during that time, and although the river was full of ice in the great frost of 1895, the ferry had continued running. In 1897 there was an increase in the number of passengers, making a total of those crossing of nearly 4½ million.

Figures were not given for the number of animals carried. Flocks of sheep and herds of cattle were carried regularly from North Woolwich railway station on their way to the Co-op abattoir at Abbey Wood. Most horses grew accustomed to the crossing but some were nervous. For these a 'tracer' horse was kept to lead them off. One skipper tells of a pig his father rescued when it fell overboard and the Co-op paid him 2s 6d. Incidentally, there was a mongrel during the 1950s who used the ferry every day to fetch his bone from a butcher in Hare Street. A ginger cat, too, used to jump the gap before the ramp was down completely to hunt the rats which were always on board.

The ferry was sometimes in the news, for good reasons.[26] Queen Victoria visited by train on Thursday 22 March 1900. The crowds were multitudinous. One journalist attempted to travel by the ferry from North to South Woolwich. The boat with a normal capacity of 1,600 was forced to take 2,000 and his complete journey took three hours. In October 1902 a court case was brought as a result of one Thomas Dunn reporting he had seen ammunition being carried on the ferry. This was strictly against the law. A ceremony took place on board *Hutton* in October 1903 when Mr R. J. Hitchcox, a member of staff, was presented with a resolution of the appreciation of the Bridges Committee for his bravery in rescuing a passenger from drowning. He was also given a medal and certificate from the Royal Humane Society. That society also gave a medal in August 1906 to Carl Mack, aged ten, who had rescued another boy who had fallen into the river at the Free Ferry.

Fog has always been a problem for the ferry; even as recently as 2 February 2008 it was closed in the morning because of persistent fog caused by a period of very high pressure. The difficulty is mainly that of having to cross shipping lanes: by law the ferry has to give way to traffic travelling up or down the river. Of old they did not always stop for fog, there is one record of a boat working all night in 1909. Even before the Free Ferry was opened there was a scheme to construct a pedestrian[27] way under the river from Bell Water Gate to North Woolwich Station. It would be of benefit to people who queued to use the penny ferry. An Act was obtained in June 1874 which allowed the promoters to raise £60,000 in share capital and to borrow a further £20,000 on mortgage. The tunnel would have to be 60 feet deep below Trinity high-water mark. There would be a toll at the entrance, with one penny charged to each pedestrian.

After land had been purchased, work began in 1876, but problems soon arose. The river bed differs on both sides. On the south it is hard chalk with a thin coating of silt, whereas the north bank has a chalk base which is broken up and covered with a fairly thick coating of silt. This proved difficult, and although Greathead had invented new tunnelling equipment which allowed for construction through waterlogged sands and gravels by using compressed air with a hydraulic lifter, this was not used. A new Act of 1879 allowed extra time for construction, but no progress was made. A further extension in 1881 gave a deadline of July 1884, but this was not met, and the project was terminated.

Another solution was proposed in 1904; this was a short electric railway,[28] called the 'North & South Woolwich Electric Railway'. The promoters were Major Lewis Isaacs, Mayor of Kensington, and Sir Robert Dashwood, with Sir James Szlumper as engineer. They required £240,000 capital. They proposed to bore the tunnel and approaches conventionally by 'cut & cover'. It would be a single tube about three-quarters of a mile long and 11 feet 6 inches in diameter One train would operate in each direction every six minutes with six cars taking up to 330 passengers paying 1d each. Electricity would be generated on the north side on a site now covered by the King George V Dock, which opened in 1921, long after this scheme was abandoned.

LCC were not in favour of this scheme and required twenty-seven clauses to be inserted in the Bill. They were concerned there would be further prohibitive claims for compensation and they wanted to protect the interests of their free ferry. At the same time, they realised some other means of crossing was necessary and developed their own plans for a foot tunnel. The N&SWER promoters declared on 22 March 1904 that they did not wish to proceed, and the Bill was killed.

WOOLWICH FOOT TUNNEL

Three months later a news article in *The Times*[29] reported that the Bridges Committee of LCC had received a deputation from Woolwich Borough Council and others in support of the construction of a footway tunnel. After consideration of a report, the committee had resolved to seek powers in the next session of Parliament, to construct it and to amend the law which regulated the working of the Woolwich steamboat ferry. A year later, on 19 June 1905, another news item reported that LCC were to be asked by the Bridges Committee to sanction the application to Parliament. They asked 'for powers to construct a footway tunnel to connect North and South Woolwich. The tunnel will be designed to supplement the facilities afforded by the Woolwich Free Ferry ... There is no other access between the north and south sides of the river nearer than the Blackwall Tunnel, about three miles westward. It is not possible to increase the frequency of the ferry service.'

Statistics were given for size and cost. The tunnel was to be about eleven feet in diameter and 500 yards long and would run underground at the same point where the ferry crossed. Therefore, no land would need to be bought, it was already owned by LCC. It would be of similar design as Greenwich Foot Tunnel. Cost was estimated at £145,000 with an annual cost of maintenance of £2,500. It was anticipated that by opening the foot tunnel the costs of maintenance of the ferry would be reduced by £7,000, thus giving a net saving of £4,500 on combining the two services. More importantly, the savings would result in an annual charge of only ·017d on the rates for the first year 'and this will after thirty-five years entirely disappear'. The Act was passed in 1909 and Messrs Walter Scott & Middleton[30] began construction to the design of Sir Maurice Fitzmaurice. The site was slightly upstream of the proposed N&SER tunnel. Lord Cheylesmore, Chairman of LCC, performed the opening ceremony on Saturday 26 October 1912. Will Crooks was responsible, as Chairman of the Bridges Committee, for seeing the project through to fruition.

The tunnel is 504 metres long and, like Greenwich Foot Tunnel, is at present (2010) being upgraded. In recent times it has not been used very much and was 'out of sorts'. There are to be new lifts, CCTV, new signing, and adjustments made to allow use of mobile phones, and the tiled lining will be refurbished. Completion date is scheduled for March 2011, with the minimum amount of closure while the work proceeds.

With the opening of the foot tunnel, the Penny Ferry finally closed down. The Barge House Ferry, the ancient ferry, had already been discontinued. Now the people of Woolwich had a choice of two free crossings from both sides. Apart from the knitting grannies (who probably did not exist), it was workmen and children who benefited the most. Whole families would spend hours making the journey backwards and forwards, and still do. But children were allowed on board unaccompanied. *The London Magazine* in 1896 commented, 'if there is any place in the boat where they ought not to be ... the boys of a certainty will discover it.' They chased round the decks evading the crews but sometimes were allowed to watch the gleaming steam engines driving the paddle wheels.[31] Mothers found that by wrapping them up warm the chill river air was a cure for their offspring's whooping cough. Sometimes their games could last all day at weekends or in school holidays. A favourite game was to go across by ferry, then run fast through the tunnel to get back to the other side before the boat returned. One young lad's Grandad[32] warned him about 'across the water, 'cos they don't even speak the King's English over there'!

Alfie and the Ferryboat (1968) is a picture book by Charles Keeping which tells the adventure story of one such child. Alfie lived in a little street called Hope Place behind a sugar factory (Silvertown on the north bank). He knew Bunty the sailor who stood at the corner of his street each Friday. Bunty would play scratchy records on an old gramophone he pushed around in a squeaky pram. He told Alfie stories about his travels to places 'on the other side of the world'. Alfie wanted to go on a boat to see them. One day Bunty was not there and the newspaperman said he had probably gone 'to the other side of the water'.

Alfie went off dreaming, and when a sudden fog came down, he missed his way. Then he saw a boat beside a street with people getting on it with cycles, cars, lorries and a little horse and junk cart. Alfie joined them moving down an iron gangway and nobody noticed him. There was a rumbling and a hoot-hoot and they moved over the water, passing big boats and barges. On the other side all got off and Alfie followed. He saw lights and a tower. Then he saw 'Stoker', Bunty's dog, and followed him up the hill. There was a big glass palace with twinkling lights and a sign saying 'The Other Side of the World'.

There was Bunty, who explained he was on the other side of the *river* – not the world! 'The boat you came on is the ferry that crosses the river many times a day. The other side of the world is much farther away – but one day, when you are grown up,

Approach to Woolwich Free Ferry on the south bank before the foot tunnel was constructed.
Postcard sent January 1906.

The same place after foot tunnel opened in 1912. Postcard sent in 1926.

Woolwich Free Ferry. Several mothers with babies and a group of boys with a dog are among the passengers. Postcard *c.* 1913-14.

you will go and see it. Now I must take you home'. And they went back in the ferry boat.

In the 1920s the three original paddle steamers were replaced[33] by four more similar ones, all built by J. Samuel White & Co. Ltd of Cowes, Isle of Wight. *Squires* was named after William James Squires (1850-1931), a bookseller and stationer in the town who became mayor twice and was for many years chairman of the Woolwich Equitable Building Society. *Squires* and the new *Gordon* were built identically, costing £35,000 each. They were 172 feet long, 62 feet in breadth with a draught of 4 feet 6 inches and tonnage of 625 tons. There were two pairs of coke-fired diagonal surface-condensing engines which were fired by hand to avoid excess smoke. They could get up a speed of 8½ knots by using about eight tons of coke a day and working at a pressure of 60 pounds per square inch. Their capacity was the same as that of their predecessors. In 1930 they were joined by the other two, *John Benn* and *Will Crooks*, which had exactly the same dimensions and speed, but cost an extra £2,000 each. *John Benn* was named after Sir John Benn, a member of LCC from its creation in 1889 and who served as chairman from 1904-05 and also as MP for Devonport. He is an ancestor of Tony Benn and Hilary Benn, both MPs.

Will Crooks (1852-1921)[34] was a man who did more than any other to further the cause of the East End people, especially the dockers, in that difficult time which spanned his lifetime. The River Thames was close to his heart, and he was responsible for Island Gardens at the end of the Isle of Dogs, the Tunnel Gardens at Blackwall, campaigning for the first Blackwall Tunnel, and both the Greenwich and Woolwich foot tunnels. Like John Benn, he also joined LCC when it was set up and stood as a member of the Progressive Party. Later he was one of the first four Labour members to enter Parliament. M. W. Colchester-Wemyss, a gentleman landowner of the Forest of Dean, Gloucestershire, did not know Will Crooks, but was moved to write a eulogy of him in his private diary for 8 June 1921, three days after Crooks died in the London Hospital:[35]

Woolwich Free Ferry. The new *Gordon*, which was in service for about forty years. Photo by S. W. Rawlings. From an album 1945-65. (Reproduced by Permission of English Heritage)

Woolwich Free Ferry. *Will Crooks*, *c.* 1940. (Courtesy Campbell McCutcheon)

Will Crooks, MP for Woolwich for many years, was born in Poplar of most humble parents who died when he was quite young. He had to be sent to the workhouse at Poplar where he spent his childhood. Many years later he became chairman of the Board of Guardians of that same Union. When he left it, he was apprenticed to a cooper and that was his trade in life, but as a young man he went through very hard times and tramped the country for work.

Later on he got more regular employment as a cooper, then threw himself heart and soul into the Trades Union movement, then in its infancy. Soon he became one of their leaders and was elected as a working candidate for Parliament. He was returned at the first attempt and became a quite prominent member of the House. Crooks was gifted with extraordinary eloquence and had a great sense of humour. He was always courteous to his opponents and readily listened to and appreciated their arguments, however little he might be convinced by them.

He was most conscientious and thoroughly acted up to his convictions and became most popular with every party in the House of Commons. Here was a man bred in a workhouse living on most friendly terms with ministers and men of the highest rank, made a Privy Counsellor by the king and well fitted to the rank of Right Honourable.

During the war he threw himself into the work of recruiting and addressed thousands of working men at meetings throughout the country with very great success. At the end of the war his health broke down and he never recovered. He had to resign his seat and live an absolutely quiet life. Of course, he was quite a poor man and some Parliamentary friends got up a subscription for him and only last week quite a nice little sum was handed to his wife and himself. She was a Gloucestershire woman from Maisemore [near Gloucester] and was a domestic servant in London when he first met her.

He took an active and strenuous part in the work of the world and died at a good age, having never made an enemy, I think, but having gained the affection of a very large number of people and having earned the respect of the whole country. I wish there were more like him to follow in his footsteps, but the men who are mostly in evidence now are the extremists with whom he had no sympathy.

Will Crooks, MP, with his wife. Postcard. No date.

Will Crooks is buried in Tower Hamlets cemetery with a memorial stone to him. A council estate in Poplar, where he was Mayor briefly, bears his name, as does a road in Eltham, Woolwich. (As fellow members of the Fabian Society, he would have known the Tuckers of Well Hall.) Perhaps the one tribute that would have given him most pleasure was the plaque above the bed endowed in his name at the London Hospital. 'To the memory of one who was ever a loyal lifelong friend of the hospital The Rt. Hon. Will Crooks'.

These four new paddle steamers were more 'user friendly' than their predecessors, in that they had a closed bridge for the crew, whereas before they had to stand on the vehicle deck. They were smarter, with lots of polished brass, but still no heating. A collision[36] at the south pontoon caused damage which took six weeks to rectify, while the service was closed. The *Squires* had just arrived with the mate in charge and 400 passengers on board and the mooring rope had just been made fast when the mate saw a large American ship, the *Coahama County*, steering an erratic course downriver towards them. The mate gave orders to let go the ropes and steer astern at full speed. The big ship hit the ferry on the port bow, causing it to rebound on to the pontoon. No one was injured, but if the *Squires* had still been moored she would have sunk.

Figures for the service during the Second World War, 1939-45, are not available, but the ferries carried on working in difficult conditions. The boats did not go to the relief of Dunkirk but many independent watermen did go in their small boats. During the big air raid on the docks on 7 September 1940, the ferries worked all night to evacuate the people from the Essex shore while oil was burning on the river and continued to run a twenty-four hour service, when it was needed, throughout the war. They were not allowed to use navigation lights and the wheelhouse on each boat was closed in with concrete to protect against shrapnel. Once a small bomb exploded under the stern of a boat but the damage did not stop it running. A frightening experience was when a V1 rocket just missed the bridge of another boat and buried itself in the opposite riverbank. A man recalled that in 1944 he played truant from school to go and have a look at King George V Docks because he heard the D-Day invasion fleet would be there. He travelled on the Woolwich Ferry but its crossing was stopped by a train of tugs passing downriver, 'towing what looked like a large concrete block about four or five storeys high'. Nobody on the boat could think what it was, but after D-Day, when he saw a cinema newsreel, he realised it was part of Mulberry Harbour.

After the war the Ministry of Transport included Woolwich in a report on extant ferries.[37] A description of the vessels is given, but only two of the four were in operation – the others were in reserve. They operated until 9 p.m. at twelve-minute intervals until 9 p.m. on weekdays and twenty minutes on Sundays. The only circumstances to interfere with the service were fog and river mist and river traffic. The foot 'tunnel was available for pedestrians and (except during rush hours) for cyclists.' The vehicular traffic was now much less than before the war when three vessels worked simultaneously. 'Construction of the Dartford/Purfleet tunnel may result in a diminution of through traffic but we believe there will continue to be a heavy demand for many years.' Their conclusion was that the equipment capacity and service available was adequate for present needs 'and in view of the difficulty of assessing demand after the Dartford/Purfleet tunnel is completed – we make no recommendations for this ferry'. In fact, in 1948 the total number of vehicles using the ferry was 50 per cent less than pre-war. This was explained partly by petrol rationing and shortage of new vehicles. (One coster-monger's barrow made crossings each year from 1949-51, but from 1937-39 there had been an average of thirteen in winter and nineteen in summer).

By the 1960s it was evident the ferries needed revamping. The vessels found difficulty in accommodating the big articulated lorries, and traffic congestion in Woolwich was a major problem. New end-loading vessels were planned, but first new causeways and approaches had to be constructed. At North Woolwich the construction of a new terminal caused little disruption, but at South Woolwich the need for a pier, offices, a forge, joinery, rope store and waiting rooms caused widespead demolition. The new landing stages, designed by Husband & Co.[38] and built by Marples, Ridgway & Partners, Civil Engineers, are actually fixed piers supported by piles. 'They are linked to the ferries by hinged loading ramps operated from huge hoist towers. These "link spans" have to deal with large fluctuations in the level of the river: on the north side the water is about 16 feet deep at low water spring tide and only about 5 feet on the south. But the spring tidal variation is between 21 and 23 feet and can be a formidable 30 feet. Thus passengers may travel steeply up or down on to the ferries'. To watch the loading ramps come down to match the loading platform at the end of the boat exactly is an amazing sight. A wonderful piece of engineering, as during the operation the boat is held steady by its engine, not by mooring ropes, thus allowing for a quicker turnaround.

The four paddle steamers were taken out of service in 1963 and were sold in Belgium for scrap, with only the bell from *John Benn* rescued by the Benn family. Figures recorded from the *Will Crooks* show that since 1930 she had travelled 800,000 miles over the river, carrying 50 million passengers, over 5 million vehicles and over 6 million motor and pedal cycles. It was the end of an era and they were sorely missed.

Three new diesel-powered vessels[39] came into service in 1963: *John Burns, Ernest Bevin* and *James Newman*. They were all named after Labour politicians associated with Woolwich. John Elliot Burns (1858-1943) led the dockers' strike of 1889. A student of London's history, he coined the phrase 'liquid history' to describe the River Thames. The boat which shares his name is the current flagship of the fleet. Ernest Bevin (1881-1951) became involved in trade unionism when a truck driver. He formed the Transport & General Workers Union in 1921 and later became an MP and Foreign Secretary, representing Woolwich briefly at the end of his career. James Newman (1879-1955) was a school teacher who was prominent in local affairs and served twice as Mayor of Woolwich. He received an OBE in 1948 for services to local government.

The new boats were all built at the Caledon Shipbuilding & Engineering Co. Ltd shipyards in Dundee, at a cost of approximately £268,000 each, and sailed to the Thames 'under their own steam'. They seem to be identical, with a length of 185 feet, breadth of 61 feet and draught of 6 feet. Tonnage is 738½ tons. The propulsion is by two pressure-charged Mirrlees Blackstone 500-hp diesel engines type R4/AU7M which drive two Voith-Schneider Cycloidal propellers type 20E, one at each end of the boat. These propellers were unique on the river when first installed. Shaped like a coffee table with five legs and not like usual propellers, they enable the vessels to come in to the terminals head-on at any state of the tide. Because there is a propeller at each end, the boats can travel in either direction or spin on the spot or move sideways just by altering the angle of the blades, and this is controlled by three consoles on the bridge, which is amidships. Although designed for end loading, they can be adapted for side loading. Their capacity is 500 passengers and 200 tons of vehicles, twice as much as the last paddle steamers. For the period 23 December 2007 to 14 December 2008, the Woolwich Free Ferry carried approximately 2,570,531 passengers, excluding vehicles.

Woolwich Free Ferry was transferred from the Secretary of State for Transport to 'Transport for London', under the Mayor of London as per the Greater London Authority Act 1999.[40] The Woolwich Ferry Order No. 1044 came into effect in 2000 and defined its powers. The ferry is now run by Greenwich Council, acting as agents for the Mayor of London. The present Mayor, Boris Johnson, is very keen on developing the river as a line for transport again and various schemes are proposed, including charging tolls on the ferry. This will bring a lot of opposition and will not be easy to achieve, as a new Act of Parliament will be needed. Meanwhile, a 'long ferry' commuter service has been instated between the Arsenal Pier and London, calling at Greenwich. Known as the 'Thames Clippers', it carries over 2,000 passengers a week.

Woolwich Free Ferry. *John Burns* came into service 1963, the date this photograph was taken. (Courtesy Campbell McCutcheon)

CHAPTER ELEVEN

Barking Reach to Northfleet Hope

After rounding Tripcock Ness, the Thames in its course downriver takes on a different aspect. It is wider and the banks on either side are flatter, apart from the chalk cliff at Purfleet. As there are several bends in the river, it has acquired different names for each stretch between each point or promontory, usually called a ness. The stretches between are called reaches, each with an apposite name. Where the river passes Barking on the north bank, there is Barking Reach, which ends at Cross Ness; Halfway Reach; then Erith Reach, which extends past Erith. After the turn at Coldharbour to Crayford Ness on the south bank for a short stretch is Erith Rands and from there Long Reach runs between Purfleet on the left bank and Dartford on the right to Stone Ness, which is opposite Stone and Greenhithe on the south. Further on is Broad Ness where Northfleet Hope begins and runs south past Tilbury Ness to Northfleet. The *Oxford English Dictionary* defines 'Reach' as 'a run on one tack', a term used of sailing ships. They quote a definition from a nautical dictionary of 1846, 'a vessel is said to be on a reach, when she is sailing by the wind upon any tack.' Ancillary to this the word is defined as 'that portion of a river, channel or lake which lies between two bends; as much as can be seen in one view'. The Thames, as an important navigable river needed to name each distinctive stretch.

Cross-river ferries were few and far between in this area by virtue of the land on either side being sparsely populated salt marsh and sand and shingle. The only ferries known were those which carried ancient ways as at Greenhithe for connection to the London-Dover road. For centuries man had battles against the river to preserve the banks to protect the lands. Often when there was a north-easterly gale driving down the North Sea at the same time as the high spring tides, this would work together to 'lend the imprisoned river a giant's strength; its waters would seek out some weak or neglected part of man's defences, breach it, and undo the work of centuries'. This happened at Limehouse when the river invaded the Isle of Dogs, but the river was returned to its normal course because of the Deptford Dockyard. A breach also occurred at West Thurrock Marshes, which was closed eventually, but left behind a lake which still exists, behind Stone Ness.

DAGENHAM BREACH

By far the worst, and the most difficult to contain was the Dagenham levels. In about 1621 there was a serious breach which covered the Dagenham and Havering Levels at every tide. Sir Cornelius Vermuyden[1] was called in and succeeded in stopping it. At the same time he embanked Dagenham Creek (or 'inned' it). Across its mouth he built a wooden sluice or 'clow' which let out the waters of the creek at low tide, but hinges enabled it to hold back the waters of the Thames at the rising tide. This worked for a time, but the work was not kept properly in repair, so it failed in 1707 when the sluice gave way under a forceful tide and gales. The breach at first was not serious, being only between fourteen and sixteen feet across.

However, time went on and the breach became much deeper, thirty feet and a hundred feet wide at low water, which led to a lake being formed along the land side of the embankment for 1½ miles, thus damaging valuable farming land. Gradually, by the scouring of the tides, about a thousand acres were washed into the main river and formed a bank about a mile long to nearly halfway across the river. This situation could not continue, and various attempts were made without success to bridge the gap. Old ships were filled with ballast and padded with bundles of straw and hay and sunk. The tide uprooted them. Huge wooden trunks were filled with chalk and packed into the breach, cargoes of chalk and ballast were even confiscated from passing ships to pour into the gap but one day one of the trunks lifted and floated downstream upright, as far as the Nore. An old royal ship, the *Lion*, was sunk there, but the tide smashed it to bits. After seven years with no solution found, an Act was passed enabling the breach to be mended at public expense. One Boswell was contracted for the work. He started by using some of the methods described but failed. He wanted to sink piles, but his foundations would not stay. His attempts to use pontoons of ships only achieved a deeper breach, and as a result of heavy losses sustained, he surrendered the contract.

Captain John Perry RN (1670-1732)[2] then took up the cudgels. He was born at Senckley (St Chloe), then in the parish of Rodborough, Gloucestershire, and entered the Royal Navy in his teens. He led a distinguished career in action until he lost an arm through not having treatment for a wound in time. From then on he acquired knowledge of civil engineering from organising naval dockyards.

While in the Marshalsea prison following a court martial for surrendering his ship to privateers, he wrote *A Regulation for Seamen*, which advocated replacing impressment for the navy by registering men as either naval or merchant seamen for a maximum of one year's paid service, at the end of which they would not be recalled. If this had been adopted, it would have lifted a great problem from watermen's lives. Czar Peter of Russia was living in John Evelyn's house in Rotherhithe in order to do some 'industrial espionage' in 1698, as he wanted to set up a Russian fleet and undertake various naval construction works as necessary. Lord Carmarthen, the Naval Surveyor-General, introduced Perry to the Czar, who then invited him to Russia to become Comptroller of Russian Maritime Works at a salary (unwritten) of £300 p.a.

Perry carried out his duties in Russia, but never got paid his proper salary, so returned to England in 1712. When he heard about the Dagenham breach he put in a tender, which was turned down in favour of Boswell's lower one. So when Boswell failed, Perry's tender of £25,000 was accepted. Work began in 1715[3] when the lake was nearly two miles long and the actual breach was 400-500 feet wide in some places. First of all he relieved the pressure of the water against the breach by making other openings in the bank for the waters to go through. Then he made two openings with strong sluices below the breach, and when these were working, he began operations on the breach itself. A row of strong timber piles were driven in across the gap and these were dovetailed into each other, rendering them almost impervious. The foundations of the piles were protected on the river side by clay which formed a sort of puddling which resisted the force of water. Then up steps Boswell. He petitioned Parliament that Perry's scheme was unworkable. Perry was summoned to a Parliamentary Committee where he conducted himself so expertly that at the end of the session he was told, 'You have answered us like an artist, and like a workman; and it is not only the scheme, but the man, that we recommend.'

So the work proceeded, slowly, like all piling jobs, and it came to the gap from both sides. Towards the end there was extensive violence from the force of water and accidents happened. It was thought the gap would be too deep for the piling to hold. Nevertheless, it was achieved and a stout clay bank was heaped all around the breach. The opening was stopped and the waters drained away by the sluices, leaving only Dagenham Breach, an extensive lake still used for fishing and recreation.

Three hundred men were employed in the operation and went on strike frequently for increased wages and this was a problem for Perry who far exceeded the amount of his tender in materials alone. The government did make a grant of £15,000 to him in compensation. Interested landowners also gave £1,000, but he still lost out, only gaining for himself a tremendous achievement. Perry may have received remuneration from his publication *An Account of the Stopping of Dagenham Breach*. He went on to work on the harbours at Rye and Dover, and was still writing reports at the end of his life.

FORD'S DAGENHAM FERRY

Not until the twentieth century was any attempt made to develop this reclaimed land. Then it became part of Britain's first experimental flying ground for the early planes. In about 1924 the Ford Motor Company bought 295 acres for £167,000 to relocate their British plant from Manchester. At the time, the chairman described the marsh as 'almost the worst possible choice' of site. In order to make the ground stable, about 22,000 concrete piles were sunk eighty feet deep. Henry Ford's son Edsel dug the first sod for construction of the plant on 17 May 1929. The first vehicle was rolled off the assembly line in 1931.

The enterprise continued to grow until thousands of people were employed. The majority lived in Dagenham, where large council estates were built, but a significant number lived south of the river. In 1933 Ford's instigated their own ferry (Exp. 162 499 808) for the convenience of those workers who would otherwise have travelled to the nearest ferry points, like Woolwich some distance away. The Ford's service was free. It was carried out on a shift basis between 6 a.m. and midnight between Dagenham causeway and one at Belvedere, next to Crossness, on the south bank. Latterly the ferry was contracted to R&G Passenger Launches who operated three catamarans, *Twinstar I, II* and *III* with a staff of nine, who were three freemen watermen, three boatmen licensed to work in Half-Way Reach, plus two marine engineers and a manager. At its peak the ferry was carrying more than 2,000 passengers a week. Ford's used it in advertising campaigns for staff recruitment.

Following reorganisation of the plant when Ford's gave up car manufacture to concentrate on diesel engine design, the company decided to withdraw the ferry[4] service from 30 January 2004, when only 250-300 workers were using it each week. The unions, Amicus and T&G[5] (the old Transport & General Workers Union), fought to obtain an injunction because it was impossible for North Kent workers to get to work. Instead they would have to use the Dartford Tunnel, the Blackwall Tunnel or the Woolwich ferry, none of them easy at peak times and very difficult to fit in with shift working.

As a compromise Ford's arranged for coaches to pick up workers and bring them to the river crossings. They also gave each regular ferry user £1,000 to help with the extra cost and inconvenience. To date, the ferry has not been reinstated, and the boats are sold. *Twinstar III* was sold for cruises on the Fal in Cornwall but returned to the Thames in 2008 and began operating as a charter boat for Wyndham[6] Grand Hotel in March 2009.

Ford's Dagenham Works. The company constructed a reinforced concrete jetty, an early use of such material, for large ships to berth at the works. Photo taken in the 1950s by S. W. Rawlings. From an album. (Reproduced by Permission of English Heritage)

THAMES IRONWORKS FERRY

Another major employer on the Thames from the nineteenth into the twentieth century was the Thames Ironworks & Shipbuilding Co. Ltd with extensive works at Canning Town and at the mouth of the River Lee (Exp. 162 455 817). They built paddle steamers, including the *Meteor* and *Prince of Wales*, which operated between Gravesend and Brunswick Wharf, and also supplied four steel caissons of 58 feet external diameter for the first Blackwall Tunnel. In 1860 they employed 6,000 men, although the number had diminished by the 1890s when there was a series of strikes. A photograph in the Museum of London shows men arriving at the riverbank[7] in crowded ferry rowing boats and crossing the foreshore on timber causeways to climb timber stairs to reach their place of work. With such a large workforce, the Company must have needed to give their workers free transport.

However, it was not just work which brought them. After a series of strikes, the management decided on measures to improve 'workplace morale' by implementing a works football team. The Thames Ironworks Football Club was begun in 1895 and was instantly very successful. One innovation was lighted matches at night. The first was held in December 1895 with electric lights powered by a generator and the football covered in whitewash. Then it became desirable to have professional players so the amateur team was disbanded and from it West Ham United Football Club was formed in 1900.

RAINHAM FERRY-JENNINGTREE POINT

Erith in Kent and Rainham in Essex (Exp. 162 510 810), now Greater London, had two ferry crossings between them since early times, both under the umbrella of Lesnes Abbey just over a mile from Erith church. Neither of the ferry sites now shows any vestige of a previous existence, being covered by industrial buildings, and even some of those have closed down. One ferry ran from near the mouth of Rainham Creek, which is the Ingrebourne River[8] in its lower reaches, across to Jenningtree Point (Exp. 162 505 805), and is at the end of Ferry Lane along a twisty road from Rainham church. This ferry is thought to date from pre-Roman times; at the creek mouth excavations in 1961, fragments of a Romano-British food vessel were revealed. Near the church was a Saxon settlement. The connection of the ferry with Lesnes Abbey continued until the Suppression of the Knights Hospitallers, when the lands came into the hands of Cardinal Wolsey. The first documentary reference is in the Erith parish records, probably for 1580, where it states that a duty of Erith Manor was to maintain the river crossing between the two parishes. The ferry appears on a map of 'The Libertie of Havering' in 1610.[9]

A copy of probate to Thomas Wiseman's will of 1580 shows that among other bequests he left to his grandson William Wiseman a tenement in Rainham together with the ferry, but subject to his widow's life interest. William then sold the inn, ferry and two marshes in 1598 to Sir Robert Southwell. The public house was first recorded in 1556. One Henry Bates of the 'Ferriehouse'[10] died in 1574 and William Watkin of the same place in 1590, both perhaps servants. Another servant was 'Bouncinge Bess' whose base (bastard) daughter Grace featured in a document of 28 November 1591. Among the papers of an Essex Assize Judge is a 'humble certificate of the inhabitants of Raynham', dated 4 August 1634, relating to the inn and ferry. The Ferry House was part of an auction sale of the Berwick and Moorhall Estate in 1729; in 1769 it had become the French Horn. By 1772 the ferry inn was named as The Three Crowns. On a map of 1777 the inn is the only building at the place marked as Rainham Ferry. Both the ferry public house and the ferry are listed in sale particulars of property of the Neave family in 1804. Edward Ind was the purchaser at auction in 1814 on behalf of Ind & Smith, brewers, who renamed it the Ferry Public House. When it was burnt down in 1834, Joseph Lee bought the land and paid off the existing mortgage. Then he rebuilt it and opened the new public house in 1839 when it was let to Richmond the brewers at £18 p.a. After the lease had changed hands several times, it was bought in 1876 by Ind Coope & Co. Ltd who kept it for seventy-five years. Having reverted to the Three Crowns, it was mostly demolished in the early 1970s. Prior to redevelopment in 1999, an archaeological watching brief was made. Slots dug by machine revealed some seventeenth- and eighteenth-century material, including a small figurine of about 1605, overlying a peat level. Loose wooden stakes and chalk blocks found suggested remains of an earlier structure.

A hamlet grew up at the site of the ferry by the creek, known as Rainham Ferry but usually called The Ferry. The 1881 census has twenty-one entries for the hamlet, which appears to be self-sufficient and separate from Rainham itself. The settlement was behind the inn and stretched along the riverbank for half a mile and consisted of fourteen cottages, a general store and another shop selling fertiliser, soap and candles. The inn had its own stables and gardens. Gradually the area became industrialised and a manure works, Vitriol, was set up. In the First World War TNT was manufactured there for the government, which led to a violent explosion on 14 September 1916 when inhabitants took to the river for shelter. Poisoned gas was also produced for a short time. Ferry Lane, previously a rutted cart track, was improved by the government. A copper refinery brought heavy industry to the area. In the Second World War production turned to shells and Ferry Lane was subject to strict security.

The hamlet gradually declined from the 1920s, and buildings were demolished to make way for Murex Ltd, an ironworks founded by a young mining engineer, Henry A. Green, to make metal containers, but which later concentrated on metallurgy and chemicals. The inn closed in 1951 and was taken by Murex for offices. Rainham Ferry and its hamlet have disappeared completely under the factory, which covered 60 acres.

ERITH-COLDHARBOUR FERRY

Erith's other short ferry went from the landing place at the town (Exp. 162 518 784) across to Coldharbour Point (Exp. 162 520 789) at the end of a vast stretch of marsh and sand and shingle, lately an infill site, in Wennington parish. The village[11] is on the former turnpike road to Tilbury, but is actually part of Rainham. Lesnes Abbey held lands in Aveley, and this crossing, first mentioned in 1240, was conveniently at the place where the river is narrower. Coldharbour, or more properly Great Coldharbour, to distinguish it from Little Coldharbour which was upstream towards Rainham Ferry, is said to signify a Roman settlement, although this has been disavowed by place-name experts. It was an Old English word meaning 'cold shelter' or stations on Roman roads, which have been likened in modern times to 'Little Chefs'. The Saxons applied the name to roads and settlements generally. The suggestion of this being a Roman ferry is strengthened by the finding of Roman bricks at low water. Astbury states, speaking of the two Coldharbours, 'if they do mark the sites of Roman posting stations they could have been built only for those crossing the Thames. No one travelling east or west on the north side of the river at these points would make the great detour necessary to call at either unless he intended crossing the river.'

Two tracks lead to the north from the Point. Astbury suggests that the one marking the parish boundary, with double ditches on each side and slightly raised, may be very early, perhaps Roman. This was Manor Way, leading into Rainham Marshes from Southhall Bridge. In 1557 it was described as a drove way or 'defence way for cattle', and was still being used as such in the 1950s. The marshes were renowned for fattening cattle, which were shipped out on the ferries. Almost certainly this was a way to the ferry. A map of 1777 shows one building at Great Coldharbour and another at Little Coldharbour. The first was also shown on the first edition Ordnance Survey map of the 1840s. By the way of things, this does not indicate whether the ferry was in operation then, but by the end of the nineteenth century it had indeed ceased. The old name for Erith was Erehythenasse. The 'London Loop' walk, which used to finish at Coldharbour, has now been extended along a paved way to Purfleet.

PURFLEET FERRY

At Purfleet (Exp. 162 546 785) there was a ferry across to the Kent shore at Dartford, although the town of Dartford itself is some distance away across marshes. The River Darent flows through the marshes to the Thames, and it is that river which gives the place its name. The ford refers to one over the tributary, so Darentford became abbreviated to Dartford. Tradition has it that a hermit stood sentinel over the ford, and later, when the Darent water was deeper, he served as ferryman. The first record of a hermit was made of John Soderman in 1438. Even today the first bridge is nearly two miles inland. Sometimes the Dartford/Purfleet Ferry is referred to as the Long Reach Ferry after the Long Reach Tavern at the landing place, which stood isolated on the river-wall, accessed only by tracks.

Purfleet is part of the large parish of West Thurrock which also had a ferry, to Greenhithe. Sometimes in documents the two West Thurrock ferries[12] are not defined, which can lead to confusion, considering they were also places on the Long Ferry from Gravesend to London. An early reference to the Purfleet Ferry is on a Replication document,[13] that is, a case of complaint or dispute, but unfortunately no date is given. It mentions both the Purfleet to London Ferry and the cross-river one 'may lawfully carry any horses or catell from Purfleet to Dartford Wharf or Dartford town'. It suggests the watermen would operate either one or the other ferry, according to demand, rather than keep to working either one or the other exclusively. If they could navigate to Dartford town, it is assumed the ferry could travel up the Darent if necessary to reach the town.

Originally the ferry rights were vested in the Crown until Edward III included the ferry across to Essex in an endowment to the Priory at Dartford. There was a reference to a Purfleet Ferry in 1566, and in 1577 William and Martha Meredith granted Roger Fryth a twelve-year lease. In a statute issued in the reign of Henry VIII, Purfleet was declared to be a public plying place. A covenant of 1601 contains a curious clause; stating that the crossing was 'not to include any passengers or goods in the boats prejudicial to the farmer at Purfleet ferry'. In 1610-11 Christopher Holford leased to his mother Mary lands in West Thurrock including Purfleet Ferry and ferry house for 12*d* (one shilling) for forty years. It was then in the occupation of John Richeman.[14] A settlement document of 1641 includes both the long and short Purfleet ferries. This last referred back to in a deed of 1664[15] when the same family, the Holford/Heymans, arranged a mortgage on half the Manor of West Thurrock to include the Purfleet ferries. A deed to settle an annuity of £150 dated 1677 includes 'the Purfleet ferry-house and the ferry and two passages over the Thames'.[16]

At some point the ferry must have lapsed because in 1836 there was an attempt to revive it.[17] A Bill was brought to construct a ship canal from the outlet of Dartford Creek into the Thames to Dartford, with a branch to Crayford Creek. The Dartford & Crayford Ship Canal & Kent & Essex Ferry Company were the promoters with a capital of £65,000. Following opposition, plans were altered to make a more modest scheme. Cuts were to be made to the creek itself, resulting in a shorter length (the original channels are defined on the map today by a public footpath which follows them). The Act was passed in 1840 and the ship canal was opened in 1844. This enterprise may have caused the ferry to operate again. A more ambitious scheme was introduced in 1844[18] when a railway was proposed, to run from Dartford to Romford in Essex, crossing the Thames by a floating bridge or steam ferry. It seems the plan was aborted.

Purfleet was an important place in the eighteenth and nineteenth centuries. The government sited gunpowder magazines there. They were demolished in the 1970s, except for one, which has become a Heritage Centre run by volunteers on the quayside. Nearby is the *Royal Hotel*, formerly the *Bricklayer's Arms*, which conceivably was the inn for the ferry. Surrounding the small town were chalk cliffs, which Samuel Whitbread, of the brewing family, quarried. The first cement factory opened in Purfleet in 1871. The Thames Board Mills operated here in the early twentieth century.

Cross-river ferry traffic can never have been very busy on this ferry. Some pilgrims to Canterbury may have used it, also visitors to Dartford Priory. Latterly, we are told, bare-fist fighters crossed with their followers to hold contests on the lonely Kent marshes. It was still working in 1860 when Kent Quarter Sessions were considering the various footpaths across those marshes, some the property of the Wardens of Rochester Bridge, to the ferry over the Long Reach. One unlikely passenger[19] was Count Dracula, whose creator, Bram Stoker, lived in Purfleet. Dracula studied the ferry timetable before he left Purfleet for Bermondsey.

Purfleet. Showing the chalk cliffs and the ferry landing point. Engraving for Dr Hughson's *Description of London*, 1807.

A pier was constructed at Purfleet in 1834 for the convenience of river passengers and this was used by the ferries until the first Dartford Tunnel was opened and the ferry closed through lack of trade in 1965. It soon became evident that Dartford/ Purfleet was an ideal crossing point for modern traffic, resulting in the construction of two tunnels each carrying two lanes of traffic travelling northwards and a suspension bridge for southbound traffic on the M25.

WEST THURROCK-GREENHITHE FERRY

In early times there were two ferries from West Thurrock to Kent. One was from Stone Ness to Greenhithe (Exp. 162 586 760), the other from Grays to Broadness and on to Swanscombe. Both served large numbers of pilgrims to Canterbury and Walsingham in Norfolk, although this cannot be proved. The way to the ferry on the Essex side was along an ancient track or manor way, which crossed the Mar Dyke at Stifford and then across fields to St Clement church,[20] close to the riverbank, where prayers would be said before the dangerous crossing could be made. The church was isolated and far from any habitation so is likely to have been built expressly for that purpose. It has a tall tower (seen in the film *Four Weddings and a Funeral*) which would serve as a navigation aid. From there a footpath still crosses the marshes to Stone Ness. On the other side there is a Pilgrims Road across the marshes at Swanscombe, first recorded in 1310. Originally the ferry at Greenhithe was said to belong to a nunnery at Dartford but in 1541 Henry VIII granted a lease[21] at 33s a year, when it was described as a ferry into Essex for horses and cattle. Later it belonged to the Manor of Swanscombe. On the Essex side some bishops held land in the marshes at West Thurrock in 1430, which included the ferry. Their annual rent consisted of three capons, two grains of pepper, one ploughshare and a share in some windmills at Stifford and West Thurrock.

The Lord of the Manor of West Thurrock is said to have had a view of frankpledge with the right of waifs and strays and the ferry in 1339 but no court rolls survive to

Greenhithe. Passengers waiting for the ferry in the 1950s. Photo by S. W. Rawlings. (Reproduced by Permission of English Heritage)

prove this. A ferry called Grene hithe to West Thurrock was recorded in 1415. John Beer, or Bere, of Horseman's Place near Dartford in 1542 took lease from Henry VIII of a mill called Tongemylne[22] and a ferry called Greenhithfery in Tonge and Swannescombe in Kent. It was then a parcel of the lands of the late Queen Jane (Jane Seymour). The lease was for twenty-one years at a rent of 53s 4d with increases of 33s 4d and 6s 8d. At the end of the lease, the ferry was restored by Elizabeth I to Anthony Weldon of Swanscombe in return for service of a knight's fee. A lease for land in Kent in 1670-71 refers to 'the Crosse ferry and water passage from Greenhithe to West Thurrock and was endorsed in 1729. An indenture of 1689 records[23] a lease of a manor house and land in West Thurrock including the ferry across to Greenhithe. As a result of a great flood in December 1690 the riverbanks broke down and over 1,000 acres in West Thurrock were inundated. A large shelf of material[24] was deposited in the river, impeding navigation and rendered 'a great ferry between Essex and Kent totally destroyed'. Highways too, were impassable. To make good the breach was costly and the revenue of Cobham College, the almshouse in Kent who were owners of the land, was 'utterly impaired'.

During the eighteenth century this ferry seems not to be working, although the causeway at West Thurrock leading to the ferry to Greenhithe was mentioned in a document of 1712.[25] An antiquarian in 1771 says, 'Here was formally a ferry over the Thames into Kent but of later years it has been disused'. By the 1830s it was revived. Thomas Wright in his *History and Topography of the County of Essex*, 1836, states, 'a ferry across the Thames to Greenhithe has lately been established here, which is much used for the conveyance of carriages and cattle.' In describing the Church of St Clement, A. W. Clapham mentions the ferry was still working in the 1860s carrying people, cattle and goods to Greenhithe.

The ferry was still working in the 1950s but must have closed soon after, probably when the Dartford tunnel opened. Greenhithe's history is now recognised; it was designated a Conservation Area in 1975 by Dartford Borough Council and extended in 1998. The hamlet, part of Swanscombe parish, was known for its wharves, lighterage, ship repairs and chalk quarrying. A pier was built in 1842 as a convenience for the pleasure steamers and almost all the prosperity of the place came from the river. Today Greenhithe is next to the new developments of Bluewater and Ebbsfleet.

GRAYS-SWANSCOMBE FERRY

Grays, or more properly Grays Thurrock (Exp. 162 605 776), had two ferries. It was the first port of call for the Long Ferry out of Gravesend for London, and travellers had to be rowed out from Grays Wharf to join the tilt boat in midstream until the pier was built. The Lord of the Manor owned the wharf and the cross ferry to the Kent shore. It was thought the crossing would have been to the nearest point at Broad Ness, but as the hinterland is a vast salt marsh impossible to cross, that is unlikely except perhaps in very early days before the river inundated the land. Instead, the landing place in Kent would have been slightly diagonally to the west where a piece of dry land juts out into St Clement's Reach (Exp. 162 600 761). Several public footpaths converge at this spot, including Green Manor Way, a name from antiquity.

Richard de Gray collected tolls on the wharf in 1228 when he was charging too much.[26] The de Gray family bought the manor in 1195 and continued as owners for 300 years, incorporating their surname into the name of the parish. As Lords of the Manor they had the exclusive right to provide boats for the passage of goods and people. This is first mentioned in an Inquisitiones Post Mortem[27] document of 1308-09 when there were seven tenants of the manor, which included the passage over the Thames, worth 5s per annum. The passage was still included in another Inquisition of 1335.

Later the ferry rights were leased out, often together with the wharf and some leases exist from 1553. In 1600 the lessor[28] was required 'to maintain the ferry with three sufficient tideboats at the least and one wherry with all the necessary furniture to row and sail withal, and four good sufficient and skilful tidesmen to row in passage boats, so that all passengers and wares paying their duties may have their passage and carriage at all times and tides heretofore accustomably used to serve if wind and weather do serve'. It was a 'by request' service and a lucrative asset for the Lord of the Manor. From being £13 5s 8d for rent of the ferry and ferry house in 1566 it rose to £40 and a fat lamb per year in 1613, £63 and a flitch of bacon in 1640, and to £60 plus a flitch of bacon and a half bushel of sweet oysters in 1706. Some ferrymen resorted to unfair means in order to gain more profit. Abraham Pelham, keeper of the ferry at Grays, was indicted in 1656 by William Hogg of Orsett for 'refusing to ferry over goods for the countrey unless at far greater prices than hath been accustomed'. He was declared to be 'very negligent and remiss in the execution of that employment and very extortive in exacting money from passengers'.

The last known written reference for this ferry was in 1843 when it was leased with Grays Wharf for twenty-one years.[29] In recent times the wharf, which has a public footpath to and along it, has been opened up to give public access to the river. The cross ferry is not likely to be reinstated.

CHAPTER TWELVE
Gravesend to Tilbury

THE LONG FERRY

The watermen of Gravesend have a unique dispensation from the Crown, in that they can operate one of their two ferries, the Long Ferry, in perpetuity. On 7 July 1377 the new young king,[1] Richard II (reigned 1377-1399), directed the sheriffs of Kent and Essex to erect beacons on each side of the Thames and keep them ready prepared to be fired on the approach of enemy vessels in the river. Unfortunately, the plan did not work and Gravesend was plundered and burnt by the French. Most of the inhabitants were taken prisoner. As a recompense, and to help the town to recover, the King granted the concession to the Abbot and Convent of St Mary Graces. The ferry from Gravesend to London was already in existence, being the easiest way in which travellers from the Continent who disembarked at Gravesend could reach the city. In future the inhabitants of Gravesend and Milton, its neighbouring manor to the east, should have the sole privilege of carrying passengers from there to London on one condition: they should provide boats for the purpose and carry passengers at 2d per head with their farthells[2] (bundles) or let the whole boat for 4s. It is suggested there was a hidden agenda behind this far-reaching concession. At the time there was increasing unrest among the peasant population, particularly in Kent and Essex, fostered by John Ball. This was a way to appease some of them, but the revolt broke out in 1381 over the imposition of a poll tax, led in Kent by Wat Tyler and in Essex by Jack Straw. The long-term result was that villeinage gradually died out.

Strict regulations were laid down for the working of the Long Ferry, mostly concerned with the fares charged. A King's remembrancer for 1364 records in the accounts that 20s was received for pontage and ferriage over the Thames for the year. (It is not clear if this means all the Thames, or just the Long Ferry.) In 1293 the charge for passengers from Gravesend to London was one halfpenny each but watermen often charged more and had been known to murder for their money. The Lord of the Manor of Gravesend had the right to hold Court[3] for the regulation of boats and water carriage on the Long Ferry. It was called *Curia Cursas Aquae* in Elizabethan times but was discontinued soon after. A jury presented to the justices of the assize in 1293 that 'boatmen of Gravesend, Milton and London did take from passengers unjust fares against their will, that is formerly one halfpenny, now one penny'. The sheriff was told to bring the perpetrators to court. 'Then came several boatmen of Gravesend and they could not deny they had taken one penny as charged. They were therefore in mercy. It was required of them they should take no more than one halfpenny and some of them gave bond of forty shillings for compliance with their sureties.' This did not end the matter, for in 1313[4] the boatmen, of which there were thirteen, were brought before the judges again and admonished. The fare was increased to tuppence in 1370; the concession in 1377 was merely to reaffirm this and at the same time to keep the boatmen in order.

A further regulation was made 'that no waterman should leave his boat at the opposite side of the river after sunset, but to moor it at the city side, so that thieves and malefactors might not obtain possession for the purpose of transit into the city'. (This seems an unnecessary restriction.) Henry IV in 1401 in a grant confirmed the exclusive right of the watermen and the charge of tuppence per passenger. It was questioned in the preamble to a charter made by Queen Elizabeth in 1562[5] when the parishes which constituted the town of Gravesend were made one body corporate for Gravesend and Milton. It was stated that the passage between Gravesend and London was 'not rightly governed, to the great damage of our liege subjects'. However, no proceedings seem to have been taken, the charter was surrendered and a new one issued in 1568. This confirmed all the previous grants and authority was given to the Corporation to make laws and regulations for the government of the ferry which was to be holden in fee-farm at 5s per annum. The inhabitants had become the regulators of the tide barges, the vessels used by the ferry, and they were responsible for issuing licences and regularising terms of employment. The boats were still operated and run by watermen, who were entitled to the profits.

By 1595 the regulations made by the Gravesend Corporation in 1568 were deemed inadequate.[6] The original square sail barges were uncomfortable and cumbersome and not to be relied upon in adverse weather. The Corporation of Gravesend (the Portreve) and the Lord Mayor of London agreed on some new regulations. They stated, 'Whereas the passage by the common barge has been hindered by the multitude of tilt boats, lighthorsemen (a smaller and lighter boat) and wherries, who ply and carry passengers before the common barge has departed, therefore no tilt boat shall depart until the Gravesend barge has departed – from the bridge at Gravesend to Hang-dog tree.' The days of the barge were numbered; trade was lost because of some fatal accidents caused by lack of safety precautions. A barge had overturned in 1553 when fourteen lives were lost, and five years later many vessels went down in a storm. However, some watermen were happy to hire out their barge to take part in the Lord Mayor's traditional procession from the City upstream to Westminster. Twenty-two shillings was paid for the special hire of a barge in 1574[7] and in the following year when Lord Mayor Ambrose Nicholas took to the water for Westminster.

The 1595 regulations recognised that tilt boats had come to stay; the barges could not cope with the increased number of passengers, so seven tilt boats were allowed to work in with the barges. Also it was agreed that the Lord Mayor and Aldermen of the City of London should be responsible for the return journey of the Long Ferry to Gravesend. They introduced the same restriction on vessels leaving the London landing stage at Billingsgate as at Gravesend. No other boat may leave until the Gravesend barge is 'furnished and gone[8] from the stairs at Billingsgate to Tower Wharf'. If any should break this rule they must pay tuppence to the barge owner for every passenger they had 'stolen'. The only exception to this rule was 'if any person of importance wish to hire them for a more speedy journey'! Because there were so many accidents, new regulations were brought in whereby rowers and other men employed in the river passage should be examined and certificated by the eight masters and rulers of the Watermen's Company. It was laid down that the Gravesend barge 'shall serve every tide if the wind and weather permit from Gravesend to London' and vice versa. Barge owners were to 'lay their barge to the common or usual stairs at the bridge and take all passengers who wish to go with them'. The common barge was to be rowed by four men in fair times and by five in foul weather with a steersman. They were to carry 'sufficient masts, sails and sailyards and a good and sufficient hawser and anchor for times of distress'. The fare was still tuppence. Before setting off from Gravesend, the bargeman should call passengers to his barge by giving one call in West Street and three calls in High Street, according to an old custom.

Tilt boats began as 'tide boats' which met the seagoing vessels on the tide and transported their passengers to London quicker than by barge. Later they provided a canvas cover, or tilt stretched over the deck to give protection from the weather, although it is said passengers had to bring their own straw to lie on. Tilt boats were clinker-built and varied between three and fifteen tons. They were propelled by oars, although they had a small sail and always went with the tide. The 1595 regulations stipulated that no more than thirty passengers could be carried, with a waterman and steersman with five rowers. They were not to be overmasted or sailed. The difference between the operation of tilt boats and barges was the former was not a regular service, with passengers each paying a fare, but had to be hired or chartered at no more than 15s per journey. Despite these regulations, a tilt boat carrying about forty people was overrun by a hoy in 1598[9] near Greenwich and most were drowned. On 23 December 1599 a terrible hurricane caused a tilt boat to be upturned and nineteen people lost their lives. Of the other vessels involved, the lighthorseman was to have four rowers and a steersman and to charge 8s per journey, and a wherry, the usual ferryman's boat in calmer waters upstream, was to carry no more than five passengers besides one waterman for a charge of 3s 4d. For all the vessels a waterman was allowed to row only if he had been a rower for one year as stipulated by the Watermen's Company. Initially, only seven tilt boats were permitted to work as auxiliaries to the barges and were meant for 'the nobility or worshipful'. But if bad weather prevented the barge from running, then the tilt boat could take passengers without paying the tuppence per head to the bargemen. Even with added comforts the journey was not always satisfactory because if the tide was unfavourable, watermen were only required to land within two miles of their destination. This meant a struggle, sometimes through thick mud.

Gravesend Tilt Boat. Engraving showing one of the last of the old boats before larger ones with decks were introduced. A steersman managed the principle sail. (From Hall's *The Book of the Thames*, 1859)

By about 1606, after a long struggle, the monopoly of the old open barge running the Long Ferry finally gave way to the tilt boat when the Corporation of Gravesend declined to defend its rights any longer. Another threat came from coaches on the improved roads. John Taylor, the Water Poet, wrote of the plight of the watermen in 1622, the year he made *A Very Merry Wherry-Ferry Voyage* from London to York.

> Carroches, coaches, jades and Flanders mares,
> Do rob us of our shares, our wares, our fares,
> Against the ground we stand and knock our heeles,
> Whilst all our profit runns away on wheeles.

Coaches hitherto had brought passengers from Dover to board the Long Ferry at Gravesend and this was possibly the oldest regular stage coach service. Frequently they were taking them direct to London, despite the possibility of highway bandits. Other coaches brought passengers from Rochester, Chatham and elsewhere in North Kent to meet the tilt boats at Gravesend on the tide. They became known as 'tide coaches'.

These changed circumstances caused the Lord Mayor of London and Aldermen to call for a report on the governing of the ferry at Gravesend.[10] The report was received in 1623 when it was decided to support the Corporation of Gravesend in putting in new orders for the regulation of the ferry. Mainly the orders concerned the circumstance that the Corporation did not have the power to deal with misdemeanours and disorders on the river, which often had led to people being drowned. They wanted to be in line with the City of London, which issued orders with penalties. Gravesend asked that 'some punishment might be inflicted on the delinquents for breach of the orders and refusal to pay the penalties, and that they might have such further powers as the council should deem expedient.'

Gravesend now had a firmer control of management of the Long Ferry, particularly of tilt boats. Masters had to pay 16d to the Corporation, presumably for each voyage. The tilt boats were now taken into the system, on payment of an annual rent, because the barge owners had relinquished their claims to interfere with the management of the ferry. Increased powers enabled the corporation to levy in 1628 an assessment on the people of Gravesend for £18 2s 8d and Milton for £13 13s to buy a new barge. The rights of the Long Ferry were confirmed to the Corporation in 1632, to be held in common socage (a form of tenure, in this case to the Crown) of 6s 8d. For the stairs at Gravesend £6 13s 4d was paid to the Lord of the Manor for maintenance and repair until 1677 when it was transferred to the Corporation.

A complaint was made to the Mayor of Gravesend in 1636 about John Brafferton,[11] a master of one of the five tilt boats. He was drunk 'upon the passage to London, there being between 40-50 passengers on board, when, without any extremity of weather, the boat was run ashore and the passengers to save themselves were run out of the boat to their middle in dirt and water'. He was fined £5. The names of the other masters were Thomas Bleake, Henry Bayley, Robert Harris and Robert Loveday, each paying £6 to the Corporation annually. In 1639 they ordered a new barge[12] for the Long Ferry, probably the last to be provided. Accounts show that in the 1640s the barge operated at a loss.

Lion Quay at Billingsgate Wharf, by London Bridge, situated between Lower Thames Street and the river, was used as the landing stage for the Long Ferry to Gravesend. Other services to the west beyond London Bridge used Billingsgate as well. Alderman John Wardell in his will dated 29 August 1656 gave property named as the White Bear in Walbrook to the Grocers' Company that they may pay the Churchwardens of St Botolph, Billingsgate, £4 a year 'to provide a good and sufficient iron and glass lantern, with a candle, for the direction of passengers, to go with more security to and from the water side, all night long, to be placed at the north-east corner of the parish church of St. Botolph'. Out of that sum £1 was to be paid to the sexton for taking care of the lantern. St Botolph was a patron saint of travellers and churches by city gates and bridges are often dedicated to him. Sadly, the church was destroyed in the Great Fire ten years later and not rebuilt because part of the site was needed for the passage to St Botolph's Wharf. Humpherus noted that a gas lamp was still kept up in (Lower) Thames Street by churchwardens in 1874 for the public benefit.

John Taylor in *The Carriers Cosmographie*, printed in 1637, describes the activity at the wharf. 'At Billingsgate, on every tide to be had barges, lighthorsemen, tiltboats and wherries, from London to the Townes of Gravesend and Milton in Kent, and to any other place within the said bounds, and (as weather and occasions may serve) beyond, or further. Great boats that doe carry and re-carry passengers and goods to and fro betwixt London and the Townes of Maydenhead, Windsor, Staines, Chertsey, Barkshire, Midlesex and Buckinghamshire, do come every Monday and Thursday to Queenhithe and they doe goe away upon Tuesdays and Thursdaies.' Queenhithe was above London Bridge. The Long Ferry would stop at stairs and wharves between London and Gravesend, if hailed from the bank. Fares were charged pro rata.

Tilt boats and the smaller vessels continued in service throughout the eighteenth and early nineteenth centuries, becoming bigger, to take fifty passengers, and having two sails in addition to sets of oars. The boats started from Billingsgate at high water at the toll of a bell, and from Gravesend Town Quay at low tide to take advantage of the incoming tide. The distance was 26 miles. In 1671 new orders were brought in because again complaints were being made of 'ye unreasonable demands made by divers watermen for their labor upon the river of Thames, and of their rude and uncivil demeanor towards the nobility, gentry and others … when they refuse to gratify them in their immoderate demands'. New rates were set for long and cross journeys, for example, from London to Limehouse would be one shilling by oars. The table of rates was to be set up in Westminster Hall, the Guildhall and the Royal Exchange and at all the landing places. In 1686 a new charter was introduced to govern the tilt boats, despite which, one sank in 1697[13] with fifty people drowned, including the Vicar of Harlow, Essex. An Act passed in 1737 limited the number of passengers taken to forty but still the overcrowding continued. All the boats used on the Long Ferry were busy but somewhat unstable, including the peter boats used for fishing. At this time about twenty-six tilt boats were operating, taking possibly about 300 passengers a day. When prisoners from the Battle of Culloden[14] were imprisoned in Tilbury Fort in 1746, the tilt boats did a good trade ferrying people from London to have a look at them.

With the advent of the age of steam, it was inevitable that steamers would take over the Long Ferry. The first one, a wooden paddle steamer[15] from the Clyde called the *Marjory*, left Wapping Old Stairs en route to Gravesend on 23 January 1815 at 10 a.m. under Captain Cortis. She was not then empowered to moor at the Town Quay at Gravesend so anchored just below at Milton and passengers were conveyed to their destination by watermen in their own boats. The Watermen's Company took proceedings against the owners of the steamship, the New London Steam Packet Company, and some sabotage took place. They got some concession, in that the master should always be a freeman waterman. *Marjory* was soon joined by *Argyle*, which was renamed *Thames*. She was 72 feet long, of 74 tons, a 16-hp engine and paddle wheels of 9 feet diameter. There was a main cabin with a fare of 4s and a fore cabin which was only 2s, and a stewardess! At first only one passage a day was made.

By 1820 fifteen steamers were operating on the Long Ferry. *London Engineer* was much bigger than the earlier vessels, being 120 feet long and of 315 tons. *Venus* was

Steamers off Gravesend. *Vesper* is on the right. (Engraving from *Finden's Ports, Harbours and Watering Places of Great Britain*, Vol. II, edition of 1842)

Gravesend. *Ruby* berthed at Town Pier. She was the fastest paddle steamer of her day. From an engraving of 1841.

bought in 1824 by the General Steam Navigation Company especially to serve this ferry. She was of 202 tons and had Boulton & Watt engines. In 1831 she was involved in a collision – traffic on the river was very dense then – but there were no fatalities. By 1830 fifty-seven steamers were operating the service and several steamship companies were involved. Some were now operating further than Gravesend to the coastal towns like Margate. This was a new venture, the tourist trade, and some produced guidebooks to enhance the experience for their customers. At Grays a Town Pier was built to replace the previously hazardous undertaking when passengers were conveyed from the town causeway in watermen's boats and transferred to the steamer midstream. At least one fatality occurred because of this. The last tilt boat, the *Duke of York*, was withdrawn from service in 1834 and the steamers took over the Long Ferry completely.

It happened that several companies were vying for trade, the steamers were very popular and a price war ensued. The fare was reduced to 3s, but a hundred years later, in the 1930s, the daily fare was only one shilling on weekdays and one and sixpence at weekends, and this included the fare to Margate. Some of the other companies were the Gravesend Steamboat Company, Gravesend & Milton Steamboat Company (later called the Diamond Company), Greenhithe, Northfleet & Gravesend Company (which failed), and the New Steam Packet Company (later called the Star Company). The *Ruby* was the fastest ship of her day, 155 feet in length and 272 tons. In 1832 she carried 290,000 people from London to Gravesend, and in 1834 the number was 690,000. Trade increased when Greenhithe and Gravesend both became fashionable commuter towns. The total number of passengers moving on and off the boats at Gravesend in 1830 was 29,681 and by 1841-42 this had increased to 1,141,285. However, this prosperity was not to last, for in 1845 the first railway to Gravesend was opened by the Gravesend & Rochester Railway (G&RR). In 1849 the railway was extended to a junction with a line connecting with London Bridge Station. Rosherville Gardens closed and the Long Ferry declined.

GRAVESEND-TILBURY FERRY

Less profitable than the Long Ferry, the cross-river ferry between Gravesend (Exp. 162 646 745) or Milton and Tilbury (Exp. 162 645 751) is perhaps one of the oldest ferries in the south-east of England,[16] although there is no Royal Charter extant to prove it. Certainly it existed at the time of Domesday, if not before, because hythes (landing places) were recorded at Gravesend and Milton. The Thames here offers a suitable crossing point, being narrower than elsewhere in the vicinity, with firmer ground on the southern shore and the crossings could more easily be defended. At that time, the river was about eleven feet below the present twenty-first-century level and causeways were constructed across marshes to the water's edge.

It was such an important ferry and the river was so wide, either bank was owned by a different manor and owned its part of the ferry. Gravesend on the south was held by the Manor of Parrock which was Milton, and held grazing land across the river, which led to difficulties later. On the north side the ferry was held by the Lord of the Manor of Tilbury, or more exactly, West Tilbury. William de Tyllebury held the manor in 1304 when it included a ferry of water let to fee-farm at 6s 8d a year, but there are theories it existed long before this. Gravesend, being the first important place on the river from the North Sea, had to be defended against invaders. After Edward III's return from the siege of Calais in 1346-47 with 30,000 men, the successful Essex archers crossed home by the Tilbury ferry.[17]

In the fourteenth and fifteenth centuries, temporary structures were built to guard the ferries and in 1539 Henry VIII built more permanent blockhouses on both shores. Stronger causeways were constructed at Milton and by the Three Crowns, which served as the ferry house at Gravesend in West Street. The blockhouse on the Essex bank developed later to become Tilbury Fort, causing the church of St Mary Magdalen, which served the ferry, to be demolished. Confirmation that the ferry was running at this time comes from the examination[18] in 1530 of a vagrant, John Thomas of Chelmsford, who had to give up work as a wheelwright because of 'trouble in his arms'. He then 'lived on the alms of good men' until 'at the snow last past he came over Tilbury ferry; went to Gravesend, then on to Deptford'.

George Tucker held the Manor of Milton, or Parrock,[19] from Queen Elizabeth, paying annually £41 7s 2d to the Crown, and the ferry was included in his holdings. At her command in 1588 a bridge of boats was made across the river to the fort as a passage for her troops and a barrier against the Spanish Armada. On 8 August that year the Queen landed at Tilbury and gave her famous speech. After her fleet sailed, the bridge of boats was taken down. An indictment[20] dated 29 August 1612 appears in the West Kent Quarter Sessions records for that year. It states that John Idenden and his ancestors had leased the ferry for some years to carry Gravesend and Milton people in their ferry boats at the rate of one halfpenny with a horse, but other people to pay one penny. Yet two men, Henry Tucker and Edward Fisher, both yeomen who were deputising for Idenden, had charged five Gravesend men tuppence each. Fisher was bound over for £1. The next year some other Gravesend cross-ferry men were brought before the same magistrates for 'delaying and refusing to transport passengers from thence into Essex'.

By some means the Tilbury ferry came to be administered by the fort from about 1540. The ferry house was within the fort, which meant that passengers had to enter it to access the ferry. For many generations the military commander there had collected the tolls and at the beginning of the Civil War the commander of the fort was Captain John Talbot.[21] The common people sent a petition to Charles I saying, 'there is a ferry house and a ferry kept within the fort, by the lord of the soil, to his own benefit, through which passengers, with their cattle and commodities, (as through a common road and highway) do pass from Essex into Kent.' In 1643 Parliament ordered that the tolls were to be used to settle the arrears of pay of the garrison and the fort. Charles I had cause to remember this ferry because of an event which took place in 1623. As the then Prince of Wales, Charles was travelling incognito[22] with the Duke of Buckingham to Spain to woo the Infanta. When it came to paying the ferryman, the pair had no small silver, so the Duke offered a gold piece, whereupon he presumed they were going 'beyond the sea' and took them to be spies. After landing them at Gravesend the ferryman alerted the officials who followed them. At Canterbury, the pair were arrested by the mayor just as they were about to take horse for Dover. On being questioned, the Duke was obliged to remove his false beard. Eventually they continued their journey, but the negotiations broke down and war with Spain was declared the next year. This episode is recorded in the State Papers Domestic.

An indictment[23] drawn up in 1640 stated, 'from time immemorial a wooden foot-bridge called "the Ferry bridge" 15 yards long over the Thames to the ferry in the parish of West Tilbury was used by the King's subjects. ... It had been broken and ruinous for one year so that people could not get to the ferryboate without great peril and thus could not go from thence to Gravesend in Kent. Andrew Joyner of Dunmow Bt should repair the said bridge.' A conveyance[24] was drawn up in 1678 to convey the Gravesend ferry from Lawrence Holker to George Etkins, who then conveyed the lease to Gravesend Corporation in 1679. In 1688 a further indictment[25] concerned 'Edward Clayton, yeoman of West Tilbury, the keeper of a common ferry boat belonging to Tilbury Fort in West Tilbury from time whereof the memory of man is not to the contrary, for the passage of people, horses and carts across the water, before and since 5 July extortionately took greater sums of money than the usual rates from divers persons'.

The Manor of Parrock was bought by the Corporation in 1694, thus they owned ferry rights for both the Long and Short ferries. The enterprising Governor of Tilbury Fort took the opportunity to claim his end of the ferry from Tilbury to Gravesend. In recompense for the large amount of money owed to him in back pay, he offered to operate that part of the ferry and to build a new ferry house and tavern away from the fort, for the benefit of the passengers and where his ferrymen could live 'on the spot'. Sir Bernard de Gomme, a military architect,[26] gave estimates in 1681 for extensions to the fort. They included removing the ferry house and building another on the marsh for £80. It was to be built of brick and plaster with straw thatch. The ground floor to be made of 'dry drawn deals' and the joists of oak placed twelve inches apart. A great room with a kitchen chimney, into which a little oven was to be built, the same as in the old house, was to be divided into three rooms. The stables were to have a hay loft over. The glass windows were to be Newcastle glass and all 'room doors to be provided to the inside strong locks, keys and iron bolts'. All the windows to have folding shutters and be fastened on the inside with small hinges and wooden bolts. A port hole was to be set up to the outside of the great door at the same height and dimension as the old one, with a door-latch, ketch and stock-lock, with two iron bolts against robbers. The name of this building was changed to the World's End Inn by the landlord in 1777. The present inn has been dated to the eighteenth century, and this is confirmed by the National Archives as being when the house was rebuilt, and the causeway was repaired in 1778.

A length of road had been diverted[27] to the west of the fort and in 1741 an order was made that the governor was to keep it in repair out of the profits made by ferries being 'warped across'. This was the practice of moving vessels from one place to another by means of hemp ropes or light hawsers attached by one end to a fixed object, usually

Tilbury. World's End Inn to the west of the fort, showing its isolated, bleak situation. Photo by S. W. Rawlings, *c.* 1940. (Reproduced by Permission of English Heritage)

a capstan. According to a definition made in 1769, 'warping is generally used when sails are unbent or when they cannot be successfully employed'. By this method, 5,000 troops were carried across to Tilbury on 20 July 1780 and brought back to Gravesend twelve hours later. Objections to this system made by shipping interests led in 1793 to warping being stopped in favour of rowing boats or towing with sailing boats.

Tilbury Fort came under the aegis of the Board of Ordnance but the Tilbury Ferry was still administered by the Governor. When Lord Cadogan was Governor[28] between 1751 and 1776 and owner of the ferry, the charges were threepence for passengers on foot; 1s for those with a horse, but 6s after sundown and before sun rising. The ferry was very useful to the Board, who used it for ferrying men, ammunitions and equipment from Gravesend to the fort. A tunnel company[29] was set up in 1798, promoted by the engineer, Ralph Dodd (1756-1822), proposing to pay £110 per annum in rent. Shafts were sunk, and the amount of compensation to be paid to both bodies who owned the ferry was worked out, but the enterprise was dropped in 1802 because of flooding and the pumping engine caught fire. Then a steam company in 1834 wanted to initiate a floating bridge working on chains. They reckoned without the difficulties of providing strong enough vessels to carry passengers, vehicles and horses, and above all, the strength of the tides, and the project was abandoned. Matters continued like this throughout the eighteenth and early nineteenth centuries without major changes, although Ralph Dodd was proposing a partnership between the Ordnance Board and Gravesend Corporation.

Relations were often stormy,[30] with the Board demanding better service from the Corporation. They maintained that if the ferry was under one management it would be advantageous. Accordingly, the Board leased their ferry rights[31] to the Corporation in September 1851 for ninety-nine years at an annual rent of £50. Both parts of the ferry were then sublet to William Tisdall, and passengers, livestock and goods were taken by a tug working in both directions, but no improvement followed. The Board threatened to terminate the lease[32] and as a result the whole was leased to Messrs Peto, Betts and Brassey on behalf of the London, Tilbury & Southend Railway on 18 February 1856 at £750 per annum for twenty-four years. The railway company extended their already existing railway by laying tracks to the waterside at Tilbury and sought to do the same on the south shore where the Town Pier was adapted to become the ferry landing stage.

The service began in 1855 using iron paddle steamers, the first being the *Tilbury*, but its name was changed in 1880 to *Sir Walter Raleigh*, to be in line with the other two steamers, *Earl of Essex* and *Earl of Leicester*, all favourites of Queen Elizabeth. The vessels were the same, almost 129 feet long, 20 feet in breadth, of 180 gross registered tonnage. They had an open foredeck, a saloon below and a small deck saloon aft. Business was brisk, especially at Bank Holidays, taking people to Rosherville Gardens, and taking livestock during the week. The livestock,[33] vehicles and goods were loaded into floats or barges at the causeways on either side of the river, at the World's End on the Essex side and at West Street in Gravesend and then were towed behind the passenger ferry. This system lasted until well into the twentieth century.

A strange feature of the early vessels was that there was no means of communication between the captain and the engineer. Young boys were employed to run messages between the two, and many of them grew up to become full-time crew. The paddle steamers supplemented their regular work by acting as tenders to the passenger liners as they became bigger and could not get up to London. PS *Cato* was brought in to help cope with this extra trade. She was built in 1849 and came to the Thames after service on the Mersey. All four vessels had black funnels and hulls, varnished deck houses and buff paddle boxes, a livery almost universal for all ferries on the Thames.

In 1880 the railway acquired the interests in the ferries from the Board of Ordnance and from Gravesend Corporation on condition that it used the Town Pier. The fact that, of the fourpence fare for the ferry, one penny levy was charged by the Corporation for the use of Town Pier was a bone of contention. The Corporation refused to reduce the levy so the railway company built their own West Street Pier and no longer took sheep on the ferry. However, the Town Pier was preferred, and in 1884 they bought it outright for £8,600 from the Receiver, the Corporation having gone bankrupt. Thereafter the Town Pier was used for passengers and the West Street Pier for livestock and freight. A huge increase in trade came about because of the navvies building Tilbury Docks, which opened in 1888. One newspaper report gave the numbers working there as 1,322 each day. Many of them would cross the ferry.

New steamers were brought into service. PS *Thames* was a former LNWR vessel, 106 feet long and 125 gross registered tonnage. The two *Earls* were withdrawn and *Sir Walter Raleigh* was broken up in 1905. A new paddle steamer, *Tilbury*, was built in Rotterdam and her engines were from John Penn of Greenwich. It was usual practice at that time for a vessel to be built at one place and to be fitted with engines at another. At 269 gross registered tonnage, she was the largest boat so far on the Tilbury-Gravesend Ferry and was used to cut the ribbons to open Tilbury Docks. Because of the success of this business, the railway reduced fares and also introduced workmen's returns. A single was tuppence and a return reduced from sixpence to threepence. Despite this, some passengers tried to dodge the fares and if caught they were fined from 10s up to 15s.

By the end of the nineteenth century the company had a fleet of four cross-river ferry sister ships, all twin-screw steamers: *Carlotta*, *Rose*, *Catherine*, and in 1906 TSS *Gertrude* entered service. She could carry vehicles as well as passengers. *Edith*, which

Gravesend-Tilbury. Military bridge constructed in 1914 at the government's request. From *PLA Monthly*, March 1929. (Reproduced by Permission of English Heritage)

was slightly larger, joined the fleet in 1911. The Midland Railway bought out the London, Tilbury & Southend Railway in 1912 including the Gravesend-Tilbury Ferry when there were six vessels in service. Workmen's season tickets were introduced. To assist in the movement of troops and ammunition during the First World War, the Port of London Authority (PLA) installed a temporary floating bridge made of seventy lighters across three-quarters of a mile between Gravesend and Tilbury. It had a two-lane carriageway with side barriers to take troops across. The centre section could be removed for vessels to pass through.

The Midland Railway was amalgamated into the London, Midland & Scottish Railway (LMS) in 1923. There were changes at Tilbury. A new railway station was built and a baggage hall and passenger landing stage, 1,140 feet long, were provided to take the liner traffic. The first part (east) of the landing stage was reserved for the cross-ferry service. The old landing stage was removed and a covered link bridge was provided for passengers and an open bridge for vehicles. LMS changed the colour of the funnels to a pale yellow with a black top. Two specially built car ferries were added to the fleet, *Tessa*, of 371 tons, which could carry thirty vehicles and 250 passengers, was built at Lytham, Lancashire, in 1924, and *Mimie*, of 464 tons, which was built in 1927, was capable of carrying thirty-six vehicles and 300 passengers. The name of the Tilbury landing was changed in 1936 to Tilbury Riverside.

During the Second World War (1939-45) the ferry boats were vital, although they did not take part in the evacuation of Dunkirk. They were painted Admiralty grey and the bridge was protected by a steel wheelhouse. Lights were not allowed, except in fog when a small light was permitted on the pontoons. Fog was still a persistent problem; the service was suspended for three successive days in 1935 when visibility was less than fifteen yards. Normally there were unique flickering lights, better seen in fog. They were fitted in the 1930s even before airports had them as standard. The boats were still used as tenders to larger ships. London Docks and river crossings

Car ferry SS *Tessa* used on the Tilbury-Gravesend service between 1924 and December 1964. She made the 800-mile journey by hugging the coast from Lytham where she was built. Photo taken 8 December 1964. (Courtesy Campbell McCutcheon)

The larger of the two car ferries, SS *Mimie*, on the Gravesend-Tilbury service. Photo taken at Tilbury, 8 May 1964. (Courtesy Campbell McCutcheon)

were restricted areas, requiring tickets and identity cards to be shown to policemen on guard who would ask necessary questions. The ferries generally escaped the bombing but a flying bomb in 1944 damaged two ferry boats moored to a landing stage. After the war the livery returned to the same as before, except for the deck houses, which were changed to white above the waist and brown below and the amidships were painted white.

A booklet published around 1998 by Thurrock Local History Society entitled *The Five-Minute Crossing* by John M. Ormston gives a detailed description of the way in which the steam ferries were worked. It was probably part of an oral history project. The way 'bunkering' was done is particularly interesting.

> Each morning coal was shovelled into tubs made from strong canvas sewn to an endless rope slug. Each held about 1¼ cwt. coal filled from trucks in the goods yard at the station. The tubs were brought down to Tilbury landing stage by small lorry and off-loaded near to the ferry mooring positions. Each tub was then put on a sack barrow and wheeled to the coal-hole in the deck and tipped into the bunker. Ash and clinker from the stoke-hole, after quenching, was loaded into the tubs which were hauled then from the boiler room by block and tackle through protective grating. The tubs were then wheeled along the deck, up a ramp, loaded onto a small lorry and taken to the tip. The landing stage was on the same level as the deck on the vehicle ferries, but about four feet above the deck level for the passenger vessels. The process was dirty and labour intensive and took a lot of time, being performed by a special gang. Afterwards the vessel was scrubbed down.

For passengers travelling from Tilbury to Gravesend the five-minute trip was good. They would pass through the booking hall and the ticket barrier and down the link bridge to the floating landing stage and board the boat. There were lounges fore and aft below deck. In the forward lounge the seats were of polished wood, whereas in the aft cabin they were imitation leather, whilst on the upper deck they were of the life-saving float type. Some commentators have described these cabins as 'Dickensian' as they were darkish, lit only by oil lamps. Electric light was not fitted until 1969. You could either go below to watch the engines or up on deck to watch the traffic. The captain in crossing the busy waterway would always give way to sail; there were still some sailing barges then. In fog he would go slowly and post extra look-outs. If the fog was too bad, the ferry would stop running and watermen would offer to ferry you in small launches at double the fare. Later a radar scanner and control room was fitted at Tilbury to overcome this problem somewhat. In the 1950s tea kiosks were added.

A government report, 'Ferries in Great Britain', was made in 1948[34] on those ferries still in operation. It began by quoting a previous report of 1926 when the ferry was administered by LMS. 'Charges for this ferry are high, but it appears to be used to full capacity.' They go on, 'It seems to us desirable that this ferry, the only cross-river communication remaining in the London Traffic Area which is not free, should be acquired by the public and placed on the same basis as the Woolwich Free Ferry.' The new report describes the ferry, which then had two beam-loading vessels working at half-hour intervals, one working, the other in reserve. Sometimes in summer the ferry was unable to accommodate all the waiting vehicles. The approach at Gravesend was narrow, which might have deterred some types of traffic. The inspectors declined to make any recommendations for improvement until the long-awaited Dartford Tunnel was completed.

In 1948 the railways were nationalised to become British Rail (BR) and these ferries came under the same body. At first Gravesend-Tilbury was in the Midland region but was transferred to the Eastern region later. BR took over the remaining passenger ferries, *Catherine*, *Rose* and *Edith*, plus the two car ferries. In 1953 the ferry was part of a projected package on Green Line coaches operated by London Transport.[35] They would run a 55-mile service from Gravesend to Windsor taking three hours, the fare being 6s 11d. Photographs exist of the Green Line bus, service 725, on board the ferry. Statistics published in 1953 show that the previous year the ferry carried 178,473 private cars and 47,875 commercial vehicles. A campaign to restart the project to build the Dartford-Purfleet tunnel was activated in 1953. A pilot scheme begun in 1938 was put on hold because of the war.

At its peak, before the Dartford tunnel opened and docks closed, together with ancillary factories, etc., the ferry was handling about 270,000 vehicles a year. Passengers totalled 2,750,000 a year with 6,500-8,000 per day, excluding drivers. The fares were 5d for a single passenger, 7s 6d for a car and 9s 10d for an elephant (yes!).

British Railways announced plans in 1959 to build three new vessels for the passenger ferry. They reckoned that expenditure on new vehicle ferries was not justified in view of the imminent opening of the tunnel. Parliament was asked to end the obligation to provide the vehicle ferry, but refused, with the concession that it may close only after the tunnel had been in operation for a year. In July 1960 the ferry came under the aegis of the British Transport Commission (BTC). Three new diesel-powered passenger ferries replaced the steam ferries in 1962. They had the same names, *Catherine 2*, *Edith 2* and *Rose 2* and were equipped with three hinged folding gangways on each side, which were operated hydraulically from the bridge (possibly the first vessels to have this facility). The last one proved surplus to requirements and was sold in 1967. Each could carry 475 passengers and were of 214 tons. When the Dartford tunnel opened in 1963 vehicle traffic on the ferry disappeared almost overnight, and notice was given that the vehicle ferry would close. There were objections made to the Transport Users Consultative Committee, but the Ministry of Transport gave its approval, so the last service was run on 31 December 1964. The passenger service continued in operation.

Passenger ferry SS *Catherine*, 259 tons gross, on the Gravesend-Tilbury service from 1903-62. Photographed off Tilbury, 14 August 1960. (Courtesy Campbell McCutcheon)

Passenger ferry SS *Rose* of 259 tons gross served on the Gravesend-Tilbury ferry between 1901 and 1962. Photo taken at Tilbury 11 September 1956. (Courtesy Campbell McCutcheon)

Gravesend-Tilbury ferry. MV *Catherine II*, of 214 tons gross, built in 1960, at Tilbury, 12 July 1977. Thames sailing barge *Gladys*, built 1901, is in the river. (Courtesy Campbell McCutcheon)

British MV *Edith*, of 214 tons gross, built 1960, leaving Gravesend for Tilbury. 30 July 1991. (Courtesy Campbell McCutcheon)

Gravesend-Tilbury Ferry. MV *Rose II*, of 214 tons gross, built 1961, berthed at Tilbury
Terminal next to *Dunera*, converted back to a cruise ship after a spell as troopship. (Courtesy
Campbell McCutcheon)

Alterations were made to the timetable and the landing place was moved from Town
Pier to West Street but business slackened off and went into deficit despite rising fares.
Losses continued, not helped by railway strikes, as in February 1966 when the ferry was
suspended. In January 1973 BR applied to the county councils[36] of Essex and Kent for
financial support, stating, 'if it is not forthcoming, there is a probability that we would
make a case to withdraw the service'. Dan McMillan, the Mayor of Gravesend accused BR
of deliberately trying to run the service down. The application was refused a government
subsidy on the grounds that 'the ferry grant scheme was designed to deal with situations
in remote country areas which could no longer sustain a service on a commercial basis'.
However, the councils did give grants from their own coffers. These grants, which had
only dispelled a small part of the losses, were discontinued from 1 April 1976.

BR did indeed then run down the service to cut costs. They attempted to remove
the common law obligation to operate the ferry but were unsuccessful.[37] Instead, they
resorted to curtailing the service. Where two boats were working constantly, one was
kept in reserve and that one was licensed for 200 instead of 475 passengers. They
wanted to shorten the timetable by cutting out the early morning run, 5.15 a.m. and
the last five late evening runs between 10.20 p.m. and 11.40 p.m. from Gravesend.
The average number of passengers on the former was six and on the latter, together,
twenty-six. BR believed these measures would save the cost of an entire ferry crew of
four. A court case ensued in 1977, brought against BR by the PLA and the two local
councils. The judge referred to previous cases, including that of Hammerton v. Dysart
at Twickenham, but as BR were not seeking to close the ferry and would keep the
half-hourly intervals in service, he dismissed the case. He said the 'introduction of the
new timetable would not involve BR in any breach of their common law duties to
provide a ferry service at all reasonable times'. As fifty employees of PLA were affected
by the loss of the late evening ferries, PLA were entitled to bring their own action as
they would sustain particular damage.

Concern was still being expressed about the cross-river ferry, and in 1979 the two MPs for Gravesend and Thurrock (for Tilbury) asked for a survey to be made by the county councils. Sealink UK Ltd, a subsidiary of BR, had taken on responsibility for ferry services on 1 January that year. The anticipated figures for 1979 were £365,000 working costs and £226,000 gross receipts. The MPs were hoping the county councils would reconsider giving grant aid. Replies to a questionnaire showed that some people would lose their jobs if the ferry stopped, whilst others disliked the Dartford Tunnel, which was only for vehicles anyway. There was also the cost and inconvenience of relying on others for lifts. The fares were getting high: for an adult with a cycle or moped it was 38p, a week's season ticket being £2.50 and no returns. Another report was made in 1982 when three crews were working, consisting of Master, Mate, Engineman and Deckhand, who issued the tickets. The staff had been reduced in 1981 from twenty-five to sixteen, which included a local manager, relief crewman and two clerks. This had reduced the deficit but still no grants were forthcoming from the councils or government. In May 1982, when a single journey of an adult with bike was £1 and a season ticket cost £8.50, an average of only thirteen passengers was carried on each trip. Occasionally, many more were carried as when a Romany funeral took place in April 1982. The horse-drawn wagons were troublesome on board. *The Times* reports a conversation with an old waterman: 'One time comin over to Kent from Tilbury on the ferry to Gravesend, there were so many caravans on deck that some of 'em 'ad to be 'eld in with ropes as they was leanin' out over the water.'

Catherine's passenger certificate[38] expired in 1984, the year that Sea Containers Ltd took over ownership from Sealink. *Edith 2* carried on alone. The new company inherited the legal obligation to run the Gravesend to Tilbury ferry in perpetuity. As they were primarily a cross-channel ferry company, they wished to divest themselves of this encumbrance, and offered it to the captain and his crews for nothing. Captain Alf Gates was aged fifty-seven and had been working on the ferry forty years. He was not happy, especially with the thought of bearing the costs of heavy repair bills. So in January 1985 the ferry was put up for sale.

White Horse Ferries Ltd of Swindon[39] took over in 1991, with support from the county councils and the local councils. They chartered *Edith 2* until their new catamaran *Great Expectations CD* of 68 tons was delivered in 1992. This was replaced in 1996 by a small trimaran, *Martin Chuzzlewit* built by the company at Gravesend. A new lease had been taken in 1992 with the Crown Commissioners for the part of the ferry from Tilbury at £200 p.a. The company also operated a commuter service to London. In 2000 the association of the White Horse Ferries Ltd with the ferry came to an end.

The ferry service, but not the boats, was taken up by the Lower Thames & Medway Passenger Boat Co.[40] In 2002 they bought the small, diesel-powered vessel *Duchess M*, which had been built in 1956, named *Vesta*, one of the last three traditional ferry boats on the Portsmouth-Gosport service. An unfortunate incident[41] occurred in August 2006 which led to a hearing before Dartford Magistrates a year later. The *Duchess M* was about to leave Gravesend on the evening of 30 August when PLA received a phone call from an unknown person that the vessel was carrying over ninety passengers. She was licensed for sixty plus one or two crew. However, she reported to PLA there were sixty-two passengers. Observations were made by PLA using CCTV on one of their launches and the overcrowding was confirmed. The matter was reported to the authorities who considered it a very serious offence, notwithstanding the wrong report of numbers on board could have led to serious consequences (viz. *Princess Alice*). The owner of the vessel pleaded guilty and was fined £18,000 plus £9,000 costs. The *Duchess M* continues to ply in a most efficient way in the year 2009, with her master following in the age-old tradition of being a registered Free Waterman of the River Thames.

GRAVESEND PIERS

Gravesend had always been a busy riverside port, serving not only the ferries but also the seagoing trade. At first the riverside quays sufficed to moor the vessels but as they got bigger to take more passengers, the quays became inadequate. Piers were built out into the river in the nineteenth century and three of the main ones, Town Pier, Royal Terrace Pier and West Street Pier, survive today, although only the latter is still operating as a public pier. Another served Rosherville Gardens to the west of Gravesend, but that was demolished, although perhaps the site of it can still be seen.

Gravesend Piers. From the bottom left can be seen Royal Terrace Pier, Town Pier, West Street Pier and Railway Pier. Taken from the air 1964. (© English Heritage NMR Aerofilms Collection)

TOWN PIER

The Town Quay, mentioned in the Domesday Book, was rebuilt by the enterprising Gravesend Corporation in 1829 at the bottom of the hill which was High Street, the main thoroughfare of the town. One penny was charged to every person landing or departing there. Soon afterwards the Corporation applied to Parliament for permission to build a pier out from the quay, at the same time promising to pay compensation to the watermen. They, however, when they heard the proposal had been passed, chose to riot on the night of 22 June 1833. They attacked the temporary jetty at the Town Quay and the local militia was called out to quell the riot. The pier, designed by William Tierney Clark, was opened in 1834. It is said the project bankrupted the Corporation in 1852.

When first constructed, the pier led majestically from a little square at the bottom of High Street, flanked on the east by the Three Daws Tavern. From a tall monument or beacon, wide steps led down to the landing places at the river. On either side at the end were two small pavilions. It is now reputed to be the oldest surviving cast-iron pier in the world. At first the pier was used by the large steamers on the Long Ferry. When the railway came to Tilbury with steamer connections to Gravesend, they too used the Town Pier. Alterations had to be made because the steps were dangerous; prams had to be carried up them and gangways had to be altered every two hours because of the rise and fall of the tides. Not until 1865 was the pier walled and roofed in the promenade section, thus making it an attractive building. A pontoon was added to allow for more than one steamer to call at a time.

The railway leased the pier, then bought it in 1884 when it was used for passengers only and vehicles and goods were transferred to the West Street Pier. All ferry services have operated from West Street since 1965. After a period of neglect it was decided to restore the pier as part of the general rejuvenation programme for Gravesend. The part near the entrance was made into a bar in 2006,[42] but there was a long delay caused through problems putting in modern floors and windows. Finally the pier opened as a bar and restaurant with a public viewing platform at the end in November 2007. In spring 2009 the company leasing the building went into receivership and the pier

Steamer berthed at Gravesend Town Pier. Postcard sent as a Christmas card, 1908.

Gravesend Town Pier. Steam ferry berthed in the 1950s. Photo S. W. Rawlings. (Reproduced by Permission of English Heritage)

remains unused. Gravesham Borough Council aspires to restart river services, from a pontoon to be built at the end of the pier, by 2011.

Town Pier Square, which had played an important role when the ferries were in full swing, was also restored, although not to its original state, as many of the taverns which surrounded it were demolished long ago. The square was repaved and railings and gates were installed as they were in the nineteenth century. A town with so many travellers passing through needed plenty of inns and several were situated in the square. A new development is now on the site of the Christopher Inn and the Pier Hotel. The Three Daws, which dates from 1488, is still there but has suffered in some of the fires which have devastated Gravesend from time to time. It is not known whether the secret smuggler's passages are still open beneath.

Of particular note is the Falcon at 3 East Street (now Royal Pier Road). Dating back to at least the eighteenth century, it served the 'top end of the market' or 'carriage trade'. Most of its clients were for the East India Company's ships, which departed from the Town Pier.[43] They would arrive from London in carriages piled up with baggage, chairs and other furniture, etc., which was stowed in the hold of the sailing ship, and when it was ready to sail, a gun would be fired to bring the passengers to the pier. Sometimes a band would play on the bridge or stairs leading down to the river while dinner was being served in the hotel a few yards away. The hotel servants were liveried. From being a straggling wooden structure with two large rooms with wide bay windows overlooking the river and its varied busy traffic, the hotel was partly rebuilt in red brick after being damaged by fire and a huge storm. Then more balconies were erected, as seen in paintings by James Tissot (1836-1902). This venue was one of his favourite subjects. One large painting, dated 1873, is in Southampton Art Gallery,

Gravesend. The Falcon seen from Town Pier. Watercolour in grey washes by James Tissot, *c.* 1873. (Reproduced by Permission of English Heritage)

entitled *The Captain's Daughter, or The Last Evening*. It shows a young girl looking out with binoculars whilst the captain sits behind in conversation with a sailor; in the background are sailing ships and stairs leading down to the water from the hotel. Another smaller painting, in a private collection, is *Waiting for the Ferry*, which shows a family sitting on the pier with the hotel and its nineteenth-century extension in the background. A preliminary drawing for this, without the figures, is illustrated here. The Old Falcon, as it was then called, was demolished in 1938, sacrificed to the growing demands of the port.

ROYAL TERRACE PIER

After the Town Pier was seen to be successful, a group of Gravesend investors[44] saw an opportunity to rival it by building another pier 500 yards away to the east. They were anxious to capture the ever-increasing steam packet trade. The consortium bought land from the Royal Ordnance on which one of the first blockhouses had been built. They used iron cylinders for the foundations out into the river, the first time such a method had been used. The engineer was J. B. Redman and the original cost of building was £14,000. It opened as Terrace Pier in 1844 with a more elaborate frontage than Town Pier of a low range with an open colonnade with Doric columns and two pavilions either side, one surmounted by a bell cupola, the other by a clock. The pier frontage to the river is not elegant, like its rival.

To take advantage of the superior setting of this new pier, the classic Harmer Street described in *Buildings of England, Kent* as 'nothing could be drabber', was constructed with the colonnaded Berkeley Crescent at the top, to lead downhill to the imposing pier entrance. Surrounding the entrance, the consortium laid out Terrace Gardens, now partly a car park. Close by, in the corner of the gardens, is the Chantry,[45] the oldest building in Gravesend, which was founded as a chapel in 1322, although at the time

Gravesend. Arrival at Royal Terrace Pier on 7 March 1874 of the Duke and Duchess of Edinburgh on board the Royal Yacht after their marriage in Russia. It was a ceremonious occasion with naval ships dressed overall and the Royal bargemen giving a salute. Etching by Auguste Ballin, born in Bologne in 1842, who specialised in seascapes.

the pier was built this was not realised. It had fallen into decay after the Reformation, then served as an inn and afterwards became part of the defence works built on the site, always remaining the property of the Royal Ordnance. As the chapel is so close to a landing place, it is probably another chapel set up for the benefit of travellers to pray for a safe crossing. It now houses a Heritage Centre in summer months.

Terrace Pier became Royal Terrace Pier in 1863 when Princess Alexandra of Denmark arrived to marry the future King Edward VII. It was not used for the ferries but for the river steamers and when that trade declined it was a base for river and sea pilots, who contributed £12,000 when the premises were sold to Trinity House and restored in 1894. After being used by private firms for tugs and towage, the pier and the offices were restored again in 1978 and in July 2004 they were taken over by PLA,[46] who have built a new pontoon and use the pier as a base for river pilots once more. The Doric columns are now made of glass fibre, instead of cast iron.

WEST STREET PIER

The site for the Gravesend landing place of the cross ferry as recorded in 1540 was a causeway in front of the Three Crowns public house at West Street. Flats are now built on the site of the pub, but a plaque which was removed when it was demolished is placed at ground level on the corner of the flats. West Street Pier was built in 1857 for use by the railway steamers. A pontoon and ramp were added by 1860.[47] For a long time this pier was used for livestock, goods and vehicles and became known as the Cart Ferry. From 1924 when car ownership was on the increase, it was called the Car Ferry, but when the vehicle service was closed down in 1965, foot passengers were transferred to it from Town Pier and once more it became West Street Pier.

Another pier, the Gravesend Railway Pier was built alongside in 1881 when the Gravesend Railway Company, later taken over by the London, Chatham & Dover Railway (LCDR), opened a double track branch to a station on West Street. A

GRAVESEND & TILBURY FERRY

OAP RETURN

Ticket No.   1388

Not transferable. Sold subject to
the Company's Conditions of Travel
available on request.

On 25 June 2009 the author travelled on this ferry.

substantial pier was built into the river, strong enough to take railway track. This pier was used by cross-channel ferries. Never an outstanding success, the viaducts and embankments were removed in 2006, but apparently the pier remains.

Doubt about this exists because the area in which the Tilbury Ferry still operates from West Street Pier is so unattractive that the visitor wishes to hurry away quickly. The approach from West Street is down a narrow passageway, inadequately signed, and by a closed-in walkway with no glimpse of the river, past private backyards. To arrive at the gangway wondering whether the ferry is actually still working is traumatic (at least for seventy-year-olds) with all the black paint around making an inhospitable environment. There is a little garden with information boards and seats to sit and wait, but it is not cared for enough. To cross on a ferry, especially one as historic and spectacular as Gravesend-Tilbury should be an enjoyable and worthwhile experience. The landing place at Tilbury is quite different and the people who use it to go shopping in Gravesend are obviously very happy with it.

CHAPTER THIRTEEN
Higham to East Tilbury

CHALK FERRY

East of Gravesend off the Lower Road to Rochester is a small settlement round an early Norman church called Chalk (Exp. 163 684 725). From there Church Lane leads northwards to the River Thames and after crossing the Lower Road it continues as a footpath across the marshes. However, the way is now stopped by a railway line, but if it continued, it would have reached the shore at the point where on the other side of the river a jetty is built out from East Tilbury Marshes and two other footpaths converge (Exp. 163 680 759). Whilst confirmation cannot be made, it is strongly suspected this was the way to a very ancient ferry.

The parish was named 'Chalkhythe'[1] (meaning landing place for chalk) in AD 785 and extended across the river into Essex where the manor held 120 acres of pasture. The Domesday Book in 1086 does not include this ferry (although often ferries were disregarded). It may have succumbed to the better and more convenient ferries at Gravesend and Higham, the next parishes to the west and east. Another factor in making the ferry obsolete was that the marshes were reclaimed early on, thus making lands on the other side superfluous to the manor.

HIGHAM FERRY-EAST TILBURY

Higham Ferry was also very old. It apparently crossed the river from a little creek over a mile north-west of the small settlement round the church at Church Street (Exp. 163 717 742), one of the hamlets which make up the long, thin parish of Higham. The precise landing place in Essex is not known, except that it was in East Tilbury, or Great Tilbury as it was called in former times. Most likely it was at Coalhouse Point (Exp. 163 689 762) at which two footpaths still meet. Detailed records refer to this as East Tilbury Ferry. Some historians have confused it with West Tilbury, so for the purposes of this account the name Higham Ferry will be used.

When the Roman General Plautius, who served under Emperor Claudius,[2] was in pursuit of the Britons from what became Essex into Kent in AD 43, he followed them to a crossing place of the Thames. The Britons would have been familiar with all such places and the one chosen for their escape is thought to have been from East Tilbury to Higham. From there were roads which used higher ground to cross the marshes and reach the chalk ridge at Gadshill and on to Watling Street and Dover. This became an important, much-used route[3] to the Kingdom of Mercia.

Saint Cedd (620-664),[4] who was brought up on the Island of Lindisfarne under the tutorage of Saint Aidan, was sent from Northumbria as a missionary to convert the East Saxons to Christianity. He was made Bishop of Essex and, in about 654, built a

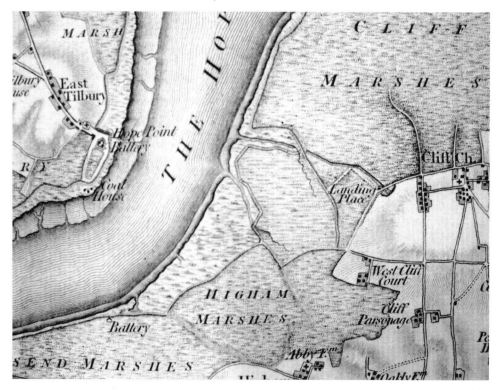

Ordnance Survey First Edition, Kent. The causeway across the Higham marshes from Abbey Farm towards the place on the river opposite Coalhouse Point is just discernible at the bottom of the map.

chapel close to the shore near Coalhouse Point. The chapel is thought to have been on the foreshore but below the present high-tide level. Some remains of Romano-British huts have been found there, one of them quite large, and pottery shards which suggest a date of mid-first century. The Church of St Catherine,[5] situated close to Coalhouse Fort, dates back to Norman times and has Kentish ragstone incorporated in its fabric. The fort dates from Victorian times. On the Kent side, the earliest part of the Church of St Mary at Higham is a Saxo-Norman chancel and would also have been attended by travellers on the ferry.

King Stephen (reigned 1135-54) gave the Manor of Lillechurch in Higham parish to his daughter Mary in 1148 in order to build a nunnery.[6] By 1280 the nunnery had moved not far away to a site near the east end of Higham church, where a priory of Benedictine nuns was set up. A footpath still connects the two places. In about 1293, in the reign of Edward I, a document[7] in the Pleas of the Crown shows that the Prioress of the Nunnery of Higham was found liable to maintain a bridge (landing stage) and a causeway from Higham down to the Thames 'in order to give the better and easier passage to such as would ferry thence over into Essex'. The document goes on to record the indictment of the Prioress's boatmen who were taking 'from persons passing over the river between Kent and Essex – for every horseman tuppence, sometimes threepence, when it should have been a penny'. Moreover, they took one penny from foot passengers when the proper fare was one farthing. The boatmen were ordered that in future they were to take no more than one penny for horsemen and halfpenny for foot passengers. The nuns were often in dispute with the town of

Gravesend over the rights to ferry people and goods over the river, but the service was still working in 1474 when the Prioress hired a replacement boat from Rochester.

The causeway begins by the church gate and runs west for a short, metalled stretch past some sixteenth-century cottages and then, after passing through a gate, becomes a green road, which is a public footpath all the way until it joins the Saxon Shore Way on the flood defences at the river side. On the way the causeway passes over a footbridge and the railway, where the path turns north-west, but for its whole length it is on the edge of access or common land, indicating it is of great antiquity. One interesting feature is that, in crossing a rough meadow between two hedges, two old oak trees in each hedge opposite each other mark the place where the path leads through the gap, about eight feet, which separates each pair of trees. Beside one pair was a pile of stones and gravel in June 2009. The way across the marshy ground seemed to be marked by thorn trees at intervals. Originally the causeway had timber foundations and was almost thirty feet wide.

Henry Yevele (*c.* 1320-1400) was a great architect of the Middle Ages, responsible for some works at Westminster Abbey, Canterbury Cathedral and elsewhere in Kent, including the gateway at Cooling Castle, about two miles from Church Street as the crow flies. He also designed parts of London Bridge of which he was a warden. Because of this expertise he was called to become a member of the Commission to arrange for the building of Rochester Bridge,[8] a very important project, over the River Medway, a tributary of the Thames. It was to supersede an early timber structure and a ferry from Rochester to Strood. In 1383 Yevele began the design and the bridge was completed in stone in 1392. It was built by private enterprise with a body of wardens as owners, Yevele becoming one of them.

On the Essex side the ferry belonged to the Manor of South Hall in East Tilbury. This manor was given to the Wardens as part of the endowment of Rochester Bridge to keep it in repair. The manor included the rights of ferry,[9] 155 acres of marshes and arable land and only one building, a blockhouse, which served as the 'ferrycote'. The wardens leased out the ferry and kept meticulous accounts, which survive in good condition, in the premises of the Rochester Bridge Trust overlooking the bridge. Microfilm copies are deposited in Essex Record Office.

Nicholas Denys made the first payment of £37 6s 8d to the wardens in 1399 for the manor and the ferry, but by the next year the amount had fallen by £4. Various leases are documented through the centuries, sometimes for the ferry with the manor, sometimes separately. The Manor of South Hall seems to have been incorporated as the Manor of East Tilbury at some point, thus leading to confusion. The ferry was described as 'a excellent source of profit' in an entry of 1449, when an allowance of 100s was made to Thomas Castell, farmer of Tilbury, because 'the ferry there was not occupied this year in summer by reason of the disturbance of the commonalty'. (The disturbance was Jack Cade's rebellion in support of the Yorkists.) In the financial year 1459/60 the wardens kept the ferry and worked it themselves. They owned two ferry boats, *Margaret* and *Margery* and it is likely they allowed the ferrymen to keep a percentage of the profits. In 1507/8 the ferry with two boats was leased to John Buckland of East Tilbury at £6 a year, with the proviso he bought a little cock boat for use at the ferry.

A survey of the Manor of South Hall made in 1575 states, 'There is excepted from the farm the ferry called Est Tylbery ferie, being indeed of very smale valewe.' The ferry does seem to have become disused, although the ferry rights remained. Gravesend being not far away and more convenient took trade away from Higham. The priory, which failed to maintain the causeway,[10] was closed down by the Bishop of Rochester in 1521. Local gossip has it that, when the Bishop came to visit, he found two nuns with child by the Vicar.[11] This was not an uncommon occurrence apparently. It is suggested that even before Henry VIII's Reformation, which began in 1530, Bishops were anxious to gain power by closing down monasteries either by fair means or foul. To appoint Vicars known for not keeping the rules of chastity would belie the hidden agenda.

Perhaps the ferry rights at Higham were lost when the priory closed, at least it does not appear to have operated from there again, although it is possible East Tilbury Ferry operated from Gravesend instead. Lady Southwell, owner of the ferry at East Tilbury, was ordered in 1627 to repair a footbridge leading[12] from the blockhouse to the ferry, which was then occupied by Thomas Walters.

The site of the priory became a farm known as Abbey Farm. A farmhouse was erected in Georgian style and incorporates stones from the priory. Fragments of a flint wall in the garden suggest it is original. After the Reformation the owners became St John's College, Cambridge, who kept it until the beginning of the twenty-first century when it was sold privately. The Church of St Mary is in the care of the Churches Conservation Trust. The hamlet of Church Street is now a Conservation Area.

CHAPTER FOURTEEN
Yantlet Creek

Yantlet Creek (Exp. 163 861 786) marked the eastern boundary of the jurisdiction over the Thames by the Lord Mayor and Corporation of the City of London, followed by the Thames Conservancy. An obelisk[1] stands about eight metres high on a substantial plinth built on a rocky shore overlooking the Thames, on the right bank at the mouth of the creek. Originally, a stone would have been placed there in 1285 when the Lord Mayor and Corporation first took over from the Crown. As Conservators of the river, they were required to make periodic inspections along its course from the London Stone at Staines to this London Stone in North Kent, a distance of about 85 km as the crow flies. On their inspection in August 1858 the party found the ancient stone completely embedded in sand and shells, therefore they decided to replace it. The inscription is now illegible, but the first edition Ordnance Survey map includes it as 'This stone is erected to mark the South Eastern Boundary of the conservation of the River Thames'. The plinth records the names of those present, probably when the stone was replaced, Horatio Thomas Austin and Warren Stormes Hale, who was a Lord Mayor and founder of the City of London School. At high water the base is covered by the tide.

On the Essex side, almost due north of Yantlet Creek, the matching London Stone there is called the Crow Stone (Exp. 175 857 852). It stands in the mud opposite the end of Chalkwell Avenue, just west of Westcliff-on-Sea. An obelisk was originally erected there in 1755, but this was removed in 1837 and placed in Priory Park, Southend, in 1950. The new stone was larger. The imaginary line between the two stones is known as the 'Yantlet Line' and is used as a boundary for various bodies, including the Port of London Authority. Seawards beyond it is the property of the Crown Estates.

Yantlet Creek is tidal for a short distance but the stone itself is cut off by marshes and access is prohibited by a notice indicating 'Danger Area'. At the water's edge, all round on the west, a public footpath follows a bank, or seawall, below which is a ditch, both part of the flood defences. The London Stone stands clear and proud above the water at high tide. A short distance away is the mouth of the Medway, with the Nore forming a promontory on its right bank at the junction with the Thames. This was where a famous mutiny took place in 1797 at a time of great unrest in Europe. Looking back from the creek along the footpath towards the village of Allhallows, the largely drained marshes look like a moon landscape, yet here families from the East End of London would come to spend their holidays in tents. Now caravan parks on the higher ground fulfil that need. The creek is below the line of sight.

All in all, not a remarkable place, nor typically English, yet it is known universally by lawyers, for a court case brought in August 1824 at Guildford Assizes before Mr Baron Graham and a special jury. The case was taken in Surrey instead of Kent to ensure impartiality. The Calendar of Treasury Books for 22 February 1743 provides the background to the case. In a report given by the Surveyor General of Crown Lands[2]

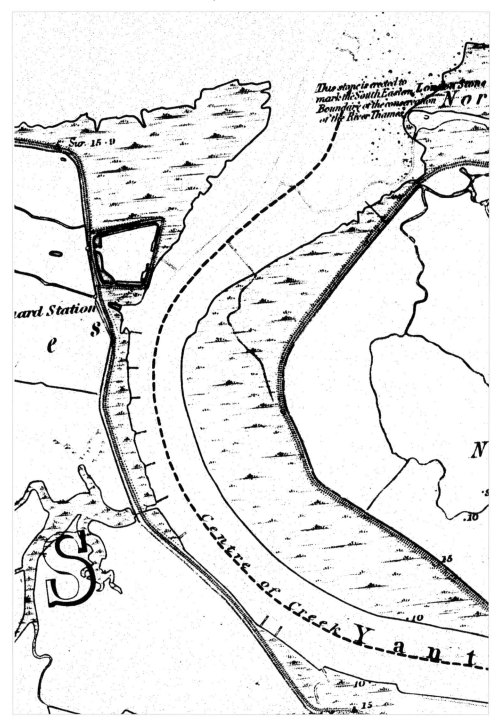

Ordnance Survey First Edition, 1869? Showing Yantlet Creek bordered by flood banks and the London Stone at its mouth.

Yantlet Creek. The London Stone marking the downstream limit of the jurisdiction of the City of London Corporation over the River Thames. Photo taken at low tide by Roger Haworth who went to a lot of trouble to obtain this image in January 2007. (Reproduced by permission via Geograph)

it states, 'His Majesty (George II), by his prerogative, is entitled to the soil of all navigable rivers as far as low-water mark and to the soil between high and low water mark in the right of his Royal Palace Manor of Westminster. The City of London is entitled to the conservancy of the water of Thames from Staines to Yantlet, but hath no right to the soil otherwise as private lords within their own manors.'

The Isle of Grain is not actually an island, but is the easternmost part of the Hoo Peninsula, separated from the mainland by Yantlet Creek on the north and by Colemouth Creek, also tidal, in the south where it joins the Medway. Neither of them are streams, as they do not flow, but inlets of the sea occasioned by the vagaries and weather of the Thames. Between them at the narrowest point on both creeks, Grain Road, which was made up of cockle shells and gravel, crossed by a bridge, Grain Bridge, from time immemorial. A map of 1580 marks this bridge but with no roads leading to it. Some said the bridge was Saxon, but in court, James Walker,[3] an engineer, swore he had seen the stones lying in the ground and from their shape he could tell they were not Saxon. At some time the bridge had fallen and a mound or embankment had been formed in the bed of the creek, causing an obstruction, which prevented the passage of boats. The place continued to be called Grain Bridge.

In August 1822, following depositions from fishermen who claimed fisheries in the creek were being destroyed, the Lord Mayor, as Conservator of the Thames, and Alderman Wood, with the water-bailiff and other officers, went to inspect. They established the creek as being within the jurisdiction of the chief magistrate of the City of London. On 18 September 1823[4] the Lord Mayor, Mr Nelson, the deputy water-bailiff, Mr James Mountague, and the City Solicitor, W. L. Newman, journeyed down the creek and had the obstruction completely removed, thus depriving the inhabitants of the village of Stoke their age-old right of access to Grain, where some of them also held land, and likewise the few people who lived on Grain. Within twenty-four hours the creek was able to take craft through from the Thames to the Medway. A peter-boat with nine persons aboard went through, followed by the water-bailiff's skiff and a four-oared boat belonging to Captain Brown, the master attendant of Woolwich Dockyard. The Conservators claimed they had made 'the free communication so essential to the interests of the public between the Thames and Medway, whereby the circuitous and frequently dangerous course round the Nore, for small craft, will be avoided, and many valuable lives saved to their families and friends, as well as a great facility afforded for the better supply of fish to the London markets'.

Nevertheless, the people of Stoke were greatly incensed by this high-handed action and, with encouragement and support from the Crown, brought the case to court. Known as Rex versus James Mountague, W. L. Newman et al, it lasted three days, 25 to 27 August 1824. Mr Baron Graham, in summing up pointed out that according to the original charter, the City of London had a right of conservancy only as far as the mouth of Yantlet Creek, not the creek itself, and that was in respect of only the fishery. He commented on the fact 'that the Corporation had never attempted to exercise an authority to the extent now insisted upon'. His Lordship also observed that 'there was by no means any satisfactory proof, within living memory that the spot in question was even a navigable waterway'. If not, then the defendants had no right to perform the act, which constituted a nuisance. (Mention could have been made that the original charter was for the Thames only and did not include the Medway.) All the defendants were found guilty. Connections with Hoo and the Isle of Grain have been strengthened over the years by a goods railway line and improved road facilities.

The City Solicitor prepared a statement asking for a retrial in which he dwelt on the fact there had been a bridge, which allowed for the passage of boats and people. (They never offered to rebuild a bridge.) A Kent jury at a Court of Conservancy backed him up in 1825 on the grounds that it was much safer for small craft to use the Yantlet/

Colemouth Creeks as a 'cut-through' than go round by the Nore. *The Times* printed a letter on 19 December 1825 from 'A West Briton' who deplored the length of time judges took before sitting a retrial. But, 'it was of little importance, whether it was decided to whom Yantlet Creek belonged, a few months sooner or later'. What did matter was the cost. In December 1826 the finance committee of the City of London disclosed in a report an excess of expenditure over income, caused by various capital outlays. They included £2,700 on Yantlet Creek and £15,000 on improvements to navigation of the river.

Was there a hidden agenda? It was well known this area was a hotbed for smugglers. Small craft could enter the creek by night, and lie unseen below the banks in this remote landscape.

Acknowledgements

While researching material for this book, I spent time in the following repositories. I thank each one for their help and courtesy.

Bath Central Reference Library
British Library
Gloucestershire Archives
Greenwich Heritage Centre
Guildhall Library
Metropolitan Archives
National Monuments Record – English Heritage
The National Archives

Help given to me by the following people has been much appreciated.

Ken Butler
Christopher French
Rigby Graham
Heatons of Tisbury
Ian Leith
Campbell McCutcheon
Jenny O'Keefe
William Tucker
Nigel Wilkins

Abbreviations

BGAS   Bristol & Gloucestershire Archaeological Society
BHO   British History Online
BL   British Library
CEN   Civil Engineering Heritage
GRO   Gloucestershire Archives (formerly Gloucestershire Record Office)
LCC   London County Council
LMA   London Metropolitan Archives
OS   Ordnance Survey*
NMR   National Monument Record – English Heritage
PLA   Port of London Authority
SHC   Surrey History Centre
TNA   The National Archives

* The first edition Ordnance Survey maps extend throughout most of the nineteenth
  century. Revisions were generally merely added to the original published maps.

End Notes

Introduction

1. Thacker, Vol. 1, p.14.
2. Humpherus, Vol. 1, p.16.
3. Act 11 Geo III c 45 GRO TS/181.
4. 14 Geo III c 91 GRO TS/181.
5. 17 Geo III c 18 GRO TS/181.
6. 2 Geo III c 28 GRO TS/181.
7. Thacker, Vol. 1, p.223.
8. PLA website.

Chapter One: Staines to Shepperton

1. Phillips, *Thames Crossings*, p.134.
2. www.adpontes-staines.com
3. Thacker, Vol. 2, p.390.
4. Thacker, Vol. 2, p.402.
5. www.everysquaremile.co.uk
6. LMA ACC/493/ED 99/1.
7. LMA ACC/493/ED/99/100.
8. LMA ACC/493/ED/101/3.
9. LMA ACC/0493/EM/025.
10. LMA ACC/493/ED/102.
11. www.meadowcroftproperties.co.uk
12. Thacker, Vol. 2, p.410.
13. VCH Surrey, Vol. 3, p.403.
14. CEH p.48.
15. Old Bailey Archive, 9.9.1896.

Chapter Two: Walton to Kingston

1. Phillips, p.147.
2. Thacker, Vol. 2, p.431.
3. VCH Middx, Vol. 3 (via British History Online).
4. Commons Commissioners, 236/u/85.
5. Phillips, p.151.
6. TNA E367/5392.
7. GRO D0873/F97.
8. SHC G85/2/1/2/21.
9. www.hamptonferryboathouse.co.uk

10. Friends of BL Newsletter 53.
11. TNA E367/409.
12. SHC QS2/1739/Xmas.
13. LMA ACC/1215.
14. LMA ACC/1215/1-46.
15. SHC QS2/6/1729/Mid47 & Mic/52.
16. http://thamesdittonisland.co.uk
17. Michael Robbins, *Middlesex*, 1953.
18. British History Online.
19. www.britishpathe.com

Chapter Three: Twickenham Ferries

1. http://wn.wikipedia.org/wiki/Trowlock_Island
2. http://richmondandtwickenhamtimes.co.uk
3. http://en. Wikipedia.org/wiki/Teddington_Lock_Footbridge
4. http://en.wikipedia.org/wiki/Earl_of_Dysart
5. Simpson and Morris, *Twickenham Ferries*.
6. Cashmore, *Ferry from Ham to Twickenham*.
7. *The Times*, 4 April 1913, issue 40177.
8. *The Times*, 13 Feb 1914, issue 40446.
9. Cashmore, *Ferry from Ham to Twickenham*.
10. Simpson and Morris, p.14.
11. Gayford, Martin, and Anne Lyles, *Constable's Portraits*. (National Portrait Gallery, 2009), p.40.
12. http:// www.twickenham-museum.org.uk
13. *The Times*, 27 Sept 1884.

Chapter Four: Richmond to Kew

1. Howard, *Richmond Bridge*, p.9.
2. Thacker, Vol. 2, p.481.
3. Calendar Treasury Books, Vol. 8, 2 June 1687, via BHO.
4. TNA T1/404/97-100.
5. LMA ACC/0397/12.
6. LMA ACC/1288.
7. Howard, *Richmond Bridge*.
8. TNA BT356/12414.
9. Thacker, Vol. 2, p.489.
10. Proceedings of Old Bailey, ref. t18070701-59.
11. Howard, *Richmond Bridge*.
12. VCH Middx, Vol. 1, p.182-191.
13. Proceedings of Old Bailey 1718, ref. T17181015-34.
14. LMA ACC/0775/431-2.
15. Bailey, *Standing in the Sun*, p89.
16. www.thamespilot.org.uk
17. www.independent.co.uk/life-style (22 June 1994).
18. Thacker, Vol. 2, p.491.
19. LMA ACC/0038.
20. TNA E134/1659/Mich30.
21. VCH Surrey, Vol. 3, p.482 via BHO.
22. Shakespeare Birthplace Trust DR37/2/Box73/61.

Chapter Five: Watermen of the Thames

1. Guildhall Library MSS. Intro to Co. of Watermen records.
2. Humpherus, Vol. 1, p.138.
3. Bell, *Great Fire of London*, p.39.
4. Public Act 29 Chas II c7.
5. Boswell, *Life of Johnson*, Vol. 4, p.26.
6. Prichard and Carpenter, *Thames Companion*, p.134.
7. Chamberlain's a/cs 1585/6 No. 185, 4 Jan BHO.
8. Holloway, John (ed.), *Oxford Book of Local Verse* (OUP, 1987), p.7.
9. Humpherus, Vol. I, p.12.
10. Strutt, *Sports and Pastimes*, p.81.
11. Act Wm III 1698. An Act for explanation and better execution of former Acts. Via BHO.
12. http://collage.cityoflondon.gov.uk/watercolour 1839
13. http://www.londongazette.co.uk/issues58753
14. Humpherus, Vol. I, p.317.
15. Guildhall Library MSS Section. Guide to records of Co. of Watermen.
16. http:// watermenshall.org/charities
17. http://guardian.co.uk/uk/2007/jan/02/british identity
18. www.riverthames.co.uk/news-section

Chapter Six: Chiswick to Westminster

1. http://en.wikipedia.org.wiki/Chiswick_Bridge
2. www.chiswickhistory.org.uk/html/150-travel.html
3. British Library newspapers, ref. Gale Doc No BC3206197461 – *The Times*.
4. 'A Pedestrian', *A Tour on the Banks of the Thames* (1834).
5. http://abcnotation.comtunepage?a=trillian.mit.edu/_ic/music/book/playford_bath_exxhf/0143
6. http://wandsworthguardian.co.uk/news/4407021.Memory_Lane_The_Thames
7. *The Antiquaries Journal* No. 89 (CUP, 2009)
8. VCH Middx, Vol. 12, p.2-13.
9. Proceedings of Old Bailey, Ref. msp 17531205-10
10. LMA B.C/B/9a,b
11. TNA WORK 6/138-141.
12. www.museumoflondon.org.uk/archive/exhibits/creative/artistloc/1900/1900
13. Exhibition catalogue Birmingham 'Sun, Wind & Rain. Art of David Cox, April 2009.
14. MacMichael, 'The Red House, Battersea'.
15. Survey of London, Vol. 23.
16. *House of Lords Journal*, Vol. 7.
17. *House of Commons Journal*, Vol. 3.
18. *House of Commons Journal*, Vol. 2, 12 Nov. 1642.
19. Survey of London, Vol. 23.
20. *Life and Times of Anthony à Wood* (OUP, 1961), p.220.
21. http://british-history.ac.uk/report.aspx?/lambeth+horse
22. http://landmark.lambeth.gov.uk/display 2639
23. http://www.bridgemanart.com/imageXCF 285168
24. BL SPR 357c3 (69)
25. *House of Commons Journal*, Vol. 85.

Chapter Seven: The London Stairs

1. Humpherus, Vol. I.
2. VCH Surrey, Vol. 2, p.107-12.
3. Brewer's *Phrase & Fable.*
4. *The Art Fund Review*, 2008/9, p.105.
5. Humpherus, Vol. I, p.80.
6. *House of Commons Journal*, Vol. 10, 1 May 1690.
7. GRO D1866/T66
8. English Folk Dance & Song Society, 'The London Wherryman'.
9. BHO, Limehouse Hole – The Riverside Area.
10. Harben, *A Dictionary of London*, 1918, via BHO.
11. http://www.the-river-thames.co.uk/police.htm

Chapter Eight: Wapping, Ratcliff and Rotherhithe

1. Trinity House Transactions, via BHO.
2. Humpherus, Vol. II.
3. Public Act 28 Geo II c43
4. Humpherus, Vol. II.
5. http://en.wikipedia.org/wiki/Thames_Tunnel
6. TNA BT31/225/717
7. http://homepage.ntlworld.com/davidlloyd/Thamessteamferry.htm
8. TNA C26/603
9. TNA BT31/225/717
10. http://www.cruising.org.uk/marina/limehouse.html
11. Proceedings of Old Bailey, ref. t18550129-311
12. http://en.wikipedia.org/wiki/Canary_Wharf_-_ Rotherhithe_Ferry

Chapter Nine: The Isle of Dogs and Greenwich

1. OED, 1933 edition.
2. VCH Middx, Vol. 11, p.19-52, Stepney – Manors & Estates. Via BHO.
3. Greenwich & Lewishham Antiquarian Society, Trans. Vol. III, no.3, p.97.
4. National Maritime Museum, ref. PTF.
5. Humpherus, Vol. I, p.144.
6. VCH Middx, Vol. 11, p.7-13.
7. Humpherus, Vol. I, p.245.
8. House of Commons Journal, Vol. 2.
9. House of Commons Journal, Vol. 3.
10. Proceedings of Old Bailey, 12.9.1764.
11. BHO, The Mellish Estate in Southern Millwall.
12. Proceedings of the Old Bailey, ref. t18380514-1345.
13. Greenwich & Lewisham Antiquarian Society, Trans. Vol. VII, p.267.
14. Act 52 Geo IIIc 148.
15. Act 54 Geo III c 171.
16. Inst. Civil Engineers. Minutes of Proceedings, Vol. LX – 326 (offprint).
17. *The Times*, 20 June 1856, issue 22399, p.11.
18. GRO 5130/33
19. NMR ADS Record ID NMR_NATINV_125382.
20. BHO, The Mellish Estate in Southern Millwall.
21. http://homepage.ntlworld.com/davidlloyd/Greenwich.htm

22. *The Times*, 15 Nov. 1892, p.8.
23. Greenwich Industrial History, Vol. 9 (Jan 2006).
24. http://homepage.ntlworld.com/davidlloyd/greenwich htm
25. Phillips, *Thames Crossings*, 1981, p.249.
26. BHO, Cubitt Town-Riverside area-Island Gardens & Greenwich Hospital Estates.
27. http://en.wikipedia.org/wiki/Greenwich_foot_tunnel
28. www.oxforddnb.com: Cubitt, William.
29. BHO, Cubitt Town-Riverside area:from Cubitt Town Pier.
30. *The Times*, 18 June 1862, p.11, issue 24275.
31. *The Times*, 5 Feb. 1863, p.10, issue 24474.
32. Johnson, Samuel, *Poems* (Yale edn, p.47). 'London' (in imitation of Juvenal's 3rd satire), pub. 1738.

Chapter Ten: Woolwich

1. Watson and Gregory, *Free for All*, p.3.
2. Act 51 Geo III c199 1811.
3. Elliston-Erwood, Woolwich & District Antiquarian Society. Vol. XXXII, 1963, p.10.
4. Elliston-Erwood, Woolwich Chamber of Commerce Review, 1952/3.
5. Act 56 Geo III c27 1816
6. www.plumstead-stories.com/story
7. Woolwich & District Antiquarian Society, Vol. XXX, p.70.
8. GRO D2427 4/1
9. http://myweb.tiscali.co.uk/tramways/Princess AliceexBute.htm
10. www.thamespolicemuseum.org.uk/museum html
11. *The Times*, 5 Sept 1878, p.9, issue 2935??(illegible).
12. http://en.wikipedia.org/wiki/Marchioness_disaster
13. *Observer* newspaper, 6 Mar 1859, in GRO D1571/x/83 (Estcourt papers).
14. Watson and Gregory, *Free for All*, p.6.
15. Act 48&49Vic c167 1885
16. TNA BT336 /10402 & 11002
17. *The Times*, 1 Oct. 1887, p.7.
18. *The Times*, 3 Mar 1894, p.5, issue 34202.
19. Watson and Gregory, *Free for All*, p.7.
20. LMA LCC/CE/GEN/3/1
21. Taylor, *E. Nesbit in Eltham* (1999).
22. *The Times*, 11 April 1898, p.9, issue 35487.
23. Proceedings of Old Bailey, ref. T18980516-396.
24. *The Times*, 19 May 1896.
25. *The Times*, 13 May 1896.
26. Each episode was reported in *The Times*.
27. Badsey-Ellis, *London's Lost Tube Schemes* (2005), p.34.
28. Ibid., p.233
29. *The Times*, 18 June 1904 and 19 June 1905.
30. http://en.wikipedia.org/wiki/Woolwich_foot_tunnel
31. Bloch, *Newham Dockland*, p.117.
32. www.eastlondonhistory.com/oiJimmy Knacker
33. Watson and Gregory, *Free for All*, pp.11-12.
34. http://eastlondonhistory.com/crooks
35. GRO D37/1/372

36. www.plumstead-stories.com/story Woolwich Free Ferry
37. TNA/MT41/21 & /83
38. Watson and Gregory, *Free for All*, p.28.
39. http://plumstead-stories.com/story
40. http://opsi.gov.uk/si/si2000

Chapter Eleven: Barking Reach to Northfleet Hope

1. Smiles, *Lives of the Engineers* Vol .1.
2. DNB Online, 2004.
3. Newcomen Society Transactions, 1951/ SB Hamilton. Capt. J. Perry.
4. *Port of London*, issued by PLA March/April 2004.
5. Union Press Release, 28 Jan 2004.
6. www.simplonpc.uk/WyndhamGrand/Wyndham-G
7. www.museumoflondonimages.com
8. Astbury, *Estuary*, p.185.
9. Seax (Essex Archives Online) D/DU 162/1
10. Bird, *The Vanished Hamlet*.
11. VCH Essex, Vol. 7.
12. *Panorama* – Journal of Thurrock Local History Society, Vol. 4.
13. TNA E321/43/22
14. Seax D/Dac 313A
15. Seax D/DWh/62
16. Seax D/DWh/137
17. *Panorama*, Vol. 4.
18. Seax Q/Rum 2/10
19. Astbury, *Estuary*, p.267.
20. *Panorama*, Vol. 4.
21. Humpherus, Vol. 1, p.87.
22. Letters and Papers, Hen VIII, Nov. 1542.
23. TNA C111/189
24. *House of Commons Journal*, Vol. 11, 18 Dec 1694.
25. Seax T/A 418/246/10
26. www.thurrock.gov.uk/heritage/content
27. *Panorama*, Vol. 11, p.71.
28. *Panorama*, Vol. 4.
29. www.thurrock.gov.uk/heritage

Chapter Twelve: Gravesend to Tilbury

1. Halsted, *History of Kent*, p.450.
2. Cooke, G. A., *Topography of Great Britain*, Kent, nd (early nineteenth century).
3. Halsted, *Kent*, p.450.
4. Humpherus, Vol. 1, p.21.
5. Ibid., p.118.
6. Ibid., p.148.
7. Ibid., p.131.
8. Ibid., p.150.
9. Ibid, p.153.
10. Ibid., p.208.
11. Ibid., p.228.

12. Ibid., p.231.
13. Bull, *Gravesham Ferries*.
14. *Panorama*, Vol. 15 (quoting Prebble, 'Culloden').
15. *Panorama*, Vol. 13, 'Steamers of Thurrock'.
16. Bull, *Gravesham Ferries*.
17. *Panorama*, Vol. 5, p.75.
18. Kent Archives Online, CCA-CC-J/Q/330/v.
19. Halsted, *Kent*.
20. Kent Archives Online CKS-Q/M/51/1612/15/5.
21. Humpherus, Vol. 1, p.245.
22. *Essex Journal*, Vol. 1, part 4.
23. Seax T/A418/119/10.
24. Kent Archives Online V6 T1.
25. Seax Q/SR459/63.
26. *Essex Journal*, Vol. 1, part 4.
27. Ormston, *The Five-Minute Crossing*.
28. Muilman, Peter, *History of Essex*, 1769-72.
29. Ormston, *Five-Minute Crossing*.
30. Bull, *Gravesham Ferries*.
31. Ormston, *Five-Minute Crossing*.
32. Bull, *Gravesham Ferries*.
33. Ormston, *Five-Minute Crossing*.
34. TNA MT41/83
35. *The Times*, 23 June 1953.
36. Tilbury/Gravesend Ferry Survey Report, Sept. 1979, pub. Essex CC & Kent CC.
37. *The Times*, 29 June 1977.
38. www.simplonpc.co.uk/TilburyGravesend2.htm
39. Ormston, *Five-Minute Crossing*.
40. http://commonswikimedia.org/wiki/File:GravesendThames340l.JPG
41. http://www.shippingtimes.co.uk/item 852_tilburyFerry.htm
42. http://www.gravesham.gov.uk/index.cfm?articleid=504
43. *The Times*, 4 July 1938.
44. *Port of London*, Journal of PLA, 2004.
45. http://www.gravesham.gov.uk/index.cfm?articleid=959
46. Plaque erected on wall.
47. http://www.simplonpc.co.uk/TilburyGravesend 3 html

Chapter Thirteen: Higham to East Tilbury

1. Bull, *Gravesham Ferries*.
2. Halsted, *Kent*, Vol. 1, p.528.
3. BGAS, Vol. III, p.143.
4. Gibson, *Northumbrian Saints*, p.36.
5. *Buildings of England: Essex*, p.339.
6. Ireland, *England's Topographer – Kent* (1830), p.201.
7. Humpherus, Vol. 1, p.17.
8. Harvey, *Henry Yevele*, p.59.
9. Essex Archaeological Society, Vol. 22, p.144.
10. Bull, *Gravesham Ferries*.
11. Ex local information.
12. Seax T/A 418/102/16.

Chapter Fourteen: Yantlet Creek

1. http://en.wikipedia.org/wiki/London_ Stone_(riparian)
2. Crown Lease BL VI p272-4.
3. Guildford Assizes, 25-27 Aug 1824. Rex v James Mountague et al.
4. *The Times*, 7 April 1952.

Bibliography

'A PEDESTRIAN', *A Tour on the Banks of the Thames from London to Oxford in the Autumn of 1829* (Printed for the Author, 1834).

ANDERSON, Jo, *Anchor and Hope* (Hodder, 1980).

ASTBURY, A. K., *Estuary: Land and Water in the Lower Thames Basin* (Carnforth Press, 1980).

BADSEY-ELLIS, Antony, *London's Lost Tube Schemes* (Capital Transport, 2005).

BAILEY, Anthony, *Standing in the Sun. A Life of J. M. W. Turner* (Sinclair Stevenson, Harper Collins, 1997).

BELL, Walter George, *The Great Fire of London in 1666* (Bodley Head, 1920).

BERRIDGE, Clive, *The Almshouses of London* (Ashford Press, Southampton, 1987).

BIRD, E. A., *The Vanished Hamlet. A Story of Rainham Ferry* (Dagenham Essex, printed by Stador Printing Services, *c.* 1972).

BLOMFIELD, David, *Tradesmen of the Thames 1750-1901* (Kingston University, 2006 thesis, uk.bl.ethos).

BULL, C. R., *The Gravesham Ferries* (Gravesham Local History Society, 1985).

CARTER, George, *Outlines of English History from 55 BC to AD 1963 with biographical summaries* (Ward Lock, 1964).

CASHMORE, T. H. R., *Ferry from Ham to Twickenham 1909-15* (Richmond Local History Society, 2006).

CROAD, Stephen, *Liquid History. The Thames Through Time* (Batsford, 2003).

DEWE, George and Michael, *Fulham Bridge 1729-1886. The Predecessor of Putney Bridge* (Fulham & Hammersmith Historical Society, 1986).

DICKENS, Charles, *Dickens's Dictionary of the Thames 1887* (Old House Books, Moretonhampstead, Devon, 1994, facsimile edition).

FARINGTON, Joseph, *The Farington Diary 1793-1821* (edited James Greig Hutchinson, 1922, original illustrated edition).

FERET, C. J., *Fulham Old & New*, Vol. 1 (Leadenhall Press, 1900).

FIDLER, Kathleen, *The Thames in Story* (Epworth Press, 1971)

FIENNES, Celia, *The Journeys of Celia Fiennes* (edited Christopher Morris, Cresset Press, 1947).

GIBSON, Edgar C. S., *Northumbrian Saints* (SPCK, 1897).

GREEN, G. W. C., *The Story of Wandsworth & Putney* (Sampson Low, 1925. Borough History series).

HADFIELD, Charles, *The Canals of Southern England* (Phoenix House, 1955).

HADFIELD, Charles, *The Canals of the South and South East of England* (David & Charles, Newton Abbot, 1969. Canals of British Isles series)

HALL, Mr and Mrs S. C., *The Book of the Thames* (Virtue, 1859).

HARRISON, Ian, *The Thames from Source to Sea* (Collins, 2004, www.getmapping.com).

HARVEY, John H., *Henry Yevele c. 1320 to 1400. The life of an English Architect* (Batsford, 1944).

HERBERT, A. P., 'No Boats on the River' with technical essay by J. H. O. Bunge (Methuen, 1932).

HERBERT, John, *The Port of London* (Collins, 1947. Britain in Pictures series).

HOSTETTLER, Eve, *The Isle of Dogs 1066-1918. A Brief History*, Vol. 1 (Island History Trust, 2000).

HOWARD, Diana, *Richmond Bridge and other Thames Crossings* (London Borough of Richmond, 1976. Exhibition catalogue).

HUGHES, Elwyn, *The Story of 'The Prospect of Whitby' at Wapping Wall* (John Conway, 1950).

HUMPHERUS, Henry, *History of the Origin & Progress of the Company of Watermen and Lightermen of the River Thames* (S. Prentice, printer, 1874-86, 3 volumes).

JOHNSON, Samuel, *The Poems of Samuel Johnson*, edited David Nicol Smith & Edward L. McAdam (Clarendon Press, Oxford, 1974. 2nd edition).

KAUFFMANN, C. M., *John Varley (1778-1842)* (Batsford, 1984).

LEGON, James W., *My Ancestors were Thames Watermen* (Society of Genealogists, 2008).

MacMICHAEL, J. Holden, 'The Red House, Battersea' in *Home Counties Magazine*, Vol. 10, 1908, pp. 38-41.

MacROBERT, Scott, *Putney a brief history*, foreword Maxwell Fry (The Putney Society, 1977, reprint of 1971 edition).

MONTAGUE, C. E., *Action and other stories* (Chatto & Windus, 1928).

MORITZ, C. P., *Travels of Carl Philipp Moritz in England in 1782* (1795, reprint OUP, 1924).

NICHOLSON, *Greater London Street Atlas* (Bartholomew-Collins, 1991. 7th edition).

ORDNANCE SURVEY, *Explorer maps* 1:25 000 Ordnance Survey, Southampton '2½" to the mile' Map numbers 160-163, 173.

ORMSTON, John M., *The Five-Minute Crossing. The Tilbury and Gravesend Ferries* (Thurrock Local History Society, 1988).

PENNELL, *The Stream of Pleasure: A Narrative of a Journey on the Thames from Oxford to London* (T. Fisher Unwin, 1891).

PEPYS, Samuel, Robert LATHAM (selected), *The Shorter Pepys* (Bell & Hyman, 1985).

PEVSNER, Nikolaus and BETTLEY, James, *Buildings of England: Essex* (Yale, 2007).

PEVSNER, Nikolaus and BRADLEY, Simon, *Buildings of England: London 1: The City of London* (Penguin, 1999).

PEVSNER, Nikolaus and CHERRY, Bridget, *Buildings of England: London 4: North* (Penguin, 1998).

PEVSNER, Nikolaus (editor), John NEWMAN, *Buildings of England: West Kent and the Weald* (Penguin, 1969).

PHILLIPS, Geoffrey, *Thames Crossings, Bridges, Tunnels and Ferries* (David & Charles, 1981).

PHILLIPS, J. F. C., *Shepherd's London ... 1800-1860* (Cassell, 1976).

PRICHARD, Marie and CARPENTER, Humphrey, *A Thames Companion* (Oxford University Press, 1981).

PUDNEY, John, *Crossing London's River* (J. M. Dent, 1972).

RIELY, John, *Rowlandson Drawings from the Paul Mellon Collections* (Yale Centre for British Art, 1977).

ROLT, L. T. C., *The Thames from Mouth to Source, illustrated ... with notes on the artists by Francis Maxwell* (Batsford, 1951).

RULE, Fiona, *London's Docklands. A History of the Lost Quarter* (Ian Allan, 2009).

RYAN, Ernest K. W., *The Thames from the Towpath. An account of an expedition on foot from Putney to Thames Head* (St Catherine Press, 1938).

SHARP, Cecil J., *The Country Dance Book Pt II. Thirty Country Dances (1650-1728)* (Novello, 1927).

SHARP, David, *The Thames Path, National Trail Guide* (Ordnance Survey, Aurum Press, 2005).

SHEPHERD, Thomas H. and ELMES, James, *Metropolitan Improvements or London in the Nineteenth Century* (Jones, 1828).

SIMPSON, D. H. and MORRIS, E. A., *Twickenham Ferries in History and Song* (Twickenham Local History Society, 1980).

SINCLAIR, Iain, *Sorry Meniscus. Excursions to the Millennium Dome* (Profile (with London Review of Books) 1999).

SMILES, Samuel, *Lives of the Engineers with an account of their principle works comprising also a History of Inland Communication in Britain* (John Murray, 1861, three volumes).

STAPLETON, John, *The Thames. A Poem* (C. Kegan Paul, 1878).

STRUTT, Joseph, *Glig-gamena Angel-ðeod. Or The Sports and Pastimes of the People of England* (Bensley, 1810, 2nd edition).

TAYLOR, John, *Travels Through Stuart Britain. The Adventures of John Taylor the Water Poet*, edited and selected by John Chandler (Sutton, Stroud, 1999).

TAYLOR, Margaret, *E. Nesbit in Eltham* (The Eltham Society, 1999).

THACKER, Fred S., *The Thames Highway. A History of the Inland Navigation* (Fred S. Thacker, 1914).

THACKER, Fred S., *The Thames Highway. A History of the Locks and Weirs* (Fred S. Thacker, 1920).

THOMPSON, A. G., *Scrap Book of London River* (Bradley, 1937).

TURNER, J. M. W., *Liber Studiorum* (various editions).

WARREN, A. P. *The Story of London's River* (Cardcraft Publishing, *c.* 1949).

WATSON, Julian and GREGORY, Wendy, *Free for All. A celebration of 100 years of the Woolwich Free Ferry* (Greenwich Libraries, 1989).

WEIGHTMAN, Gavin, *London's Thames* (John Murray, 2004).

APPENDIX
London Stairs A-Z

This list has been compiled from various sources and includes most of the stairs on both sides of the river through London.

Abbots Mill	At site of Tower Bridge?
Alderman	At East Smithfield between Miller's Wharf West and Carron Wharf East.
All Hallows	At south end of All Hallows Lane, Dowgate, 1720.
Arundel	Nobleman's house on north bank, 1758.
Battlebridge	North side of Tooley Street on south bank.
Baynard's Castle	At west end of Baynard's Castle Wharf, 1680.
Bear Garden	Pepys watched a prize fight.
Bear Key	aka Sabbs'. Site taken by Custom House.
Bell Wharf	At Bell Wharf, Thames Street, 1755.
Billingsgate	At Billingsgate Market, Lower Thames Street.
Bishop of Winchester's	Southwark.
Black Lion	At Hammersmith Terrace. Takes its name from Black Lion pub.
Black Raven Alley	
Blackfriars	At south end of Water Lane.
Blackwall	Named from a river wall. It was a slipway and common way.
Blackwell	Where George III used to inspect the navy.
Bull	Included in list of 1708.
Chalkstone	West side of Isle of Dogs.
Chelsea Royal Hospital	New pair of stone stairs and causeway built in 1690.
Cherry Garden	Bermondsey. Street with same name.
Churchyard Alley	
Cocoa Nut Stairs	Isle of Dogs. Landing place for Deptford Ferry.
Coldharbour or Cole-harbour	On lane leading south out of Upper Thames Street.
Cousin Lane	At south end of Cousin Lane in Dowgate Wood.
Crane	Greenwich. Where a treadmill crane once stood.
Cupers	In Cupers Gardens, Lambeth, nearly opposite Adelphi, 1627.
Custom House	At east and west ends of the terrace, 1648.
Dog & Duck	South bank. At entrance of Commercial Docks.
Dorset	Opposite Dorset Street, Whitefriars, 1720.
Dowgate	
Duke Shore	Where Pepys took water in 1660 for the Tower.
Dunghill	Possibly belonging to parish of St James, Garlickhythe.
East	Later, East Lane Stairs. Bermondsey.
Ebgate	
Essex	Nobleman's house on north bank.

Falcon	Out of Shoemaker Row, Aldgate, 1755.
Fishmonger's Hall	On south side of Upper Thames Street, 1720.
Fleur de Luce Alley	Demolished for erection of Cannon Street Station.
Frying Pan	Ref. Hospital of Bridewell, 1676.
Garden	Greenwich. Near pier in Cutty Sark Gardens.
Globe Stairs Alley	Rotherhithe. Blue Anchor Road.
Gully Hole	
Holy Ghost	
Horn	Rotherhithe. North of Nelson Dockyard Dry Dock.
Horseleydown	Old and New Stairs. Still extant?
Horsey	In St Katherine's pool in Thames, Trinity House, 1635.
Hospital	Greenwich. For Greenwich Hospital.
Hungerford	Number 4 was the blacking warehouse where Dickens worked.
Irongate	Leading down from the Irongate at bottom of Little Tower Hill, 1664.
Ivy Bridge	Near St Dunstan's.
Kidney	Limehouse. Watermen always at hand here to convey fares.
King Edward's	At Wapping.
King Henry's	At Wapping.
King's	A gate at Westminster beyond the Star Chamber led to stairs.
King's Arms	West side of Isle of Dogs.
Lambeth	For passengers not using the Horseferry.
Limehouse Hole	Limehouse.
Lower Custom House	Near Traitor's Gate, 1746.
Marygold	Bermondsey. Near Paris Garden. Bought by Waterman's Co., 1697.
Masons	
Millwall	West side of Isle of Dogs.
Old Bargehouse	Southwark.
Old Palace or Privy	At Whitehall. Where the famous were brought for burial in abbey.
Old Swan	At south end of Swan Lane leading down to the river.
Orchard House	On Orchard Wharf by East India Docks.
Palace	In New Palace Yard. Westminster by the Turk's Head tavern.
Palace or Privy	At Whitehall, abutting on Scotland Yard.
Paris Garden	Bankside.
Parliament	Used by Westminster School scholars for rowing.
Paul's	At south end of Paul's Wharf in Castle Baynard Ward, 1758.
Pelican	Popular place to pick up flotsam and jetsam.
Pickle Herring	South bank. The quay was renowned for the English Delft pottery.
Puddle Dock	Puddle Wharf was an ancient free landing place.
Queen's	Later called Stone Stairs with paved alley leading to Custom House.
Queenhithe	At south end of street called Queenhithe, east of Queenhithe.
Queenhithe Little	West of Queenhithe Stairs at east end of Brook's Wharf.
Sabbs'	aka Bear Key Stairs.
Salisbury	At south end of Salisbury Court, 1755.
Says Court	aka W. Greenwich. Deptford.
Somers Quay	Approached by Dark House Lane out of Lower Thames Street.
Somerset	Double staircase in front of Somerset House.
St Katherine	In precinct of Hospital of St Katherine, 1686.

St Mary Overy   Southwark
St Saviour's Mill   South bank, Bermondsey.
Steelyard   South of Steel Yard Wharf in Dowgate Ward, 1748.
Stew Alley   At south end of Stew Lane in Queenhithe Ward, 1816.
Swan   Used when rapids at London Bridge made navigation
                         difficult.
Temple   South of Thames Street at No. 22 on east side of
                         Billingsgate, 1585.
Three Crane   At south end of Queen Street in the Vintry.
Three Mariners'
Tower   On Tower Wharf. First mention of wharf 1436.
Trigg
Wapping Old & Wapping New   Between Nos 288 and 304 High Street.
Watergate   At Deptford Strond.
Westminster Hall   Stairs led down to river from some low houses.
Wheatsheaf Alley   In Old Swan Lane.
White Fryers   At south end of Waterman's Lane, west of Whitefriars Dock.
White Swan   South out of Thames Street, 1755.
Whitehall or Queen's   Westminster.
Willow Bridge   West side of Isle of Dogs.

Index

Also available from Amberley Publishing

Thames & Medway
Pleasure Steamers
From 1935

Andrew Gladwell

ISBN: 978-1-84868-694-6

£14.99 PB

Available from all good bookshops, or order direct
from our website www.amberleybooks.com

Also available from Amberley Publishing

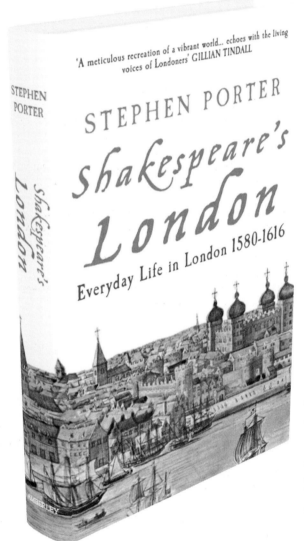

'A meticulous recreation of a vibrant world... echoes with the living voices of Londoners' GILLIAN TINDALL

STEPHEN PORTER

Shakespeare's London

Everyday Life in London 1580-1616

Stephen Porter

ISBN: 978-1-84868-333-4

£20 HB

Available from all good bookshops, or order direct
from our website www.amberleybooks.com